Dominique Charpin is Professor of Ancient Near Eastern History and Director of Studies at the École Pratique des Hautes Études, Sorbonne, Paris. An internationally recognized authority on the Ancient Near East, his books include *Lire et écrire à Babylone* (2008) and *Hammu-rabi de Babylone* (2003), both written and published in French.

'A first-rate study of this important Babylonian ruler by one of the world's leading Assyriologists.'
Andrew R George, FBA, Professor of Babylonian, School of Oriental and African Studies, University of London

'A thorough introduction to the life and times of one of the most prominent rulers in the history of ancient Mesopotamia, presented by one of the masters of Old Babylonian studies. In addition to detailing Hammurabi's military and political achievements, Dominique Charpin lucidly sketches the society and economy over which he ruled and of course discusses his famous "Law Code." Numerous translated excerpts from the original documents afford the reader a vivid picture of life in Babylonia.'
Gary Beckman, Professor of Hittite and Mesopotamian Studies, University of Michigan

HAMMURABI of BABYLON

DOMINIQUE CHARPIN

BLOOMSBURY ACADEMIC
LONDON • NEW YORK • OXFORD • NEW DELHI • SYDNEY

BLOOMSBURY ACADEMIC
Bloomsbury Publishing Plc
50 Bedford Square, London, WC1B 3DP, UK
1385 Broadway, New York, NY 10018, USA
29 Earlsfort Terrace, Dublin 2, Ireland

BLOOMSBURY, BLOOMSBURY ACADEMIC and the Diana logo
are trademarks of Bloomsbury Publishing Plc

First published in Great Britain 2012 by I.B. Tauris & Co. Ltd
Paperback edition first published by Bloomsbury Academic 2021

Copyright © 2003 Presses Universitaires de France
Translation copyright © 2012 I.B.Tauris & Co Ltd

The right of Dominique Charpin to be identified as the author of this work has been asserted by Presses Universitaires de France in accordance with the Copyright, Designs and Patent Act 1988.

All rights reserved. No part of this publication may be reproduced or transmitted in any form or by any means, electronic or mechanical, including photocopying, recording, or any information storage or retrieval system, without prior permission in writing from the publishers.

Bloomsbury Publishing Plc does not have any control over, or responsibility for, any third-party websites referred to or in this book. All internet addresses given in this book were correct at the time of going to press. The author and publisher regret any inconvenience caused if addresses have changed or sites have ceased to exist, but can accept no responsibility for any such changes.

A catalogue record for this book is available from the British Library.

A catalog record for this book is available from the Library of Congress.

ISBN: HB: 978-1-8488-5752-0
PB: 978-1-3501-9778-7
ePDF: 978-0-8577-2486-1
eBook: 978-0-8577-3199-9

To find out more about our authors and books visit
www.bloomsbury.com and sign up for our newsletters.

Contents

List of Illustrations	vi
Time Chart	xii
Glossary	xiv
Preface	xxxiii
Abbreviations	xxxv
Maps	xxxvii

Part One – The Conqueror · 1

	One	From the Accession of Hammurabi to the Death of Samsi-Addu (1792–1775)	23
	Two	From the Death of Samsi-Addu to the Victory over Elam (1775–1764)	35
	Three	The Great Conquests (1764–1759)	55
	Four	The End of the Reign (1758–1750)	69

Part Two – Politics · 73

	Five	The King and the Gods	75
	Six	The Government of the Kingdom	91
	Seven	War and Peace as Means of Conquest	113

Part Three – The Administrator · 143

	Eight	Hammurabi, the Legislator, and the Judge	145
	Nine	Hammurabi and his Subjects: Observations on Babylonian Society	161
	Ten	The Palace Economy	183

Conclusion	199
Notes	203
Bibliography	213
Index	221

Illustrations

Maps

Map A	Upper Mesopotamia in the time of Hammurabi	xxxvii
Map B	Lower Mesopotamia in the time of Hammurabi	xxxviii
Map C	Towns named in the Prologue to the Code of Hammurabi	xxxix

Illustrations

Fig. 1 When a new floor of pounded earth was being laid in the temple of Šamaš at Larsa (Tell Senkereh) tablets dating from the time of Hammurabi were used as material for ballast. Here they are being delicately excavated. — 5

Fig. 2 The ruins of the stepped tower (the *ziggurat*) at Eridu (modern Tell Abu Sharein). Because of the encroaching desert, this ancient Sumerian settlement was gradually abandoned over the years. Under Hammurabi it retained importance only as a religious centre where the worship of Enki/Ea was conducted. — 11

Fig. 3 A letter from the archives at the palace of Mari, sent from Babylon to the king of Mari by his envoy Yarim-Addu. He informs his master about the current political developments, since Hammurabi has made an alliance with the king of Malgium (see *ARM* 26/2: 373). — 13

Fig. 4 Hardly anything remains today of the staged-tower (the *ziggurat*) at Babylon, made famous by the narrative in the Bible (Genesis 11:1–9). — 18

Fig. 5 A plan of the palace of Mari, showing the rooms where the tablets were found; from J. Margueron in K.R. Veenhof (ed.), *Cuneiform Archives and Libraries* (Leiden, 1986), p. 146. — 21

Fig. 6 The ruins of the stepped tower, the *ziggurat*, at Kiš, in the background. Now it is a grazing ground for the local animals. — 25

Fig. 7	The site of Uruk (Warka) is dominated by the ruins of its stepped tower (the *ziggurat*) which was built at the end of the third millennium.	28
Fig. 8	The victory stele of Samsi-Addu, now in the Louvre. The king stands upright, in profile, striking the brow of an enemy with an axe and pressing him to the ground with his left foot. His face is not preserved, which is particularly disappointing since this is the only surviving representation of the king. The campaign he undertook with the king of Ešnunna against the kingdom of Arbele is mentioned in the inscription on the back.	29
Fig. 9	The statue of 'Baal of thunder', found at Ugarit, is now in the Louvre. The God of the Storm is here shown battling with the God of the Sea, symbolically represented by waves under his feet. The mythical narrative is recorded in Ugaritic on tablets dating from the thirteenth century. But now, thanks to the Mari archives, we know that it was documented at Aleppo five centuries earlier. The weapons with which the God of the Storm was supposed to have overcome the God of the Sea were sent from Aleppo to Zimri-Lim as a sign of support.	36
Fig. 10	The Jebel Sinjar as seen from the south. Although the mountain is not particularly high, rising to about 1,200 metres, it presents a significant barrier to communication.	39
Fig. 11	A view of the island of 'Ana (ancient Hanat) in 1985, at the time when it was being submerged by the Euphrates as the Haditha Dam was constructed. Rescue excavations were undertaken in the years before this happened but they never managed to reach the levels contemporary with Hammurabi.	47
Fig. 12	A view of the palace in the lower town of Šubat-Enlil (Tell Leilan). The archives that were found here in the course of excavations in 1985 and 1987 can be dated for the most part to the 25 years following the death of Hammurabi. They are particularly important for providing information about the history of Syria for several decades after the archives of Mari become silent.	51
Fig. 13	The façade of the temple of Šamaš at Larsa. The monotony of brick has been relieved by a pattern of	57

half-columns, some of which are shaped spirally.

Fig. 14 The slowly flowing River Balih, a tributary of the Euphrates, played an essential role in the environment, not only for the transhumance of sheep and cattle farmers but also for the settled population of the region. — 63

Fig. 15 The statue of the goddess found shattered in the palace of Mari. She holds a vase-fountain from which floods of little fish would spurt as a traditional sign of fertility. It is now in the Aleppo Museum in Syria. — 64

Fig. 16 Modern Tell Afar, at the eastern end of Jebel Sinjar, now dominated by a fort from the Ottoman period, is perhaps the site of ancient Karana. — 70

Fig. 17 The figurine of a man in an attitude of prayer said to have come from Larsa. He intercedes with the god Amurru on behalf of Hammurabi, the king of Babylon. — 79

Fig. 18 One of the inscribed clay models of a liver from the Louvre. Thirty or so of them have been found in the Mari excavations but how they were used is not altogether clear. Objects like this are valuable supplements to the information from literature about the importance of hepatoscopy in the period of the Amorites in revealing the will of the gods. — 84

Fig. 19 The head of a god in clay. A deity depicted anthropomorphically is often given the traditional emblem of a horned tiara. — 87

Fig. 20 Music played an extremely important role in the life of the palace and also in the life of the temples. This depiction of a harpist on baked clay is now in the Louvre. — 93

Fig. 21 The relative luxury of life in Amorite palaces can be seen from the splendid bathroom at Mari. — 95

Fig. 22 This tablet, one of the largest found in the archives of the palace of Mari, measuring 23 x 16.5 cm, has five columns on each side. It lists more than 500 persons in the harem of King Zimri-Lim to whom rations of oil were dispensed. — 97

Fig. 23 The sacred area of the pre-Sargonic palace at Mari. Several centuries later, in the reign of Zimri-Lim, the chapel consecrated to Belet-ekallim, 'the Lady of the Palace', was sited on the same spot. — 102

List of Illustrations ix

Fig. 24 A mural painting from 'Palm Tree Court' (Court 106) 103
in the palace of Mari depicting a procession in
preparation for a sacrifice. People are processing in two
registers, with the sacrificial bull in the lower register,
behind a much taller figure, who is probably the king. It
is dated as being in the time of Yasmah-Addu.

Fig. 25 Canals were used both for irrigating the agricultural 105
land and for transport by boat; a photo taken in the
region of El-Hibbah in the south of Iraq.

Fig. 26 Excavations at Tell Harmal were begun in 1948 by Iraqi 106
archaeologists to reveal the ancient small town of
Šaduppum. The site has been the subject of much
restoration work. This photograph shows in the
background the plans of the 'temple of the lions',
dedicated to Bel-gašer the local god, with the splendid
house of the governor in the foreground.

Fig. 27 The impression of 'Seal I' of Mukanništum, the steward 108
of the king of Mari. The inscription reads: 'Mukanništum,
son of Habdi-bahati, servant of Zimri-Lim'.

Fig. 28 A haematite cylinder-seal representing the king as 'the 108
warrior with a mace'; see D. Collon, *Cylinder Seals III.
Isin-Larsa and Old Babylonian Period*, (London, 1986),
pl. I, no. 388.

Fig. 29 One of the sites for bitumen near Hit, on the Middle 115
Euphrates. The possession of this town was of crucial
importance in negotiations between Zimri-Lim of Mari
and Hammurabi of Babylon.

Fig. 30 A general view of the ruins of Mishrife, ancient Qatna, 123
showing part of the imposing glacis going round all
four sides of the town.

Fig. 31 The site of ancient Kurda is almost certainly to be 129
located at the modern town of Beled Sinjar, lying just to
the south of Jebel Sinjar.

Fig. 32 The obverse of the surviving half of a four-column 136
tablet from Mari recording the treaty between Ibal-pi-El
II of Ešnunna and Zimri-Lim. It begins in the left
column with the list of deities Zimri-Lim invokes for
the king of Ešnunna.

Fig. 33 Ur (modern Tell Muqayyar) showing the remains of 147
the famous *ziggurat* in the background. In the

foreground is the building called Dublamah, where those under trial took the oath prescribed by the judges.

Fig. 34 The 2.25-metre high basalt stele of the 'Code of Hammurabi'. The text is written in horizontal columns on the front and on the back. In the twelfth century BC it was pillaged from Babylonia, probably from Sippar, by the ruler of Elam and taken to Susa in southwestern Iran as booty. French excavators found it there just over a century ago. At the head of the stele Hammurabi stands before the enthroned sun-god Šamaš, the god of justice, whose rays stream from his shoulders. The damage that can be seen at the base has destroyed the last few columns on the front. There is no trace of any dedicatory inscription, although the erasure must have been made deliberately to make room for such a secondary inscription. 153

Fig. 35 A clay image of a carpenter apparently making a plough is one of the few representations of craftsmen to have been found. Now in the Louvre. 167

Fig. 36 A typical tomb-chamber excavated at Tell Khoshi, probably the site of ancient Andarig. It is a good example of a vault constructed with inclined courses of baked bricks. 170

Fig. 37 A plan of the small fortified town of Šaduppum (modern Tell Harmal; see photograph in Fig. 26) where extensive excavations have been conducted by Iraqi archaeologists. The temple (marked with A), consecrated to the principal deity of the town, Bel-gašer, is separated from the residence of the governor of the locality by a street. 176

Fig. 38 Traditional reed buildings, known in Arabic as *zarifeh*, are common in Southern Iraq. As early as the fourth millennium BC they feature in Mesopotamian iconography. 179

Fig. 39 A letter from Larsa, now in the Louvre, from Hammurabi to Šamaš-hazir. It was first copied by F. Thureau-Dangin. 185

Fig. 40 A palm-grove in the region of Nasiriyeh. Palm trees have the advantage of hardly ever being affected by salinity in the irrigation water. Today, as in ancient times, various kinds of vegetables are grown in the shade between the trunks of the trees. 188

Fig. 41 A reconstruction by Seton-Lloyd of the temple of the goddess Kititum at Nerebtum. The archives found in this building illustrate various aspects of the economic life of a Mesopotamian temple. 191

Fig. 42 The stairway leading up to the main temple of Šamaš at Larsa. This photograph shows the restoration undertaken by the Cassite kings in the second half of the second millennium, after the building which had been erected in the time of Hammurabi had fallen into ruins. 193

Time Chart

Sovereigns of the First Dynasty of Babylon

1894–1881	[Sumu-abum]
1880–1845	Sumu-la-El
1844–1831	Sabium
1830–1813	Apil-Sin
1812–1793	Sin-muballiṭ
1792–1750	Hammurabi
1749–1712	Samsu-iluna
1711–1684	Abi-ešuh
1683–1647	Ammi-ditana
1646–1626	Ammi-ṣaduqa
1625–1595	Samsu-ditana

Principal Events in the Reign of Hammurabi

1792	Accession to the throne
1787	Raid against Uruk and Isin
1784	Victory over Malgium
1783	Capture of Rapiqum
1779	Accession of Ibal-pi-El II to the throne of Ešnunna
1777	King of Malgium buys peace from Samsi-Addu, Ibal-pi-El II and Hammurabi
	Death of Samsi Addu
1775	Accession of Zimri-Lim to the throne of Mari
	Kingdom of Upper Mesopotamia falls apart

1772–1771	Ešnunna attacks Mari and the Habur triangle
1765	Elamite victory over Ešnunna
1764	Hammurabi and his allies are victorious over the Elamites
1763	Annexation of the kingdom of Larsa
1762	Ešnunna at war with Babylon
1761	Capture of Mari and Malgium
1759	Destruction of Mari and Malgium
1757	Victory over the Gutians and Turukkeans
1756	Flood destroys Ešnunna
1755	Victory over Šubartum
1750	Death of Hammurabi

Glossary

Letters marked with diacritics are listed alphabetically after corresponding ones without diacritics, e.g. s, ṣ, š and t, ṭ. But in the ordering of entries in the Index (pp. 213 ff.) these diacritics have been ignored. Individual lexical elements of personal names have been separated, except for that of Hammu-rabi, which is better known to the general reader with no hyphen.

Adab (Bismaya)	A town situated on the former course of the Tigris. Archaeological findings were made at the site at the beginning of the twentieth century.
Adad (Addu)	A storm god with principal temples at Aleppo, Arrapha and Karkar.
Agade	See Akkad.
Akkad	The ancient name of the whole territory of Central Mesopotamia, from Babylon to Ešnunna. The kings 'of Sumer and Akkad' had united the wider territory of Southern and Central Mesopotamia. The same Akkadian word also denotes more specifically Agade, the ancient city founded by Sargon in the twenty-fourth century as the capital of his empire. It was somewhere near modern Baghdad but, although it survived longer than the Empire of Sargon, its precise location is unknown.
Akkadian	The language, classified as Eastern Semitic, used throughout Mesopotamia and beyond during virtually the whole of its ancient history. From the end of the third millennium onwards Babylonian, the language of Central and Southern Mesopotamia, can be distinguished from Assyrian, which was first attested in

	Assur and subsequently, from the middle of the second millennium, in the whole of Northern Mesopotamia.
Alalah (Tell Atchana)	A town situated on the River Orontes in Northern Syria. It was first excavated by British archaeologists from the 1930s onwards, with operations suspended during the War. The archives from the seventeenth century were found in Level VII.
Aleppo	See Halab.
Ammi-ṣaduqa	King of Babylon (1646–1626) and great-great-grandson of Hammurabi. The well-preserved text of the *mîšarum* he proclaimed when he was king is taken as the model for those proclaimed by other kings.
Amorites	An Amorite-speaking people from Western Syria who invaded Mesopotamia at the end of the third millennium. After the demise of the kingdom of Ur (2002) Amorite warlords established several dynasties, firstly at Isin and Larsa, and then at Babylon, Halab, Qatna and Ekallatum. They and their language gradually assimilated with the native Akkadian population. Amorite is classified as a North-Western Semitic language and is attested especially in personal names and some technical terminology between the end of the third millennium and the beginning of the second millennium.
Amud-pi-El	King of Qatna, son of Išhi-Addu.
Amurrum	A deity whose name is identical with the region of Syria that was the original homeland of the Amorites.
An	One of the two principal deities of the Sumerian pantheon; see Enlil.
Andarig (perhaps Tell Khoshi)	Capital city of a kingdom south of the Jebel Sinjar. After the principal king Qarni-Lim (1775–1765) was murdered, he was succeeded by Atamrum (1765–1763).
Anšan (Tall-i Malyan)	Ancient capital of Elam, situated close to the city of Shiraz in Iran.
Apil-Sin	King of Babylon (1830–1813) and grandfather of Hammurabi.
âpilum	A type of prophet. The Babylonian word literally means 'respondent'.
Arrapha (Kirkuk)	Capital of a kingdom that Samsi-Addu annexed as his own for a few years.
Asqur-Addu	King of Karana (1764–1762).

Assur (Qala'at Šerqat)	A city-state situated on the right bank of the middle Euphrates. In the first half of the second millennium it was not of any major political importance but was the base for long-distance trade with Anatolia. The famous Old Assyrian archives found in the commercial quarter of Kaniš (Kültepe) show in great detail how the Assyrian merchants conducted their affairs. Assur was the principal god associated with the city of Assur.
Ašlakka	An important town, not yet identified, at the centre of the Habur triangle. At the beginning of his reign as king of Mari, Zimri-Lim conquered it and installed Ibal-Addu as king. When he rebelled against Mari at the end of 1763 Zimri-Lim conquered the town again.
Ašnakkum (Chagar Bazar)	Capital of an important kingdom in the Habur triangle.
Atamrum	Coming originally from Allahad he took refuge at Ešnunna. There he sided with the emperor of Elam, who gave him a large number of troops to invade Northern Mesopotamia. After the murder of Qarni-Lim at the beginning of 1765 he became king of Andarig, but then he joined forces with Zimri-Lim once he realised that Elam was going to be defeated. Eventually he associated himself with Hammurabi. At the end of 1763 he died suddenly.
Atra-hasis	One of the heroic personages in the Babylonian legend of the Deluge. His name can be translated as 'exceedingly wise'. The text of the legend is found on a series of tablets written towards the end of the Old Babylonian period as well as from later 'Ninevite' versions, which were prepared for the library of Assurbanipal at Nineveh.
awîlum	A word occurring very frequently in the Code of Hammurabi. Essentially it means 'a man', but in different contexts it can also mean a person in general, or more specifically a free man (in contrast to *wardum*), or even someone enjoying a privileged position at court (in contrast to an ordinary subject of the king).
Aya	A goddess, spouse of Šamaš.
bâbtum	A word denoting both a designated area of a Babylonian town and the assembly that was in control of regulating affairs in that area.
Babylon	A city situated on the ancient course of the Euphrates. The

	name is attested as early as the Agade period (*c.* 2300) and it was the residence of an *ensi*, a governor in the Ur III period. When the Amorites arrived at the beginning of the nineteenth century they made it the capital of the First Dynasty of Babylon.
Bahdi-Lim	Governor of Mari in the time of Zimri-Lim.
bâ'irum	One of two categories of soldier referred to in the Code of Hammurabi (see *rêdûm*). The word literally means 'a fisherman', which when applied to a soldier becomes a marine, because supposedly he caught his fish while patrolling the southern marshes in his boat and fulfilling his military duties.
Balih	A tributary of the Euphrates flowing into the left bank. The valley it formed was known as the region of Zalmaqum, where Harran was one of the principal towns.
Belet-ili	One of the names, literally meaning 'Lady of the Gods', for the mother goddess of the Sumero-Akkadian pantheon. Alternatively she is known as Nintu.
Benjaminites	A confederation of five of the Amorite tribes living in various territories of the Near East. Not all of them were sedentary, as some were always on the move with their flocks along the Euphrates valley in Western Syria. The name Benjamin literally means 'a son of the right' or 'someone from the south' and is identical to the name used in the Bible to denote the most southern of the twelve tribes of Israel. The element meaning South, *yamin*, is cognate with the name Yemen, in the south of the Arabian Peninsula.
Bensim'alites	An important element of the Amorite population to which both Yahdun-Lim and Zimri-Lim, kings of Mari, belonged. They exercised sovereignty over the Bensim'alites, who in the time of Zimri-Lim were still nomadic, leading their flocks in the pastures of the Habur triangle. The element *sim'al* means both 'left' and 'north', and so the literal meaning of the name, 'a son of the left' or 'someone from the north', distinguishes the Bensim'alites from the Benjaminites.
Borsippa (Birs Nimrud)	A town, 20 kilometres south-west of Babylon, where the principal temple of Nabu, the Ezida, was located.
Burundum	A region which must have been situated to the north-east of Zalmaqum, on the right bank of the Upper

	Tigris. It is mentioned as one of the regions conquered by Hammurabi in 1761.
cuneiform	A system of writing attested from the end of the fourth millennium onwards, first used to write Sumerian and subsequently Akkadian as well as several other languages from different groups, such as Elamite, Hurrian and Hittite. The name is derived from *cuneus*, the Latin for 'wedge', since the signs it uses, which may indicate whole words (logograms) or a syllable of a word (phonogram), consist of wedges clustered in different formations. Most cuneiform inscriptions are imprinted onto soft clay tablets which are then hardened by drying. Stone was also often used as a more permanent writing medium, as for example when inscribing the stele with Hammurabi's laws.
cylinder seal	Small cylinder of stone engraved with images and perhaps also an inscription to identify the owner. Once a scribe had completed writing a clay tablet the seal would be rolled over the still moist surface. The seal impression marked the end of a document, confirmed that the words that had been written were genuine and authenticated a legal decision. Boxes, jars and gates were sometimes secured with clay over which a seal has been impressed and clay envelopes as well as the tablet contained in them are similarly sealed. Cylinder seals from the Old Babylonian period were usually engraved with an image and an inscription to identify the owner. The images and inscriptions are inscribed in mirror format so that they could be properly seen in the seal impression.
Daduša	King of Ešnunna until 1779, when his son Ibal-pi-El II succeded to that throne. After attacking the kingdom of Upper Mesopotamia he concluded a peace treaty with Samsi-Addu, and then in 1780 joined him in the campaign against the kingdom of Urbilum.
Dagan	The principal god in the area of the Middle Euphrates with temples at Tuttul and Terqa. He became assimilated with the Sumerian god Enlil.
Damkina	Spouse of the god Enki (Ea).
Der (Tell 'Aqar, close to Badrah)	Capital of a kingdom in the east of Babylonia on the route from Malgium to Susa. It is to be distinguished from two other towns with the same name, the one in

	the Balih valley, and the other on the Euphrates, a few kilometres downstream from Mari.
Dilbat (Tell ed-Deylam)	A town located 30 kilometres to the south of Babylon devoted to the god Uraš.
Diyala	Tributary of the Tigris along which the kingdom of Ešnunna extended. One of the main routes from the Iranian plateau to the Mesopotamian plain passed through the Diyala valley.
Ea	See Enki.
Ebabbar	The Sumerian name, meaning 'the shining temple', for the temple of Šamaš at Sippar.
Ebla (Tell Mardikh)	Located 60 kilometres to the south of Aleppo and capital of a vassal kingdom of Aleppo in the seventeenth century. The name is not attested in documents from the time of Hammurabi.
Ekallatum	Town on the middle stretches of the Tigris, almost certainly to be located on the right bank about 30 kilometres north of Assur. Samsi-Addu, after he had established the kingdom of Upper Mesopotamia, chose Ekallatum as the capital and placed his son Išme-Dagan on the throne there.
Ekur	The Sumerian name, meaning 'the mountain temple', for the temple of Enlil at Nippur.
Elam	Area in the west of modern Iran with Anšan (modern Tall-i Malyan) as the capital. The Sumerian name for the emperor of Elam was *sukkal-mah* but this was generally abbreviated to *sukkal*.
Emar (Meskene)	Town on the right bank of the Middle Euphrates. Situated as it was on the border of the kingdom of Aleppo it became an important crossroads for trade.
Emeslam	The Sumerian name for the temples at Kutha and Maškan-šapir.
Emutbalum (also Yamutbal)	Name of an Amorite tribe which settled in the lower valley of the Tigris around Maškan-šapir and which gave its name to the surrounding area. The name was used to refer to the whole of the ancient kingdom of Larsa after it had been annexed by Hammurabi.
Enki	Sumerian god of wisdom and of subterranean water courses, who was venerated principally at Eridu and Malgium. The Akkadians identified him with Ea.
Enlil	One of the two principal deities of the Sumerian pantheon.

	His temple, the Ekur, was at Nippur; see An; Dagan.
eponym	The name of a person or place used to denote a distinct period of time. In Assur a series of names of eponymous magistrates denoted a sequence of years. But in Babylon during the reign of Hammurabi every year was given a name commemorating a significant event accomplished in the year that had just passed (see 'Year name').
Eridu	Ancient Sumerian town which gradually became depopulated because of the desertification of the environment. But because it was the cult centre for Enki/Ea, it always retained its religious importance.
Erra	Deity of the underworld identified with Nergal with a principal temple at Kutha.
Esagil	See Marduk.
Ešnunna (Tell Asmar)	Capital of the territory of Warum in the Diyala basin, with Tišpak as its principal deity. It played an especially important political role in the period of Hammurabi, during which time the names of three successive kings are recorded: Daduša, Ibal-pi-El II and Ṣilli-Sin.
Eštar	Goddess of love and war, to be identified with Sumerian Inanna. She was a principal deity at Uruk together with An, and at Agade and Nineveh. At Zabala she was known as Sugallitum and at Kiš she functioned alongside the warrior god Zababa. At Mari the ritual of Eštar was enacted at the winter festival. It is one of the very few Old Babylonian rituals where the text has been preserved and the festival was an occasion for the king to assemble all his vassals together in his presence.
E'unir	Sumerian name for the temple of Enki at Eridu.
Ezida	See Borsippa.
Gilgameš	Legendary king of Uruk and a Sumerian hero. A series of legends written in Sumerian narrate his famous exploits. Some of them were assembled together into one legend written in Akkadian in the Old Babylonian period. But the most famous version of the Gilgameš legend was compiled in the second half of the second millennium and is known from a series of first millennium tablets, in particular those compiled and conserved in the library assembled by Assurbanipal in Nineveh.
Girsu	Sumerian town situated on the lower reaches of the

	Tigris. Its former importance had greatly declined by the beginning of the second millennium.
Gula	Principal deity of Isin, also known as Nin-karrak and Nin-Isina. She was particularly associated with health and had the dog as an animal attribute.
gur	Measure of capacity, approximately equal to 300 litres.
Guti	Mountain dwellers in the Zagros. They were resident in the kingdom of Gutium and were regularly used as mercenary troops by the kings of the surrounding areas.
Habiru	Wandering bands of migrants who were occasionally used as mercenary troops.
Habur	Tributary on the left bank of the Euphrates. The numerous streams flowing down from the mountain of Ṭur Abdin and feeding the upper course of the Euphrates produce the Habur triangle, a very fertile area of piedmont.
Halab (Aleppo)	Capital city of the kingdom of Yamhad. The ancient name is preserved in Arabic for modern Aleppo. Three of the kings of Halab, Sumu-epuh, Yarim-Lim and Hammurabi, were contemporaries of Hammurabi of Babylon.
Hammurabi of Aleppo	Ascended to the throne in 1765, son of Yarim-Lim.
Hammurabi of Babylon	King of Babylon (1792–1750), son of Sin-muballiṭ.
Hammurabi of Kurda	Ascended to the throne in 1769. His relationship with Zimri-Lim of Mari was marred by conflict.
Hanat ('Ana)	An island in the Euphrates which formed the capital of the upper region of Suhum.
Harradum (Khirbet ed-Diniye)	Small town in the region of Suhum which was excavated by a team from France between 1981 and 1988.
Haya-sumu	King of Ilan-ṣura in the heart of the Habur triangle. He was one of the principal vassals of Zimri-Lim, who gave him two of his daughters in marriage, and one of the principal channels for authoritatively relaying orders from Zimri-Lim for the region.
Hiritum	Town between the Tigris (near Upi) and the Euphrates (near Sippar) still yet to be discovered. In 1764 the Elamites failed in their attempt to take it by siege. Hammurabi's victory at Hiritum marked the beginning of the successful expulsion of the invading Elamites.
Hit (Hit)	Town on the Middle Euphrates that has kept its ancient

	name. Under Zimri-Lim it was attached to the kingdom of Mari and was coveted by Hammurabi for its rich supplies of bitumen. It was to here that those condemned to be subjected to the 'ordeal by the river' were taken.
Hurrians	Mountain dwellers in the north and north-east of Mesopotamia.
Ibal-pi-El	Influential nomad chief from Mari, with the same name as the king of Ešnunna, his contemporary. He commanded the troops sent to Babylonia to resist the invasion of the Elamites and during this time sent several letters to Zimri-Lim at Mari.
Ibal-pi-El II	King of Ešnunna (1778–1766), son and successor of Daduša.
Ida-maraṣ	Ancient name for the western part of the Habur triangle.
Ilan-ṣura	Important capital in the Habur triangle, where Haya-sumu was king.
ilkum	Babylonian word meaning 'the service', usually military service, demanded from an individual by his king in return for which he was given a subsistence field.
Inanna	Sumerian name for the goddess Eštar.
Ipiq-Eštar	King of Malgium. In 1764 he made an alliance with Hammurabi and joined him in the capture of Larsa.
Isin (Išān Bahrīyat)	Town in the centre of Sumer, where Gula was the principal deity, and capital of the kingdom of Isin. That kingdom was first annexed by Rim-Sin in 1794 and then in 1763 by Hammurabi, when he conquered the kingdom of Larsa.
Išhi-Addu	King of Qaṭna, father-in-law of Yasmah-Addu and an ally of Samsi-Addu.
Išme-Dagan	Oldest son of Samsi-Addu, who was installed on the throne of Ekallatum by his father. Soon after his father died (1775) he was obliged to leave his capital and take refuge in Babylon. He was able to occupy his throne in Ekallatum again when the Elamites had taken Ešnunna. But he began to have very serious troubles with the Elamites and once again, in 1763, sought refuge in Babylon. Hammurabi was able to take control of the whole region in 1761 and he allowed him to return to his throne.
Jebel Sinjar	Mountain separating the valley of the Habur from that of the Tigris.
Kahat	Important town in the south of the Habur triangle,

	perhaps Tell Barri.
Karana	Town on the south of the Jebel Sinjar close to Tell Rimah (modern Qaṭṭara), perhaps Telafar.
Karkar	Town situated on the lower reaches of the Tigris, where the principal god was Adad, perhaps Tell Jidr.
kârum	A word literally meaning 'quay', which is used also to denote the commercial district occupied by the merchants of a town and also the scheme of organisation into which they arranged themselves. A team of merchants comprised five men, and a chief merchant controlled the activities of all the teams.
Kazallu	Town in Central Babylonia which was the base for the tribe of Mutiabal. Control of the town was a matter of dispute between the kingdoms of Larsa and Babylon. When the Elamites invaded the inhabitants sided with them. As a result, the town was captured by Hammurabi in the course of his victory in the war against Elam.
Keš	Sumerian town close to Nippur, where the principal deity was a mother-goddess who was known by different names, including Mama, Nintu and Ninmah. Its exact location is not known, but it should not be confused with Kiš.
Kingdom of Upper Mesopotamia	Extensive kingdom founded in Northern Mesopotamia by Samsi-Addu, stretching from the banks of the Tigris (Ekallatum, Assur) to the banks of the Euphrates (Mari). It dissolved after the death of Samsi-Addu.
kispum	A ritual in which food and drink was offered to the deceased relatives of a family.
Kiš (Tell Uhaimer and Tell Ingharra)	A town with two focal points situated 25 kilometres to the east of Babylon. The god Zababa was venerated in Tell Uhaimer and the goddess Eštar in Tell Ingharra. It should not be confused with Keš.
Kurda (Beled Sinjar)	Important town to the south of the Jebel Sinjar. The two kings there, who were contemporary with Hammurabi of Babylon, were Bunu-Eštar and Hammurabi of Kurda.
Kutalla (Tell Sifr)	Small settlement near to Larsa. A cache of archives from the period of Hammurabi was found there by nineteenth-century excavators.
Kutha (Tell Ibrahim)	Town situated to the north-east of Babylon where Erra, god of the underworld, was venerated.
Lagaš (al-Hiba)	Important Sumerian town on the lower reaches of the Tigris.

Larsa (Tell Senkereh) Town in the south of Sumer, where Šamaš was the principal deity, and the capital of the kingdom of Larsa. Rim-Sin, king of Larsa (1822–1763), annexed the kingdoms of Uruk and Isin, but was finally defeated by Hammurabi.

Lipit-Eštar King of Isin (1936–1926). The Laws of Lipit-Eštar, written in Sumerian, are attributed to him.

Lu-Ninurta (Awil-Ninurta) A high-ranking Babylonian nobleman who was a close companion of Hammurabi. It was he who wrote the large number of letters to Šamaš-hazir.

Malgium Town situated on the ancient course of the Tigris above Maškan-šapir. It had often attracted the attention of others but was finally conquered by Hammurabi in 1759. The exact location of the place is not known.

Mankisum (perhaps Tell Kurr) Town on the middle reaches of the Tigris. Control of the town was a matter of dispute between the kingdoms of Ekallatum, Ešnunna and Babylon.

Marad (Tell Wanna wa Ûadūum) Town to the south of Babylon where the god Lugal-Marad was venerated.

Marduk Principal god of Babylon, whose temple was called Esagil, meaning 'temple of the lofty peak'.

Mari (Tell Hariri) Town situated about 15 kilometres on the Syrian side of the present border with Iraq. During early excavations at the palace there led by André Parrot (1933–1939), a large archive of approximately 20,000 tablets was discovered. It is this archive, more than any other, that has provided us with information of detailed historical events in the time of Hammurabi.

Maškan-šapir (Tell Abu Duwari) Town situated on the ancient course of the Tigris where Nergal was venerated. Under Rim-Sin it was the principal town in the north of the kingdom of Larsa. It was captured by Hammurabi to open the way for his assault on the capital city, Larsa.

Me-Turan (Tell Haddad and Tell es-Sib) Town halfway along the Diyala valley belonging to the kingdom of Ešnunna. The construction of a dam meant that this double tell had to be flooded, and the Department of Antiquities of Iraq made it the subject of a rescue archaeological operation from 1977–84. One house in the town must have belonged to an exorcist, as an exorcist's library was found there.

mina See shekel.

mîšarum	A decree proclaimed by the king to restore a balance in economic and social affairs. The proclamation of *mîšarum* would normally be made on the king's accession and possibly also later in his reign. The most complete text of a proclamation we have is that made by Ammi-ṣaduqa, the main point of which is an amnesty for debts, both those owed to the palace and any not yet paid that had been incurred to ensure a person's livelihood.
muškênum	An ordinary subject of the king, of a lower social status than *awîlum* but higher than *wardum*.
Mutiabal	Name of the tribe inhabiting the region of Kazallu.
Mutu-Numaha	Younger son of Hammurabi. He was sent as a Babylonian prince to spend some time at Mari.
nadîtum	A woman who had been consecrated to the principal deity of a town and who was prohibited from having children. We know more about those who were consecrated to Šamaš at Sippar and whom lived in the *gagûm*, a secluded area usually translated as 'cloister'.
nawûm	The Babylonian term for the land frequented by nomads, as well as for the nomadic groups to be found there, and also for their flocks which they pastured there.
Nabu	Son of Marduk and the protective deity of scribes, whose principle temple was at Borsippa.
Nahur	Important town in the Habur triangle which has not yet been located.
Nanna	Sumerian moon-god who was principally associated with the town of Ur. Akkadians venerated the same moon-god under the name of Sin.
Naram-Sin	King of Agade (*c.* 2254–2218), who became the subject of historical legends which began to be put into writing in the Old Babylonian period. He is to be distinguished from a king of Ešnunna in the nineteenth century who had the same name.
Nergal	God of the underworld who was also known as Erra. His principal temples are at Kutha and Maškanšapir.
Nineveh	Town situated on the left bank of the Tigris opposite modern Mosul. An important cult of Eštar was based there.
Nintu	See Belet-ili.
Ninurta	God associated with warfare. He was the protector of Nippur and his principal temple had been built there.

Nippur (Nuffar)	Sumerian town where the temple of Enlil had been built.
Old Babylonian	Four centuries covering the period 2002–1595, from the collapse of the dynasty of Ur to the death of Samsu-ditana, the last king of the First Babylonian Dynasty. Old Babylonian is the name used to refer to the language recorded on documents from this period.
Palmyra	See Tadmor.
Qabra	Town situated in the valley of the Little Zab to the east of Assur. Samsi-Addu and Daduša launched a joint campaign and captured it in 1780.
Qarni-Lim	King of Andarig (*c.* 1775–1765).
Qaṭna (Mishrife)	Town in Central Syria close to Homs, which was the capital of the kingdom of Qaṭna. The kings there that were contemporary with Hammurabi were Išhi-Addu and Amud-pi-El.
Qaṭṭara (Tell al-Rimah)	Town on the south-east of the Jebel Sinjar excavated by a team from Britain (1964–1971). Several sets of archives were recovered there, including around 200 tablets in the palace from the time of Hammurabi. The mound has also been identified with ancient Karana, but identifying it with Qaṭṭara is more plausible.
Rapiqum	Town on the middle Euphrates between Hit and Sippar. It became involved in several confrontations between Babylon, Ešnunna and the kingdom of Upper Mesopotamia.
Razama	Town to the north-east of the Jebel Sinjar. In 1765 it was besieged by troops from Elam and Ešnunna led by Atamrum.
rêdûm	A Babylonian word literally meaning 'follower'. The original task of a *rêdûm* was to act as an escort, somewhat similar to a duty sometimes assigned to today's policemen. In time he became used more as an infantryman.
Rim-Sin	King of Larsa (1822–1763), who enjoyed considerable military success in the earlier part of his long reign, annexing the kingdoms of Uruk (1803) and Isin (1794). Less is known about the later period, but it ended when Hammurabi annexed Larsa (1763).
Samsi-Addu	Founder of the vast kingdom of Upper Mesopotamia, after he had managed to conquer first Ekallatum and then Assur on the Tigris. He almost certainly originally came from the region of Agade. Towards the end of his reign he placed his two sons on two thrones; Išme-

	Dagan at Ekallatum and Yasmah-Addu at Mari. He died in 1775.
Samsu-iluna	King of Babylon for 38 years (1749–1712), son and successor to Hammurabi. He was unable to maintain control of all the territory his father had passed on to him and parts of it seceded in phases. In 1738 he lost the south of Sumer (the regions of Ur, Uruk and Larsa), and in 1719 he lost the centre (the regions of Nippur and Isin). To maintain Babylonian control consistently over the area of the Middle Euphrates (from Mari to Tuttul) was also too much for him.
Sargon	King of Agade (c. 2334–2279). Some of his legendary accomplishments were put into writing in the Old Babylonian period.
shekel	A unit of weight approximately equal to 8 grams; 60 shekels (480 grams) equal 1 mina; 60 minas equal 1 talent (just under 30 kilograms).
Sin	Akkadian name for the Sumerian god Nanna.
Sin-bel-aplim	Court official of Hammurabi in control of foreign diplomatic relations.
Sin-iddinam	The secretary of Hammurabi at the time war broke out with Elam. It is possible that he is the same person who was appointed to be governor of the Lower Region of Larsa after that kingdom had been annexed by Hammurabi.
Sin-kašid	Benjaminite king who founded a dynasty at Uruk around 1865 and built a palace there. After he had concluded an alliance with Sumu-la-El, the king of Babylon gave him one of his daughters in marriage.
Sin-muballiṭ	King of Babylon (1812–1793), father of Hammurabi.
Sippar-Amanum (Tell ed-Der)	Town, sometimes known as Greater Sippar, where Annunitum was the chief deity. It was situated on one of the ancient tributaries of the Euphrates, about seven kilometres from Sippar-Yahrurum. Both towns are often called simply Sippar.
Sippar-Yahrurum (Abu Habbah)	Town situated on one of the ancient tributaries of the Euphrates. It was often simply called Sippar, like Sippar-Amanun, which was only about seven kilometres away. Šamaš was the chief deity of the town.
Suhum	Area on the middle reaches of the Euphrates downstream from Mari. Hanat was the chief town of the Upper

	Region, the region higher upstream, and Yabliya the chief town of the Lower Region. It was an area where conflicts frequently erupted with Mari, Babylon and Ešnunna.
sukkal-mah	Official Sumerian title for the emperor of Elam at the beginning of the second millennium, which is often abbreviated to *sukkal*.
Sumer	The ancient name of the territory of Southern Mesopotamia. When that territory had been united politically with Central Mesopotamia, with Nippur as its centre, the kings were known as kings 'of Sumer and Akkad'.
Sumerian	Earliest language attested in cuneiform. The language has an agglutinative structure with a marked tendency towards monosyllabic elements. It is a language which is not with any certainty affiliated to any other. Towards the end of the third millennium it ceased to be used as a spoken language but continued in use for writing scholarly and religious texts as long as there were scribes who maintained the tradition of writing cuneiform.
Sumu-abum	Traditional founder (1894–1881) of the First Dynasty of Babylon, according to the later lists of kings. In fact he was a powerful Amorite nomad chief who was a contemporary of Sumu-la-El, but he never took up residence in Babylon.
Sumu-ditana	The eldest son of Hammurabi. As a prince of Babylon he was sent to spend some time in the kingdom of Mari.
Sumu-Epuh	Founder of the Amorite dynasty at Aleppo in the nineteenth century. He died in 1778.
Sumu-la-El	King of Babylon (1880–1845) and the actual founder of the First Dynasty of Babylon (see Sumu-abum). It was he who built the palace which came to be occupied by Hammurabi. He eventually annexed the smaller kingdoms surrounding Babylon, such as Sippar, Kiš and Marad.
Susa	Capital of the region in south-western Iran now known as Khuzistan. The sovereign was generally affiliated to a side-branch of the ruling dynasty at Anšan. In the twelfth century an Elamite sovereign deposited booty there, plundered from Babylonia, which included the stele on which the Code of Hammurabi is inscribed.
Suteans	Nomads who controlled the routes in the Syrian Desert from west of the Euphrates over the steppe.

Ṣilli-Sin	King of Ešnunna (1763–1762). He had simply been the head of a section of the army at Ešnunna but, once the Elamites had been repelled, he took the throne. He entered into an alliance with Hammurabi, who gave him one of his daughters to marry. The alliance was shortlived and Ṣilli-Sin was defeated in 1762.
Ṣiwapalarhuhpak	Emperor (*sukkal*) of Elam. His name must have sounded particularly complicated to the ears of Semitic-speaking people, for more than one scribe at Mari records it as Šeplarpak.
Šaduppum (Tell Harmal)	Small town belonging to the kingdom of Ešnunna, situated in the suburbs of modern Baghdad. Excavations by Iraqi archaeologists began there in 1945 and have yielded many documents from the Old Babylonian period, including letters and administrative and school texts. Two copies of the Laws of Ešnunna attributed to Daduša were also found there.
Šamaš	God of the sun and controller of justice and divination. His two main sanctuaries, each known as Ebabbar, were at Larsa and Sippar.
Šamaš-hazir	Manager of the administration of the royal domain in the region of Larsa after 1763. The stream of letters he received from Hammurabi and Lu-Ninurta provide important insights into social affairs and economic matters in Larsa after it had been annexed.
Šehna	An alternative name for Šubat-Enlil.
Šerda	Goddess, wife of Adad.
Šibtu	Daughter of Yarim Lim, king of Aleppo. He gave her to Zimri-Lim, king of Mari, as a wife.
Šitullum	Town on the Tigris, at the southern end of the kingdom of Ekallatum, perhaps near Tikrit.
Šubartum	Region in northern Iraq which became the focal point for several campaigns by Hammurabi towards the end of his reign.
Šubat-Enlil (Tell Leilan)	Town situated in the centre of the Habur triangle. Samsi-Addu used this name for the town of Šehna, when he selected it to be his principal residence at the end of his reign. But it fell victim to the assaults of many attackers, including some from Ešnunna and some from Elam, and in 1728 it was destroyed by Samsu-iluna.

šukallum	A palace official who was in very close contact with the king. The term is sometimes translated as 'vizier' or 'first minister'.
Šušarra (Tell Shemshara)	Town in the upper valley of the Little Zab. In the late 1950s Danish and Iraqi archaeologists worked there, and some 200 tablets were found in the archives dating from the time that Samsi-Addu incorporated it into the kingdom of Upper Mesopotamia. The town was destroyed in 1779.
Tadmor	Town in the Syrian desert, better known by its Classical name, Palmyra, but which has kept its ancient name in Arabic. It was frequented by Suteans in the Old Babylonian period.
talent	See shekel.
tamkârum	The Babylonian word for a merchant. Merchants were grouped into a kind of guild supervised by the head *tamkârum*, who was a dependant of the king.
Tašmetum	Goddess, wife of Nabu.
terhatum	A payment made by the family of the husband-to-be to the father of his bride-to-be.
Terqa (Tell Ashara)	Town on the Middle Euphrates about 70 kilometres upstream from Mari. It was a very important provincial centre for the kingdom of Mari and the site of an important temple of Dagan.
Tilmun	An exotic location referred to in Mesopotamian literature. It is located in the Arab-Persian Gulf and in the Old Babylonian period is to be identified with Bahrain. Maritime trade was being regularly conducted between Tilmun and the merchants of Ur.
Tur Abdin	A peak in the eastern projection of the Taurus Mountains where the sources of the tributaries of the Habur can be found.
Turukkeans	A semi-nomadic people coming from the Zagros who used to make terrifying raids against the settled population. Some of them were deported to Babylonia at the end of the Hammurabi's campaign in 1757.
Tuttul (Tell Bi'a)	Town situated at the confluence of the Balih with the Euphrates. A German archaeological team excavated the site (1980–1997) and they discovered a palace of Yasmah-Addu, king of Mari, with an archive of 300 tablets.
Ṭab-eli-matim	High-ranking official in the court of Hammurabi, probably functioning as the 'overseer of the barbers'.

Ugarit (Ras Shamra)   Town on the eastern coast of the Mediterranean, just north of the modern port of Lattakia, Syria. It was occupied as long ago as the sixth millennium but the excavations there, which have been being conducted since 1929, have essentially concentrated on material from the fourteenth and thirteenth centuries. In 1765 Zimri-Lim, king of Mari, is said to have stayed there for more than a month.

Upi   Normally identified with Opis of Classical literature, a riverside town on the Tigris, but still without any certain location. In the time of Apil-Sin it was attached to Babylonia but then became part of Ešnunna. Hammurabi devoted much effort to seeing it reconquered.

Ur (Tell Muqayyar)   Town in southern Iraq. It had been an important capital until the collapse of the Third Dynasty of Ur, but it was later able to remain significant as a port on the Gulf and as a religious centre. The principal deity venerated there was Nanna (Sin) in the temple Ekišnugal. The Third Dynasty of Ur was founded by Ur-Nammu in 2110 and lasted for just over a century until 2002. The five kings of the dynasty had managed to accumulate a vast territory under their control, even more extensive than that of Sumer, and they established a remarkably impressive system of central planning for maintaining an efficient administration.

Urbilum (Arbele)   Capital city of a kingdom located in modern Iraqi Kurdistan.

Ur-Nammu   King of Ur (2110–2093), founder of the Third Dynasty of Ur. A code of laws written in Sumerian is attributed to him.

Uruk (Warka)   Town in Sumer. In about 1865 Sin-kašid founded an independent dynasty there, which lasted until it was brought to an end by Rim-Sin in 1803.

wardum   The Babylonian term for a servant, someone of a lower social class. The word is also used to refer to a servant of the king, who would have been a high official at court.

Yabliya (Tell Jodefiyeh and Shishin)   Principal town of Lower Suhum.

Yagid-Lim   Father of Yahdun-Lim and grandfather of Zimri-Lim, kings of Mari.

Yahdun-Lim   King of Mari (*c.* 1810–*c.* 1794). Although he is recorded as being the father of Zimri-Lim he is more likely to have been his uncle or his grandfather.

Yamhad   A kingdom with its capital at Aleppo.

Yamut-Bal	See Emutbalum.
Yarim-Addu	Envoy sent by Zimri-Lim to Hammurabi of Babylon at the time of the war with Elam. He sent numerous reports back to the king of Mari about the situation as it developed.
Yarim-Lim	King of Aleppo (1778–1765).
Yasmah-Addu	King of Mari (about 1792–1775), son of Samsi-Addu. It was in his reign that the kingdom of Mari was integrated into the kingdom of Upper Mesopotamia.
year name	A significant event that occurred in a year was used as the name for the next year. It was a convenient way of dating documents, where an abbreviated form of the official year name is often found. In the Old Babylonian period these names were generally written in Sumerian, but in Mari they were written in Akkadian.
Zababa	Warrior god, protector of the town of Kiš.
Zabala (Tell Ibzaykh)	Town close to Larsa where Inanna was venerated.
Zalmaqum	Region of the upper valley of the Balih. Harran was the capital of one of the four kingdoms of Zalmaqum.
Zarpanitum	Goddess, wife of Marduk.
ziggurat	The principal religious sanctuary in a Babylonian town, constructed as a stepped tower. The ziggurat at Babylon was known in Sumerian as Etemenanki and was located next to Esagil, the temple of Marduk.
Zimri-Lim	Last king of Mari (1774–1761). He is presented as the son of Yahdun-Lim and, like him, as belonging to the tribe of Bensim'al. When the kingdom of Mari was annexed by Samsi-Addu he went into exile, but with help from Aleppo he came back to reconquer it in 1775. Because of the importance of the town of Hit, which he very much wanted to keep, there were years of tension between him and Hammurabi about fixing the border between Mari and Babylon. In 1764 he joined forces with Hammurabi to repel the invading Elamites and also sent troops to help him in the battle for Larsa in 1763. His archives recovered from the palace of Mari are one of our richest sources of information for reconstructing the events of the reign of Hammurabi. There is no mention of him after 1761.

Preface

It was the chance discovery of a stele, now commonly known as the 'Code of Hammurabi', by French archaeologists working at Susa (a site in southwestern Iran) at the beginning of the twentieth century that has enabled the name of King Hammurabi to be known by the public at large. Very few other names of figures from pre-Classical history could be cited so widely. Since that discovery, the stele has been conserved in Paris at the Louvre. To mark the centenary of its discovery and of the publication of the text of the Code by Father Vincent Scheil, a new exhibition room was inaugurated in the Louvre, offering visitors an opportunity to view and appreciate this famous object.

That the contributions Hammurabi made to ancient history were important is indicated by the length of his reign, which lasted from 1792–1750 BC, a total of 43 years. What is a little curious is that there is no book in French, the title of which indicates a description of the life and times of this prestigious sovereign of Mesopotamia. The present work seeks to fill this vacuum. However, honesty compels me to warn the reader that even now the state of our sources is still limited and so it is not possible to write a proper biography of Hammurabi. More and more details of his involvement in the international politics of the day are being discovered through specialist research. Reports sent from Babylon by foreign ambassadors describe certain aspects of his personality in a most striking way, but his private life remains almost completely inaccessible.

We do not intend to use Hammurabi here as a pretext for painting a complete picture of Mesopotamian civilisation in the first half of the second millennium BC. Rather, we shall seek first to review the decisive moments of political history in the Near East during his reign in the first half of the eighteenth century. Then we shall pay attention to those aspects of Babylonian civilisation adopted by the king which help to explain Hammurabi's actions, not just in the sphere of politics but also in his juridical, social and economic activities. For this we shall use frequent citations from government documents, and in particular from official correspondence found in the palace of Mari, a site in the east of Syria. French-speaking scholars have been publishing a great number of these texts over the last few years, but the material has generally been restricted to a rather narrow group of specialised research workers. Important citations from documents kept in the British Museum in London, including recently published documents and some letters from King Hammurabi himself, will also be used. Because of uncertainties and complexities in the original documents, there was never any question of 'letting the texts speak for themselves', so our primary desire has been to make the reader aware of the exceptional richness of the documentation now at our disposal.

In a book about Charlemagne a reader does not expect to be told about the status of the Pope, or to be given a definition of the Byzantine Empire, or to be told where to find Aix-la-Chapelle on a map. But facts like these do need to be explained for someone wanting to begin to learn about the life and times of Hammurabi. To assist readers, therefore, a glossary has been provided which gives a brief definition of the most important names and technical terms cited in this book.

In conclusion I wish to thank those who have enabled the publication of this work to be completed. Over the years in my work I have had an amicable and trusting relationship with Jean-Marie Durand, who has entrusted me with the publication of many previously unpublished documents from the archives of Mari concerning the history of Babylon under Hammurabi. Thanks are also due for various reasons to those who have read my work before publication, in particular to my wife, Nele Ziegler, herself an Assyriologist, and to my father, Bruno Charpin, who was happy to play the role of the frank listener. Christine Kepinski-Lecomte allowed me to reproduce some of her photographs, which she took during her excavations in Iraq. And I do not forget my students in the Sorbonne, who indirectly contributed to this project by attending my lectures and taking part in my seminars.

I am not so insensitive as to finish this preface without referring to the suffering that the people of Iraq have endured in recent years and in an even more crucial way as time moves on. I had the good fortune to discover the country almost 30 years ago, and now to see it so ravaged is a source of great bitterness to me. Perhaps all we can do is hope for the speedy return of better days which will be worthy of the prestigious history of this land to which our own Western culture owes so much.

Francueil, France

Abbreviations

This list gives fuller bibliographical information for explanatory material, secondary references and sources of citations, for which an abbreviated format has been used.

AbB	*Altbabylonische Briefe* (Leiden, 1964–2005). 14 vols., proceeding
ARM	*Archives royales de Mari* (Paris, 1950–2009). 30 vols., proceeding
CDOG 2	D. Charpin, 'Ḫammu-rabi de Babylone et Mari: nouvelles sources, nouvelles perspectives' in J. Renger (ed.), *Babylon: Focus mesopotamischer Geschichte, Wiege früher Gelehrsamkeit, Mythos in der Moderne*, pp. 111–130 (Colloquen der Deutschen Orient-Gesellschaft 2. Sarrbrücken, 1999)
CT	*Cuneiform Texts* (British Museum, London). 58 vols.
CTN IV	D.J. Wiseman and J.A. Black, *Literary Texts from the Temple of Nabû* (Cuneiform Texts from Nimrud IV. London, 1996)
FM	Florilegium marianum (Paris, 1992–2011): 12 vols., proceeding
LAPO 16-18	J.-M. Durand, *Documents épistolaires du palais de Mari* (Littératures du Proche Orient 16–18. Paris, 1997–2000)
'Lettres et procès'	D. Charpin, 'Lettres et procès paléo-babyloniens' in F. Joannès (ed.) *Rendre la justice en Mésopotamie*, pp. 69–111 (Paris, 2000)
MARI	Mari. Annales de recherches interdisciplinaires (Paris, 1982–1997). 8 vols.
RA	*Revue d'assyriologie et d'archéologie orientale.*
RIME 4	D.R. Frayne, *Old Babylonian Period: 2003-1595 BC* (Royal Inscriptions of Mesopotamia: Early Periods 4. Toronto, 1990)
VS 17	J.J. van Dijk, *Nicht-kanonische Beschwörungen und sonstige literarische Texte* (Vorderasiatische Schriftdenkmäler 17. Berlin, 1971)

Dates

Except when reference is being made to modern studies, dates should usually be understood as BC.

Transcription of names

Assyriologists are accustomed to a system of transliteration for the phonetic transcription of Semitic names into Roman script. Here it has been partially simplified, and the following is an approximate guide to pronunciation:

g is hard, as in *gutter.*
ū as *oo*, in *boot.*
š as *sh*, as in *shoot.*
ṣ as *ts*, as in *shoots.*
ṭ more emphatic than *t*, compare *tt* in *shutter* with *t* in *shooter.*

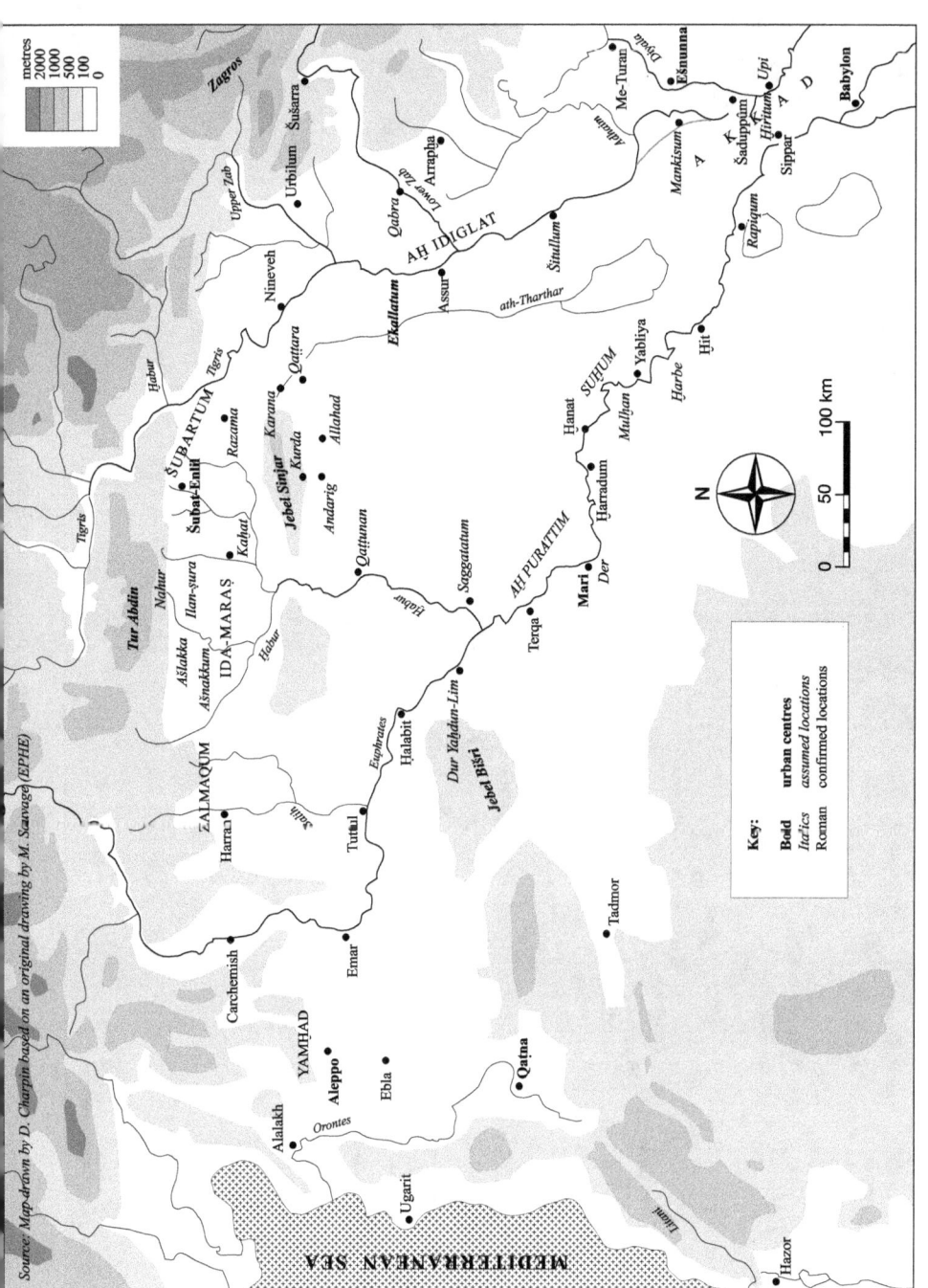

Map A Upper Mesopotamia in the time of Hammurabi

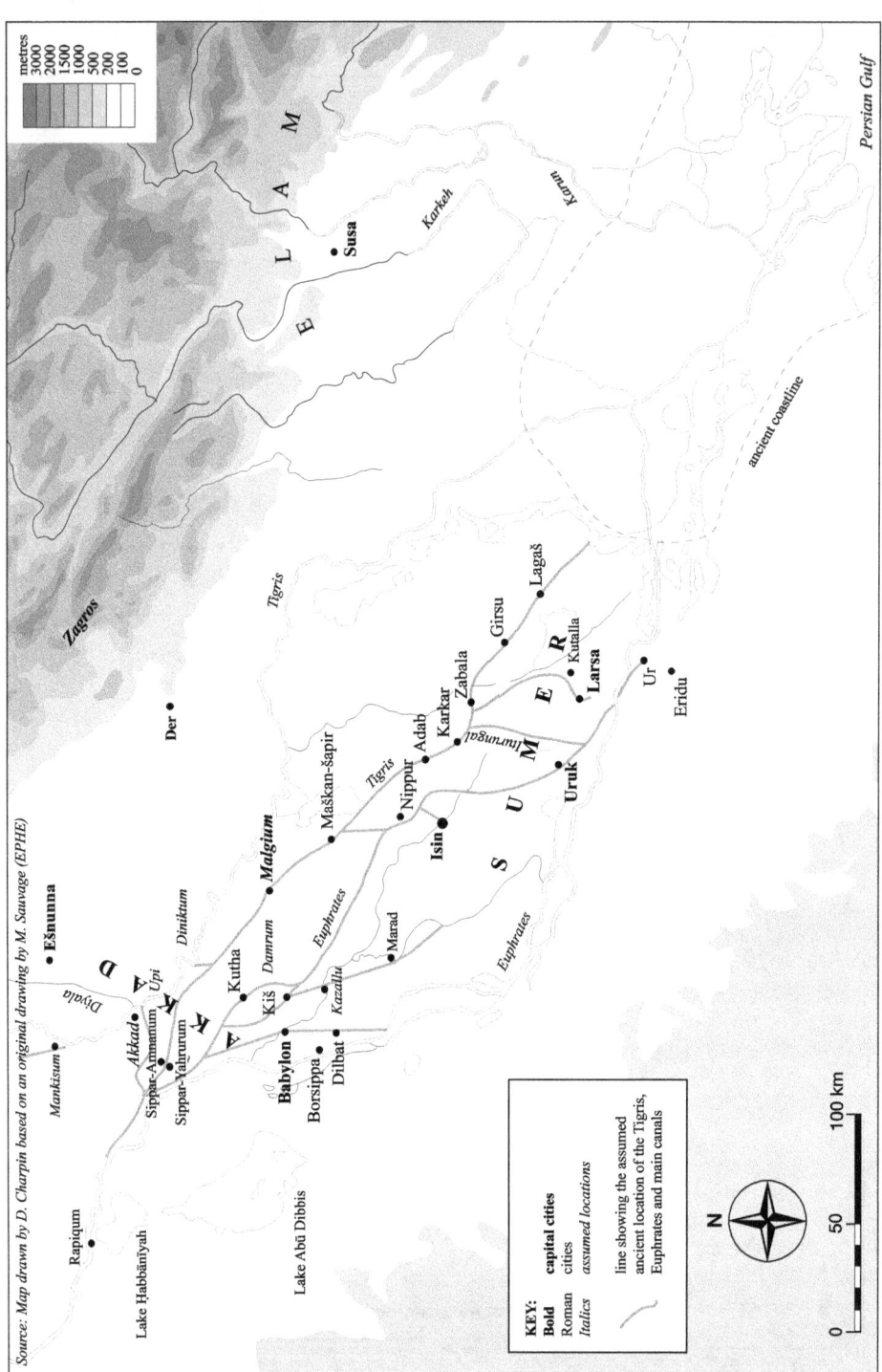

Map B Lower Mesopotamia in the time of Hammurabi

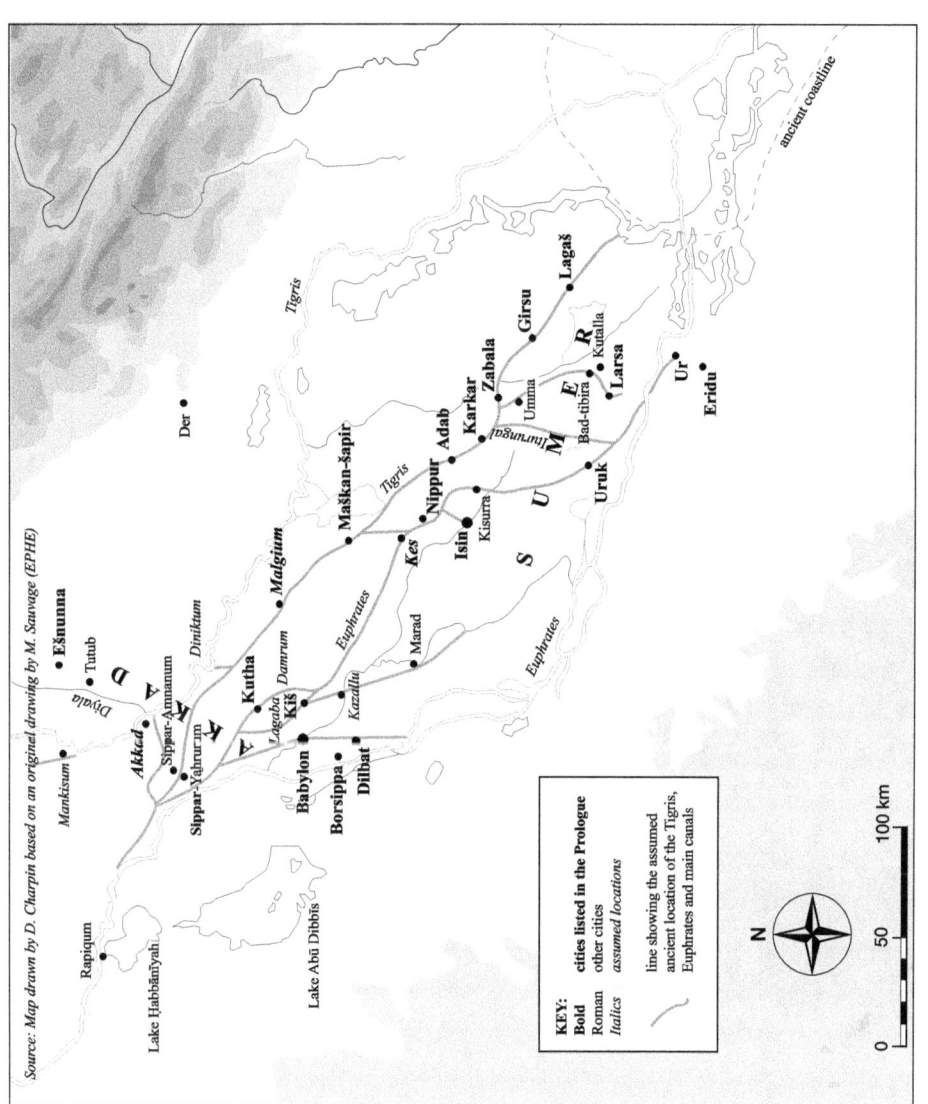

Map C Towns named in the Prologue to the Code of Hammurabi

Part 1

The Conqueror

The long reign of Hammurabi, some 43 years, saw a profound transformation in the Babylon that his father had bequeathed to him. From a mediocre power, land-locked in a Near East dominated by a few superpowers, Hammurabi created a kingdom, exerting supremacy over the whole of Mesopotamia. Now a new synthesis of this history can be attempted, based on the considerable influx of new information which has been published in the last 20 years and which derives in particular from the very rich archives of Mari.

His reign can be divided into four phases. Insofar as concerns the kingdom of Babylon the first 18 years are still rather poorly known. They seem obscured under the shadow of the vast kingdom which covered the whole of the north of Mesopotamia, from the middle reaches of the Tigris to the middle reaches of the Euphrates, created by the great Samsi-Addu of Ekallatum. The second phase opened up with the death of Samsi-Addu (1775), when there was an attempt by the king of Ešnunna to reclaim his heritage. He failed in this attempt and Hammurabi, fighting together with the emperor of Elam and the troops from Mari, contributed to his downfall. But once the Elamites had annexed Ešnunna, they wanted Babylon to submit as well, but Hammurabi, with the support of his Syrian allies, managed to repulse them in 1764. What followed was a brief but successful phase of his reign in which Hammurabi launched political offensives in all directions. It culminated in the capture of Larsa in 1763, and then in 1761 of Mari, which was destroyed several months later. The final ten years of his reign was a period of consolidation of his previous conquests.

INTRODUCTION

The Relationship between the Historian and the Sources

To place him in a wider historical context, Hammurabi compelled the world of his time to recognise Babylon as a superpower in the Near East. But to appreciate this fact it is important to present the sources which have made it possible to reconstruct the events of this period. The traditional aim of historical research has been to narrate the past as elegantly as possible. Any allusions to the documentary sections of the dossier compiled by the researcher have had to be unobtrusive. But in recent years a more clinical and frank approach has become acceptable, in which it has become obligatory for the historian to show readers the documentation available. However skilfully an investigation may be conducted, it may suffer from the inevitable limitations imposed by the documentation, particularly when we are dealing with material from so long ago. The art of good scholarship lies in being able to surmount these obstacles, while openly acknowledging their existence. These problems are primarily associated with the significance of writing within the social and cultural practices of a given period, but also with the risks involved in the conservation process itself.

The Nature of the Sources

All the sources available for writing a history of the reign of Hammurabi are a result of the efforts of archaeologists, which is also true for writing any general history of Mesopotamia. The discovery of primary material has the great advantage of being unlikely to be as biased as a later, traditional narration of events would have been. But even though we now have access to contemporary epigraphical material, original texts written on materials such as stone, metal and especially clay, interpreting them presents a plethora of obstacles. The Mesopotamian documents about Hammurabi at our disposal can in general be described as basic, for we have no narrative history or more sophisticated description of events. There is no ancient biographer or even a chronicler of his reign. No-one undertook to string together isolated occurrences into a progressive story. For that matter, neither do we have any comprehensive description of the institutions of ancient Babylon. There is no Babylonian counterpart to Thucydides or Titus Livy. We have to imagine trying to reconstruct the development of the institutions of ancient Greece just from the surviving decrees, without any recourse to the Constitutions collected by Aristotle and his pupils. Mesopotamian archaeologists have to survive with no traveller and geographer such as Pausanias (second century AD) as their guide. They have no narrative of an itinerary offering a description of visits to sites. It is as though they had to solve a giant jigsaw puzzle unsure of the overall picture or whether they had the right number of pieces.

A historian of Classical Antiquity is accustomed to categorising sources as epigraphical documents or literary texts. These literary texts were repeatedly copied, from the period of Late Antiquity until the end of the Middle Ages, sometimes through the intermediation of Byzantine and Arab sources, and particularly through the efforts of those working in the *scriptoria* of Western monasteries. At long last they appeared in print through skills acquired from the technical advances of the Renaissance. But, as for texts of the pre-Classical period from the ancient Near East, it is only the Bible that has been the object of such an unbroken tradition.

The difficulties associated with dealing with epigraphical material should not be overlooked. The researcher is always at the mercy of whatever the excavator happens to find, and experience has shown that archaeological discoveries are most often achieved not by rational planning, but by a succession of fortunate coincidences. André Parrot, for example, began excavating the palace of Mari (Tell Hariri) in Syria, not very far from the border with Iraq, in 1933. But it was bedouin, who happened to unearth an ancient statue while digging a family grave, that led him to start work there. The discovery of the archives that came from his excavations there have provided an abundance of information about the life and times of Hammurabi. On more than one occasion a government's decision to construct a dam was the impetus for an archaeological rescue dig. It was better to recover at least something of what was concealed on a site before allowing it to be submerged forever. Of course there have been excavations that have been undertaken with advance planning and are properly programmed, but they are rare by comparison. One such excavation was the remarkable investigation of the Diyala valley, to the east of Baghdad, undertaken by Americans in the interwar years. Instead of just concentrating on Ešnunna (Tell Asmar), the main town of the region, they were able to establish what was happening in the whole region.

Sometimes the first results of a dig seem to have been clearly inadequate from some perspectives, but the discovery and publication of new texts can help to correct some deficiencies. The archives from the palace of Mari have enabled us to fill in a great many details of the middle years of the reign of Hammurabi of Babylon, the years coinciding with those of the last sovereign of Mari, Zimri-Lim (1775–1762). But unfortunately we have no similar material with which to reconstruct precise details of the events at the beginning of his reign. It is also important to remember that we can place these Mari documents into a particular archaeological context, which is not always the case. It is never without significance to know the different literary genres found at one particular location. What is most deplorable is that clandestine digging has had such a ravaging effect and has so often has robbed us of crucial information. Documents frequently arrive on the market deprived of their archaeological context and even of details about the site where they were found. They are then randomly scattered all over the world to be incorporated into private and public collections. This illicit activity still continues apace, and whatever the legal and moral questions it raises we must highlight the fact that it produces an irreparable loss of information.

The archival documents on which we rely for our information frequently have the drawback of being terse in style. In sale contracts there is never any statement to say why some patch of ground is being sold or the purpose for which the purchaser is acquiring it. Letters provide us with much information and, although they are less stereotyped, they are sometimes very difficult to understand. Background details are not always explicitly stated, for these were perfectly well known to sender and addressee alike. All too often the allusions in them give only a vague idea of what is implied.

The normal way in which Babylonians wrote to one another was to use the cuneiform script imprinted on a clay tablet. Clay had the advantage of being easily accessible, even though it took some time while it was carefully worked, cleaned, shaped and made ready for writing. The written document was put out in the sun to dry and to make it durable. There are certainly considerable advantages in such a durable medium, not all of which could have been foreseen when it was being used. An outbreak of fire, provided it is not too violent, serves to increase its durability, and flood water does not cause lasting damage. A tablet discovered in damp surroundings can be put out to dry immediately after it is excavated and the information recorded on it is preserved. Hardly any other medium in the history of writing has been so tough and so cheap, but a clay tablet is not very versatile and poses some restrictions in communication. A correct estimate had to be made for size when shaping the tablet so that the text to be inscribed would fit. This must have been particularly difficult for a scribe to whom a letter was being dictated. Any correction could be made only at the time of writing, while the clay was moist, and once it had dried no changes would have been possible. When a document became obsolete it was easily recycled by soaking the hardened clay and kneading it again into shape. We are probably often dealing with archives written on recycled clay. Usually the tablets that were kept in an archive date only to the period immediately before the building in which they were stored was destroyed, and all earlier documents have become lost. But, fortunately for the historian, obsolete texts were sometimes thrown away, and often a very useful archive can be reconstituted from discarded tablets which were used by ancient builders as filling during renovation work. A high level of archaeological and epigraphic expertise is required to recover and process such material.

The script in which Akkadian was written consists of a series of wedge-shaped signs. It is known as 'cuneiform', a name derived from the Latin word *cuneus* ('wedge'). The signs were impressed upon the surface of a clay tablet with a stylus made from a reed. Differently angled wedges were combined to form specific signs. The script was probably invented for writing Sumerian and the earliest evidence for it can be dated to the end of the fourth millennium. Sumerian does not seem to be related to any other known written language and died out as a spoken language towards the end of the third millennium. But for more than 2,000 years it was used in religious and scholarly circles. It must have had a status similar to that of Latin in Western mediaeval and modern civilisation.

By stages, from the second half of the third millennium onwards, Akkadian, a member of the large family of Semitic languages, the best known of which are Hebrew and Arabic, replaced Sumerian. From around 2,000, two branches

Fig. 1 When a new floor of pounded earth was being laid in the temple of Šamaš at Larsa (Tell Senkereh) tablets dating from the time of Hammurabi were used as material for ballast. Here they are being delicately excavated.

of the language can be distinguished, Assyrian in the north and Babylonian in the south. When writing Akkadian, two different techniques are combined. Some cuneiform signs function as whole words, the 'ideograms', and others indicate just a syllable of a word, the 'syllabograms'. This leads to a measure of superfluity, and it has been calculated that the language could have been adequately written with about 80 syllabograms. Old Babylonian documents use about 120 signs. Disregarding very rare signs, there are about 50 ideograms that occur with varying frequency according to the genre of text being written. Obviously it was not the easiest script to learn, but it would be easy for those of us used to the alphabet to exaggerate this difficulty. Several members of the ruling class could read and write, but they would normally have had professional scribes in their service, who unavoidably act as a screen, intermediaries for the modern historian of their versions of ancient events. They reveal only as much information as they have filtered out, and when reading their versions this aspect of their writing should not be forgotten.

The invasions of the Amorites began in about 2000 and from then onwards there were significant modifications to the population of central and southern Mesopotamia. Although as yet we have no single text in Amorite, the extent of their influence can be seen from the frequent attestation of people with Amorite personal names. In the regions to the north and north-east of Mesopotamia Hurrian was spoken, and we find a number of Hurrian names as well as a letter and some incantations written in Hurrian in this period.

More often than not a cuneiform document is discovered as a clay tablet in a poor state of preservation. It cannot be published until much meticulous work has been done by a trained epigraphist on the unclear traces of the signs. Usually supplementary information has to be adduced from elsewhere for this task to reach a satisfactory conclusion. If the tablet has been broken, piecing together the fragments that remain can be a frustrating puzzle in itself and any attempt to restore the text of lacunae is fraught with uncertainty. But even when a satisfactory text has been established, the translator faces other kinds of problems. Despite the wide range of Akkadian literature now at our disposal, a newly discovered text will often contain rare words which raise philological problems. It is not unusual for the meaning of such words to remain imprecise or doubtful. Over the course of time documents will need to be re-edited, not only because subsequent closer examinations of the tablets, usually referred to as 'collations', establish better readings, but also because proposals for corrections to the original publication and a revised translation arise from the later discovery of related documents. For example, there were about 1,300 letters from the royal archives of Mari published between 1936 and 1993, but now, thanks to J.-M. Durand, new translations of them with commentaries are available.[1]

While it is clear that a historian of Ancient Babylonia needs to become competent in both epigraphy and philology, we must also be aware that history cannot be properly written from documents alone, for there are other sources of information available which can and must be used. Many Assyriologists have developed the habit of referring to iconographic examples simply to illustrate an allusion in a text. They have left the language of iconography encrypted and not allowed the images to speak on their own terms. It is true that we do not have so many bas-reliefs, stelae or statues sculpted in the round but we do have a number of clay figurines and many cylinder seals, which together provide a wide range of iconographic material. Understanding the language of iconography is far from easy, as can be seen from the uncertain significance of the common motif of the ring and the rod in the hands of a god who is being addressed by the king. Other questions such as this still have to be answered adequately.

The monuments unearthed from archaeological excavations have an intrinsic importance for the historian who wishes to understand the civilisation of Ancient Mesopotamia. Without reference to the structure of a palace it would be impossible to reach a full understanding of the nature of royal power, but this involves more than an architectural description. To assign a date to the end of a known level of occupation is also possible with archaeological evidence of destruction and this can be important for understanding events about which the texts are silent. Archaeological surveys over a wider region are also important in this connection. Mapping the surface finds of pottery from all the recognisable sites in a particular area can produce a reasonably precise pattern of sedentary occupation. When the information gleaned in this way is combined with what can be deduced from texts we are able to establish the beginnings of a historical geography. This is how the location of some sites was fixed well before any excavation began there. Research based on regional surveys has also been able to identify ancient waterways, which were different from those of today. An important task of such research has been to trace the courses of the Tigris and the Euphrates in the second millennium BC.

Combining information from texts with that from non-written sources is far from easy, but if it should happen that different types of evidence complement one another, that is a particularly precious occasion for the historian. Usually references to events in texts cannot be observed from the archaeological record and, conversely, texts will be silent about objects and phenomena discovered by archaeology.

COMMEMORATIVE TEXTS

It is convenient to classify the texts available to us as commemorative, archival or pedagogic documents. Commemorative texts include royal inscriptions, laudatory hymns and lists of year names.

Year Names

The simplest way to identify a particular year was to count the years of a sovereign's reign, but no such system is attested in Babylon until the second half of the second millennium. Before that the custom was to identify each year by an event that had occurred in the preceding year. There are lists of successive year names that establish their relative order, and, fortunately for our purposes, for a long time we have known the names for all 43 years of the reign of Hammurabi. So while we do not know any precise dates we can be certain of the relative chronology of these events. In this book we have decided to use what is termed 'middle chronology' as the basis for specifying dates. This assumes that the Old Babylonian period lasted from approximately 2000 to 1600 BC, and that the reign of Hammurabi is to be dated in the middle of these four centuries, from 1792 to 1750.

The king was accustomed at the end of the year to meet with his advisers when events of the old year would be proposed as names for the new year. When a choice had been made a tablet announcing the name of the new year would be sent from the chancellery to the main towns of the provinces. Sometimes the name was so long that it was shortened for the purposes of everyday use. The name chosen might refer to some kind of activity that the king had undertaken in the past year, which might well be a military expedition, such as the one commemorated in the name for Hammurabi Year 32.

> The hero, who proclaims the triumphs of the god Marduk, by his mighty strength overcame in battle the army of Ešnunna, of Šubartum and of Gutium, and fought against Mankisum and the land along the banks of the Tigris as far as Šubartum.[2]

According to the middle chronology 'Hammurabi 32' equates to 1761, so we know that he won these battles in the preceding year, 1762. Year names are essential evidence for reconstructing events of such political and military significance. But it can happen that military victories are not necessarily commemorated in a year name and preference was given to formulating some other achievement. In other year names, large construction works judged by the king to have been significant, such as excavating canals and building temples, are commemorated, and there are also references to statues, valuable materials and precious objects given as offerings to the gods.

Royal Inscriptions

Hammurabi is the first sovereign of his dynasty for whom we have any royal inscriptions, but there are only about 20 of them, not very many in view of his long reign. Moreover, only three of them refer to military activity, so they are not especially instructive for reconstructing political history. The rest are concerned with his building activities to keep temples, town walls and fortresses in good order, or his excavation work on the canal system. They are not all in the same format. They were written on stelae, bricks, clay cones and stone tablets. Some were used as foundation deposits, with a message addressed to the gods that were venerated in the buildings in which the documents were placed. They can be seen as underlining the piety of the sovereign and his zeal to obey the instructions the gods had given him. They also served to leave a permanent written record of the king's achievements for his descendants after his death, so that one of them could refurbish his work and prevent his name from being forgotten whenever that was necessary. For him it meant that he was remembered for more than fourteen centuries after his death. He is still remembered even today, and this legacy will be considered later in the conclusion of this book. Eleven of the inscriptions of Hammurabi are written in Sumerian and six are in Akkadian. Three others are 'bilingual' but this is an imprecise use of the term, for we have a Sumerian version on the one hand and an Akkadian one on the other.

Two of the inscriptions were found at Babylon, but the clay tablets were fragmentary. In the first millennium a scribe copied one of them still to be seen in the temple of the gods Enlil and Ninurta and he deposited his copy in the temple of Nabu at Borsippa. It is that copy that has survived. Excavations at other towns, such as Sippar, Kiš and Borsippa, as well as at Larsa and Zabala in the old territory of Sumer, have produced other inscriptions. When we have a corresponding year name it is possible to date the events commemorated in the inscription. The bricks found at Kiš refer to the year we know as 'Hammurabi 36' for the restoration of the stepped tower, the *ziggurat* for the god Zababa.

Here we must mention the 'Code of Hammurabi', perhaps the most important of the commemorative inscriptions. The diorite stele is inscribed with a prologue, nearly 300 legal provisions and an epilogue, and this text will be discussed in Chapter 8. It has been kept in the Louvre ever since it was discovered in 1901–2 by a French archaeological expedition working at Susa, in modern Iran. Originally it was doubtlessly displayed in Sippar, but in the twelfth century, during a raid on that city by the Elamites, it was captured and removed to Susa. A fragment of a second monumental stele of Hammurabi, but in granite, was also found at Susa. Hammurabi probably gave instructions for this stele to be inscribed and erected after his victory over Larsa.

A partially legible impression of the royal seal of Hammurabi was found at Mari. It had been used to seal a package which would almost certainly have contained a gift from the king of Babylon 'for Zimri-Lim', as is written beside the seal impression.

Royal Hymns

Royal hymns are sometimes addressed to the gods and sometimes to the king. Those addressed to the gods conclude with an intercessory prayer for them to show favour to the king. Those praising the king allude to him in the second or third person, and occasionally in the first person. Fragments of bilingual inscriptions on basalt monuments from Ur and Kiš are ascriptions in praise of Hammurabi. We also have two clay tablets which contain copies of a bilingual hymn originally written on the lower part of a royal statue. There is a fragment of a hymn in Sumerian dedicated to Hammurabi which seems to be an acclamation addressed to the king on the occasion of a visit to the temple E-abzu, the temple at Eridu for the god Enki. A hymn written in Babylonian addressed to the goddess Belet-ili refers to an expedition against the region of Šubartu, apparently a military campaign undertaken by Hammurabi towards the end of his reign.

ARCHIVAL TEXTS

Juridical Texts

Excavations of palaces and temples as well as of simple houses have revealed archives of an official and a private nature. But whatever their nature, the texts can be classified as juridical, administrative or epistolary. Most of the juridical texts are in the form of contracts. Some contracts were issued for a particular circumstance on a particular occasion and had a limited validity. These include contracts for renting land or materials, for hiring workers and for loans. Once any obligation had been discharged at the time appointed for settlement, the document would normally have had to be destroyed. By chance some were kept and have been retrieved from excavations. They could well not have been discovered and form a tiny proportion of all the contracts that were actually drawn up. Other contracts are permanent, where no time limit was envisaged. Such documents had to be preserved from the day of enactment so that if there was any future disagreement they could be produced as legal proof. They refer to the transfer of goods and property to a person or to his estate, such as the sale of slaves and animals and of houses, fields and orchards. Contracts involving marriage or adoption give an idea of the practice of family law.

An agreement that results from a court case may also be regarded as a permanent contract. An obligation is placed on those whose dispute has been resolved never to contest the rights of the opposite party in the future. As if to reinforce the seriousness of the agreement, the main body of a juridical text is usually followed by an oath in the name of the local god and the king. It concludes with the names of the witnesses to the agreement and the exact date.

Fig. 2 The ruins of the stepped tower (the *ziggurat*) at Eridu (modern Tell Abu Sharein). Because of the encroaching desert, this ancient Sumerian settlement was gradually abandoned over the years. Under Hammurabi it retained importance only as a religious centre where the worship of Enki/Ea was conducted.

The name of the month, the day of the month and the name of the year are all given.[3]

The scribes who drew up these juridical texts followed fairly fixed forms which accorded with local practice. They always used just one tablet. It was left in the sun to dry, and then it was covered with a thin layer of clay, just a few millimetres thick. This formed a sort of envelope on which a copy of the text was written. The cylinder-seals belonging to the person who was receiving or the one who was transferring the goods, as well as of some of the witnesses, were rolled along the edges of the envelope while it was still moist. This meant that if there was ever any dispute, the envelope would be broken open and reference would be made to the original text of the tablet, which could not have been modified.

Administrative Documents

Many phrases in administrative texts are stereotypes. Often they seem to have something of a laconic character, and this makes them monotonous to read. To extract worthwhile historical information from them, they must be arranged into a series according to date and subject matter. When those giving details of the 'meal for the king' from the archives at Mari were published, they naturally raised much interest about the kind of food that was eaten in the palace. But there were thousands of them with a repetitive content, so at the time it seemed unnecessary to publish them all.

For several years nothing more was done and then it was decided to arrange them in chronological order. Opinions have now changed, for gaps appeared in the calendar and these gaps could be explained by the occasions when the king was not resident in his palace. It suggested the possibility of synchronising the date and duration of the gaps with known periods of absence, such as when the king was occupied with a military expedition.

While administrative and juridical texts are obviously important for understanding economic and social history, they can to no small extent also illuminate political history. In the date, the name of the sovereign who exercised power in the place where the contract was made is given. A set of texts from a given location arranged chronologically can show when and for how long a sovereign included that place within the boundaries of his kingdom. Such historical-geographical information gathered from the occurrences of the year names of Hammurabi enable us to trace his conquests over a good part of the Near East.

Letters

Typically letters will contain dialogues, recorded in direct speech with interesting anecdotes and so generally exhibit a much more lively style than that found in administrative and juridical documents. While first impressions seem to suggest that they have been written down by dictation word for word, this is not always the case. Historians have to undertake a critical textual analysis. They face a further handicap in that a letter will not normally contain the date or place of writing. This information was obvious to the messenger and would be most easily told to the addressee orally. Now, however, advanced research has provided an approximate date for some letters, especially when found together with dated administrative documents and contracts in an archive. Some of the letters from the Mari archives can even be dated to a specific month. Many of the letters we have were exchanged between individuals, such as the correspondence circulating between the merchants, but, as will be seen from later chapters, the diplomatic correspondence, letters sent from one king to another, is the richest source of information for the political historian. To show that the letter was genuine and ensure confidentiality, an envelope would be used on which the name of the addressee was written and the seal of the sender impressed.

Fig. 3 A letter from the archives at the palace of Mari, sent from Babylon to the king of Mari by his envoy Yarim-Addu. He informs his master about the current political developments, since Hammurabi has made an alliance with the king of Malgium (see *ARM* 26/2: 373).

PEDAGOGIC TEXTS

The texts that have been traditionally defined as 'literary', 'religious' or 'pedagogic' in fact had a wider context than they have normally been allowed in the scribal schools. They derive from a corpus of material that was gradually developed over the years to facilitate the skilled teaching of scribes and other experts, such as diviners, exorcists and healers.

By analysing what was actually written on the exercise tablets with information from texts describing life in the schools, it has been possible to discover the stages by which a scribe learned to write. First he was taught to hold a stylus correctly and then he would practise writing the three basic cuneiform signs: the vertical wedge known as DIŠ, the horizontal wedge known as AŠ and the angular wedge known as U. He would move on to simple signs such as A or BAD. The next stage involved copying syllabaries, such as the series known as a-a me-me. Simpler signs, such as A, KU and ME in various combinations, would then be supplemented in the syllabus by the more complex signs. This led to copying such series as tu-ta-ti, nu-na-ni, bu-ba-bi, etc., comprising signs not associated by their shape but by the sounds they represented. Every consonant was listed followed first by the vowel u, then by a, and then by i. He then learned how to write the names of people and other proper names, many of which would have standard forms and would have been well known to a young scribe of the time. In Sumerian as well as in Akkadian, personal names could always be seen as a meaningful combination of words, and this accelerated acquisition of vocabulary must have been a pedagogical advantage.

A further extension to vocabulary was achieved by using the so-called 'lexical lists'. They are something like an encyclopaedia, such as the names of all kinds of animals, plants and other objects in the series known as ḪAR.RA. The teacher used to dictate these lists to his pupils, evidencing an interest in actual objects such as one finds in traditional societies. The correct pronunciation of each Sumerian ideogram, as well as the corresponding word in Akkadian would be enunciated by the teacher and repeated by the pupil until they could be recited by heart. During the Old Babylonian period the series stretched to about 3,300 lines, which were divided into six sections.

Once the student had mastered how to write the signs, he had to learn the different phonetic values they could indicate, and this was the purpose of the series Proto-Ea. From this the student would proceed to the list named Proto-Lu, which was concerned with the titles and names of professions, terms for family relationships and descriptions of human beings. This series dates back to the beginnings of cuneiform writing, and it is because of its antiquity that it appears to be out of step with what was in fact the real social situation pertaining in the Old Babylonian period, for some of the titles listed were in fact no longer current at that time. In those days the teachers were not afraid to be seen as conservative. There were other lists to be copied after Proto-Lu. When the scribe had reached this stage, he was ready to begin the study of mathematics by learning tables of multiplication and tables of reciprocals.

Scribal training also involved learning the standard phrases used in contracts and other juridical documents. What was customary in the legal parlance of Nippur is reflected in one of these established collections of legal expressions. Model contracts, for which we have no date or list of witnesses, were also copied as exercises. In another document a young scribe proudly boasted of being able to write

> contracts for formalising marriages and for business partnerships, for selling houses, fields and slaves, for deposits of silver, for leasing cultivation fields or palm-groves, and tablets for contracts of adoption.[4]

A scribe who was more advanced in his training learned to make copies of literary texts. This means that the corpus of Sumerian literature coming from the Old Babylonian period was not written from a desire to protect it from oblivion but, more prosaically, because teachers required a selected anthology to include in their educational syllabus. Copying out proverbs, which were short and easily memorised, served as introductory exercises in writing literature. Hundreds of such lenticularly shaped tablets have been found, between 5 and 13 centimetres in diameter, which are examples of such exercises for beginners. On them a teacher has written out two or three lines of a proverb and a scribe has then had to copy what he wrote. Sometimes the teacher made it more complicated by requiring the scribe first to memorise the text he had written on the obverse of the tablet, and then to write it out again on the reverse from memory. It is easy to distinguish the writing of the master from that of the pupil, which is often hesitant and has mistakes. The aim was first to let the scribe learn to copy out short extracts from a literary text and ultimately to write out the whole composition. A scribe was sometimes expected to repeat a phrase that his master dictated to him and then to write down, but it could also happen that he was presented with a whole text that he was required to copy accurately. He would have to check carefully, sign by sign, ensuring that it corresponded exactly to the original.

Various different genres of literature have been copied in this way but classifying these genres poses problems. Categories generally considered obvious in the world of today are not necessarily the same as those used by the scholars of the ancient world and they need to be adapted by specialists reading Sumero-Akkadian literature. Then, the concept of 'great literature' was an anthology of what we would now classify as myths and epics. The myths describe activities of the principal deities of the Sumero-Akkadian pantheon. The most famous epic concerns the exploits of the hero Gilgameš. It comprises different episodes in Sumerian which are integrated into a continuous narrative in Akkadian, and then many manuscript copies were made in the first millennium. The story of *The Deluge* has also been incorporated into the epic of Atra-hasis, narrated in Babylonian. In a series of legends recalling the memories of the times of the kings of Agade, Sargon and Naram-Sin figure as the protagonists. There was obviously considerable popular interest in traditional dialogues, proverbs and riddles, judging from the number of such texts.

Copying out letters written in Sumerian formed a part of the syllabus, particularly those of historical significance. Although some of the details may well be apocryphal, correspondence of some of the early rulers, notably those from the Ur III Dynasty and also of the Amorite kings of Larsa, has survived for our attention through the scribal schools. Trainee scribes were also required to copy royal inscriptions, and what we have mostly comes from the excavations at Nippur. Very many earlier Old Akkadian inscriptions were copied onto tablets from twenty-fourth and twenty-first century statues and stelae still to be seen in the courts of the great sanctuary of Ekur. Usually the scribes copied the archaic forms of the signs, but some preferred to write in a more up-to-date style. The original sculptures are now lost, but on the tablets we find a note about the kind of object from which the copy was made and where precisely it had been inscribed, such as on the shoulder of a statue. The catalogue is another type of text that provides us with information about scribal training. Several examples have been found, some of which simply list the manuscripts found in the house of some savant. As such these are a valuable complement to the corpus of Sumerian literature actually discovered by archaeologists. But many of the catalogues seem to be duplicates, and so it has been proposed that they constitute a sort of school curriculum.

At first sight Akkadian seems to have played a relatively reduced role in the training of the scribe. This impression arises because so much of our evidence comes from Nippur and Ur and therefore it reflects the literary tradition of the southern part of the country into which Sumerian influences had penetrated deeply. It would be wonderful to have a complete inventory of what had been found from a site where the tradition of copying literary texts in Akkadian was well developed, such as Šaduppum (Tell Harmal) in the lower valley of the Diyala. Duplicates of Sumerian literary texts are found more often than duplicates of Akkadian ones. This is why it has been proposed that Akkadian literary texts may be considered as examples of what scribes could produce at the end of their training as their 'masterpieces'. Because identical model letters have been found at various archaeological sites, we also know they had to practise writing letters in Akkadian.

Since scribes were required to learn skills that could be applied to practical problems, their training was not limited to belles-lettres and the like. If required to record a contract for inheritance, it would not be enough for them just to have learned by heart the requisite legal phrases. They would need to divide up the area of land as specified to be shared by the beneficiaries. This demanded competence in arithmetic, and so the mathematical tables for calculating surface areas and weights would also have formed part of their curriculum. Some scribes developed other skills such as music and singing. They learned the different musical styles and were able to sing the songs they wrote.

Legal, medical and omen literature of the Old Babylonian period was normally formulated in a series of conditional sentences. If a specified set of circumstances existed then a specified set of consequences would follow. If some criminal act had been committed, or if certain symptoms were associated with a disease, or if an omen had been consulted and a particular result had been obtained, then the appropriate penalty for the criminal, the correct prognosis for the invalid and the proper decision to be made in the light of the omen could be determined. The most famous examples of this type of literature are the collections of law. The oldest Old Babylonian collection is that of Lipit-Eštar of Isin, drawn up in Sumerian, on which two Akkadian collections, attributed to

Daduša of Ešnunna and to Hammurabi of Babylon, were dependent. An important series of omens, referred to by the opening words šumma izbum, 'if a malformed birth', describes unusual human and animal births. Such anomalies were regarded as an ominous message from the gods. Occasionally propitious omens occurring in everyday life are mentioned, but at this time no systematic collection of them had been made. They were collected later and referred to as šumma âlu, 'if a city'.

Various texts concern religion, the most important of which are categorised as liturgies, magic and exorcism, or divination. An important set of texts which was discovered in the house of an exorcist at Me-Turan focused on his activities. The house of the chief lamentation-priest Ur-Utu excavated in 1975 at Sippar Amnanum (modern Tell ed-Der) contained some 2,000 of his tablets, but somewhat surprisingly very few of them relate to activities which could really be described as religious. We are obliged to assume that usually instructions for the correct observance of rituals were given orally seeing that so few ritual texts from the Old Babylonian period have been found. Of the three rituals that are attested, one concerns the diviner, the second the cult of the ancestors (known as *kispum*, from Mari) and the third the festival for the goddess Eštar (also from Mari).

Not every scribe necessarily followed the same curriculum. A clerk in a warehouse would need to know only a basic set of signs, just enough to write out receipts and expenditures. This was a far cry from the expertise of someone able to compose a Sumerian hymn in praise of his sovereign. They may have both received the same initial training, but the one was able to continue his studies much further than the other. Another view is that there were different streams of instruction for different careers, but there is no compelling evidence either way. What is clear is that the training was not devised just for the members of the clergy, for that would ignore the needs of countless bureaucrats who were indispensable for the efficient conduct of palace affairs. It has sometimes been assumed that the development of competence in Sumerian literature was the preponderant aim of the educational establishment, but it could well be that the documents that have survived are a non-representative sample of what actually existed. The possibility remains that in fact there was a choice of syllabus open to trainee scribes determined by practical considerations about their intended work.

Geographical Distribution of the Texts

The first major excavations at Babylon were undertaken by the German Oriental Society (*Deutsche Orient-Gesellschaft*) between 1899 and 1917. Most of their discoveries came from the upper layers of the mound and are therefore

Fig. 4   Hardly anything remains today of the staged-tower (the *ziggurat*) at Babylon, made famous by the narrative in the Bible (Genesis 11:1–9).

dated relatively late, in the first millennium. The branch of the Euphrates that crosses the site prevented any excavation of the deeper layers where the evidence for earlier occupations could have been found. But it was possible to undertake excavations of the Old Babylonian levels between 1907 and 1912, in the area of the site knows as Merkes, following some accidental damage to a dyke upstream from Babylon which caused a temporary drying out of the soil. Those excavations had to be conducted at a depth of 12 metres. Only three small areas could be exposed where a few houses were located. This section of the city was named 'the new eastern town'. The archives that were discovered come mainly from the end of the first dynasty (seventeenth century BC).

The palace of Hammurabi has not been found, but even if it had been found the discoveries may not have been as spectacular as generally expected. Sumu-la-El (1880–1845) first built the palace there, but it was subsequently abandoned by Hammurabi's son, Samsu-iluna (1749–1712). The name of his thirty-fourth year commemorates the building of a completely new royal palace. Although the old palace continued to be used, its precise function is unknown. The excavations at Mari, which will be discussed in more detail later, show that stores of obsolete tablets were kept only in very exceptional circumstances, so it is highly possible that no tablets from the reign of Hammurabi were kept in his abandoned palace. Why we now know so much about Zimri-Lim, a sovereign from Mari who did not have nearly the same intrinsic importance as his contemporary Hammurabi, is simply because he happened to be the last occupant of the palace before his capital city was destroyed.

The palace archives at Babylon may well have been lost forever, but we surmise that the contents would have been very similar to those of the archives at Mari. Some thousands of letters sent to the king from foreign rulers, provincial governors, official office holders and members of his family would have been there. Hammurabi, like his contemporaries the kings of Mari, probably had the letters which he received while travelling brought back to his palace. There would have been large sets of administrative documents concerned with the daily needs of those residing in the palace, such as the lists of the rations provided for the women of the harem and their households. But it is only on the basis of the rich finds from Mari that we can make these assumptions.

The documentation that we do have comprises a large number of letters written by Hammurabi which were found some way away from Babylon. From these we can gain many exceptionally valuable insights into the history of his reign. When it comes to reading letters from antiquity often the question of authenticity arises, but for these letters their archaeological context proves that they are genuine. As it is we have at our disposal more than 200 letters sent by Hammurabi. Hammurabi is concerned for the most part with problems arising in the management of the royal domain which needed a decision from the king. They reveal many interesting points about why and how the sovereign intervened in the administration of the royal domain and ensured that justice was done. Invariably they are full of administrative formulations and are hardly distinguishable either in content or style from some letters written by Lu-Ninurta, one of the ministers of Hammurabi. This suggests that the scribes were trained not to write down a message precisely as it was dictated to them but rather to formulate the letters according to the intention of the sender.

In contrast to the dearth of material from Babylon, the finds from other towns in the kingdom of Hammurabi have been richer. Archives have been found at places such as Sippar, Kiš and Dilbat, though most of what we have has come from ancient illicit digging at these sites. Some documents from the ancient city of Larsa can be dated to before the time when it was conquered by the soldiers of Hammurabi, and his conquest did not automatically mean that the keeping of written records stopped. But record keeping was interrupted at Mari by the Babylonian conquest, for Hammurabi made a systematic destruction of the palace there after he had removed from it anything that was of interest to him. Even so, many archives remained in place in the chancellery. Fortunately for our purposes, the administrative documents had no interest for the conquerors. Thousands of letters were found addressed to the kings

Yasmah-Addu and Zimri-Lim. Several of them are concerned with Babylonia and a few were written by Hammurabi himself. Most of them are reports sent to the king of Mari by his envoys, giving an account of their mission and general information about the situation in Babylonia. One letter is obviously concerned with the gathering of military intelligence. Soldiers had been detailed to help the Babylonian allies in some military expedition and one commander of his troops writes to his king:

> I have managed to win to my cause two of the servants of Hammurabi by means of ... They have not refused to tell me anything they have heard in the palace, whether secret or about palace affairs, and they have given me full details.[5]

The treaty of alliance between Babylon and Mari against Elam is a rare instance of a diplomatic document found there which is not a letter.

****

The advantage in investigating this period of history is this rich array of written material; we have tens of thousands of cuneiform tablets from the time of Hammurabi. Not all of them have been formally excavated, for clandestine activity either in times past or more recently has had a part to play. Much of the material that is deposited in museum stores has so far been published only as hand copies. This still needs to be fully edited and much still remains unpublished. And what has been published in transcription and translation still often needs more work in order to gain access to the rich information it contains. By contrast the documentation we have for the third millennium consists mostly of administrative texts and a few letters and contracts. In the first millennium, administrative documents were written in Aramaic on perishable material which has long since been lost. We do have a vast number of texts from the Old Babylonian period but much has been lost, for it was the normal practice to remove the contents of buildings, including the archives, when they were abandoned voluntarily. Only in an unexpected event such as a fire or a war are texts likely to survive. Mari is one example, after the attack by the Babylonians. In the south of Mesopotamia from 1740–1738 BC, during the reign of the son of Hammurabi, Babylonian cities were themselves attacked, and there many texts concerned with his father have survived.

Fig. 5 A plan of the palace of Mari, showing the rooms where the tablets were found; from J. Margueron in K.R. Veenhof (ed.), *Cuneiform Archives and Libraries* (Leiden, 1986), p. 146. A little before the palace was destroyed the archives from the chancellery were reassembled and placed in labelled cases in a small room (here numbered 115) more or less in the centre of the building. Thousands of letters were discovered there which had been exchanged between Yasmah-Addu and Zimri-Lim, kings who were contemporaries of Hammurabi. Other archives seem to have remained in situ. The queen's archive was found in Room 52 (in the northern central block) and documents concerning the kitchens in Room 5 (in the western central block).

Chapter 1

From the Accession of Hammurabi to the Death of Samsi-Addu (1792–1775)

It is in the Agade period, around 2200, that we first find a reference to the city of Babylon. A little later, during the third dynasty of Ur in the twenty-first century, we know that it became the official residence of the 'governor', which is the usual translation of the Sumerian word *ensi*. In Akkadian the name for the city of Babylon is *bâb ilim*, 'the gate of the god'. The year 2002 marked the end of the third dynasty of Ur and then, after the last king of Ur had disappeared, Amorite nomads originating from Syria took advantage of the political vacuum to install themselves in Southern Mesopotamia. Several dynasties were soon established, of which the best known are those at Isin and Larsa. A century later, other Amorite chiefs seized power in five or six towns in the north and centre of Babylonia. For several decades those chiefs enjoyed a measure of independence, but one by one their towns were gradually annexed by Sumu-la-El (1880–1845 BC). More than a century after the earlier Amorite invasions he chose Babylon as his royal seat and it is this event that can be taken to mark the actual founding of the first dynasty of Babylon. Traditionally, however, according to ancient lists of kings, it is Sumu-abum who is reputed to have founded the dynasty.[1]

Hammurabi was the fifth in the succession of kings of this dynasty. His predecessors belonged to a section of the tribe of Bene Yamina and, just like other nomads of the ancient world, even after they had become settled they did not lose their sense of tribal affiliation. It is clear from the alliance which Sumu-la-El concluded with Sin-kašid, the king of Uruk, that one reason that motivated him was that the two of them were apparently ethnically the same. Later we know that King Ammi-ṣaduqa (1646–1626), a descendant of Hammurabi, enacted a funeral ritual known as *kispum*, during which he was required to recite the names of his dynastic ancestors, and the names he lists are the same as those given by Samsi-Addu as being his forefathers. The Amorite kings evidently maintained a tradition of recalling the precise details of the roots of their community.

The reign of Hammurabi began in 1792 and lasted for 43 years. We do not know exactly when he was born but he must have been a very young man when he came to power. It was considerably longer than the reigns of his father Sin-muballiṭ, who occupied the throne for 20 years (1812–1793), and of his grandfather Apil-Sin, who reigned for 18 years (1830–1813).

Before the beginning of the eighteenth century there is no evidence of anyone else called Hammurabi, but then it suddenly becomes more frequent. No less than three other monarchs of the period have the same name, and we know of at least two private individuals who were given the same name as these kings. The father of one of them was even coincidentally called Sin-muballiṭ, the same as the father of King Hammurabi of Babylon. The meaning of almost all Akkadian personal names, like those from other parts of the Ancient Near East, can be deduced with reasonable certainty, and it is possible that Hammurabi means 'Grandfather is great'. But another possible suggestion is that the name was pronounced *Hammu-rapi*, and then it would mean 'Grandfather is the healer'.

Babylonia and the Near East in 1792

The capital of the kingdom of Babylonia was the city of Babylon. The kingdom extended to the north to the twin cities of Sippar, situated on a branch of the Euphrates that eventually joined the course of the Tigris. Sippar-Yahrurum, also known as Sippar of Šamaš, the god to which it was devoted, was seven kilometres upstream from Sippar-Amnanum, also known as Great Sippar, which was under the protection of the goddess Annunitum. To the east there was Kiš, 25 kilometres from Babylon. It was an important agglomeration of communities with two focal centres: one consecrated to the god Zababa and the other to the goddess Eštar. Not too far away from there was Kutha, where Erra, the god of the underworld, was the tutelary deity. To the south-west of Borsippa was the sanctuary of the god Nabu, patron of the scribes. Dilbat, the domain of the god Uraš, and Marad, under the patronage of the god Lugal-Marad, marked the southernmost limit of the kingdom.

The kingdom of Babylonia had been established for less than a century when Hammurabi acceded to his throne to take up his place in the dynasty. As far as politics were concerned, it held only modest sway. Some frontiers had already been extended through the efforts of the grandfather and the father of Hammurabi. Apil-Sin had been particularly successful in annexing the towns

Fig. 6 The ruins of the stepped tower, the *ziggurat*, at Kiš, in the background. Now it is a grazing ground for the local animals.

of Upi and Mankisum, on the bank of the Tigris, but various neighbouring sovereigns had eventually managed to counteract his advance, thus the region was no longer controlled by Babylon at the beginning of Hammurabi's reign. On several occasions his father Sin-muballiṭ, on the strength of the alliance he had made with the king of Uruk, tried to extend his power southwards, keeping the sovereigns of Isin and Larsa in his sights. But he was unable to build systematically on the occasional successes of his sporadic attacks.

If we picture the scene of international politics in 1792 as a chessboard at a complex stage of the game, then the kingdom of Babylonia was a low-value piece. The Suti, a group of nomads, wandered in the desert to the west. To the south there was the ancient territory of Sumer, where for several decades power had been shared among three kingdoms. Isin had long been the rival of Larsa, and Uruk had recently been showing signs that its power was waxing. Isin and Uruk had together formed an alliance against Rim-Sin of Larsa, and Hammurabi's father, Sin-muballiṭ, joined that coalition. But it must have failed, for in 1810 Rim-Sin had gained the upper hand and was able to seize Uruk in 1803. A little later, in 1794, he annexed Isin and so secured for himself the whole of the ancient territory of Sumer. Rim-Sin may well have been at the zenith of his power, but the geopolitical situation of his kingdom was inherently weak. His territory stretched like a ribbon for more than 200 kilometres from north to south, with its northern border marked by the town of Maškan-šapir. But it was at the mercy of Babylon and Malgium, kingdoms situated further upstream on the Euphrates and the Tigris, and in this position it was a most attractive target to attack.

At present we know comparatively little about the kingdom of Malgium, which lay to the east of Babylonia. As yet its capital, which would have been on the ancient course of the Tigris, has not been found. Der, a town situated further to the east at the foot of the Zagros mountain chain, was the capital of another independent kingdom. It must have been an important centre of power but it has not yet been excavated, so it remains to be seen what is to be discovered there. To the north-east was the mighty kingdom of Ešnunna, with the valley of the Diyala at its centre. It separates the Mesopotamian plain from the Iranian high plateau. The area is reasonably well-known because excavations have been carried out at several smaller towns in the kingdom as well as in the capital. It was governed by King Daduša, who at this time also controlled a small section of land along the Tigris around Upi (known later as Opis) and downstream as far as Mankisum.

The extensive territory to the north of Babylonia was controlled by the formidable Samsi-Addu. In 1807 he marched from his own town of Ekallatum, on the right bank of the Tigris, north of Assur, and extended his domination over Assur. Then he moved north-westwards to take possession of territory to the south of Jebel Sinjar. He crossed the mountains of this massif and took control of the region called the Habur triangle. This fertile region of the piedmont is irrigated by the River Habur and its tributaries which run down from Tur-Abdin, an easterly extension of Taurus. Samsi-Addu made Šehna, modern Tell Leilan, one of the key towns of his kingdom and renamed it Šubat-Enlil, 'Abode of Enlil'. Recent American excavations there have confirmed the importance of this site. Just before 1792 Samsi-Addu significantly developed his plans for expanding his territory by advancing against Mari. By conquering it he had given himself a base on the Middle Euphrates, and could claim to be uniting the lands between the Tigris and the Euphrates. This territory is now often referred to as the kingdom of Upper Mesopotamia. Samsi-Addu reorganised the administration of his territories soon after Hammurabi came to the throne of Babylon. His oldest son, Išme-Dagan, he placed on the throne of Ekallatum, and his younger brother, Yasmah-Addu, he made king of Mari. Samsi-Addu himself assumed the title of Great King and stayed for most of the time at Šubat-Enlil, in the centre of the Habur triangle. The frontier between his territory and Ešnunna was on the Tigris, downstream from Mankisum.

Babylonia, surrounded by three more powerful neighbours, the kingdoms of Larsa, Ešnunna and Upper Mesopotamia, fits into this context as something of a middle-ranking power. Some other distant great powers were to play an important part in deciding the destiny of Hammurabi. Yamhad and Qatna, two kingdoms to the west, were rivals for the control of Western Syria. Aleppo was capital of the kingdom of Yamhad, the more northerly territory, which bordered the kingdom of Upper Mesopotamia with the boundary marked by the Euphrates running between Karkemiš and Emar. The kingdom of Qaṭna to the south, with its centre at Tell Mishrife near the modern city of Homs, was the principal focus of contention for Yamhad. The kingdom of Elam, in southwestern Iran, on the eastern edge of the ancient Near East, had a formidable influence on political affairs. The ruler of Elam resided at Anšan, modern Tall-i Maliyan in the province of Fars. He was referred to by the Sumerian title *sukkal-mah*, which is usually translated as 'emperor'. His younger brother, who had been made king of Susa, supported him. What has emerged in the last few years from a closer study of the archives of Mari is that Elam wielded far greater weight in Mesopotamian politics than had previously been thought: the emperor of Elam was generally recognised as the supreme arbitrator by the kings of the region.

A Modest Beginning to his Reign (1792–1775)

After he had come to the throne Hammurabi proclaimed a *mîšarum*, a word which is usually translated as 'amnesty'. It involved measures such as the remission of debt; this and other implications of a *mîšarum* will be discussed in Part III. This measure was commemorated in the name of his second year. What we know of the political events in the kingdom of Babylon for the first fifteen years of the reign of Hammurabi is somewhat limited. One reason for this is that the archives of Mari for these years are much less detailed. Yasmah-Addu occupied the throne of Mari at this time but it is the documents from the time of his successor, Zimri-Lim, that provide us with the kind of fuller information we need. Mari, as part of the kingdom of Upper Mesopotamia, was controlled by Samsi-Addu, a man keen to enter into diplomatic contracts with neighbouring foreign potentates.

Most of the year names for this first period of his reign mention Hammurabi's building works or offerings to particular deities. The names concerned with political and military matters are for Years 7, 8, 10, and 11, when it appears that he was concerned with expanding his territory. He advanced not only southwards to Isin and Uruk and northwards to Rapiqum, along an axis formed by the course of the Euphrates, but also eastwards, towards Malgium on the Tigris. The name he chose for Year 7 shows his pride in having conquered Uruk and Isin. Uruk had been under the control of Rim-Sin for the previous 15 years and Isin for six years. To be told that the old enemy should have so quickly ceded these two very important towns to his northern rival invites a measure of suspicion from a historian. In fact we learn from private archives that what is commemorated in the year name is a brief raid on the cities. Some elements of the population of

Fig. 7 The site of Uruk (Warka) is dominated by the ruins of its stepped tower (the *ziggurat*) which was built at the end of the third millennium.

Isin were forced into exile and settled for a few years in the Babylonian town of Marad. Uruk and Isin were soon back under the control of Rim-Sin.

In the name for Year 10 (1783), commemorating an event which occurred in 1784, Hammurabi boasts about the destruction of Malgium, a site which has never been certainly identified, and its surroundings. What is known is that it lay upstream of Maškan-šapir on the Tigris, where the road from Babylon to Der crossed the river. It has recently been suggested that Hammurabi placed an intrinsic value on the possession of Malgium in order to control the headwaters of the Tigris. In theory he could already threaten to withhold the water supply of Larsa, since he controlled the Euphrates upstream. But their primary source of water was from the Tigris, so once in control of Malgium he could play a trump card in his struggle with his rival. Just how much serious damage was done is impossible to tell but, since Malgium appears later in our sources as an independent kingdom, conquest seems too strong a term. It was not until much later, in 1760, that Malgium was definitively suppressed by Hammurabi. That first assault by Hammurabi against Malgium may have been a stimulus for Daduša, the king of Ešnunna, to launch an attack against Mankisum, which then belonged to Samsi-Addu. Yasmah-Addu wrote to his brother Išme-Dagan saying that Daduša had tried to persuade the king of Babylon to join him in the operation:

> The master of Ešnunna has begun to move all his troops and his servants and his well-to-do citizens. Now he is at Upi and he has written several times to the master of Babylon to join him in the attack on Mankisum. But the master of Babylon has not agreed.[2]

In the event the might of Išme-Dagan's soldiers forced Daduša to withdraw on that occasion. When he was finally able to overcome Mankisum he commemorated it in a year name.

In the following year, 1783, according to the name for Hammurabi Year 11 (1782), he captured Rapiqum and the surrounding area. The town was situated on the Euphrates north of Lake Ḥabbânîyah, and at the time it was being fought over with claims by Babylon, Mari and Ešnunna. With the victory of Hammurabi, the governor, who was apparently a dependent of the king of Ešnunna, was brought down. Hammurabi owed his success largely to the alliance between Ekallatum and Babylon, and also to the support he had received from Samsi-Addu. The alliance that united Babylon and Ekallatum can be deduced from the record of a trial that took place in Babylon at the end of Year 10, when an oath was sworn before the god Marduk and the Kings

Fig. 8 The victory stele of Samsi-Addu, now in the Louvre. The king stands upright, in profile, striking the brow of an enemy with an axe and pressing him to the ground with his left foot. His face is not preserved, which is particularly disappointing since this is the only surviving representation of the king. The campaign he undertook with the king of Ešnunna against the kingdom of Arbele is mentioned in the inscription on the back.

Hammurabi and Samsi-Addu. The victory was short-lived because Daduša of Eshnunna, after his success at Mankisum, soon took back control of Rapiqum and then commenced a campaign against Mari. Assembling 10,000 soldiers, he advanced up the Euphrates and invaded the region of Suhum as far as Hanat. He seems to have been halted when he made a peace agreement with Samsi-Addu, but we have no details of that agreement. Had the alliance between Daduša and Samsi-Addu made them turn their attention to their southern neighbour, Hammurabi would certainly have felt under threat. But in fact they decided to make for the region east of the Tigris and undertook a campaign together against Urbilum (Arbela, modern Erbil). In fact from his new alliance with Ešnunna Samsi-Addu seems to have wanted to allow Hammurabi to derive some advantage. He abandoned not just Rapiqum to his control, but also Hit. This meant that now, with these two Euphrates towns in his possession, the frontier between Babylon and Mari was situated between Harbe and Hit.

From two administrative documents dated in Years 12 and 13, we learn that for the second time Hammurabi proclaimed a *mišarum*, an edict of grace. The first document tells of someone who had been obliged to sell some land he had inherited and was able to reclaim it again 'according to the edict of the king'. He claimed that most of what he had sold should be given back to him and that the purchaser should keep only a fraction of what he had bought. The second document refers to a loan of one-third of a mina (about 165 grams) of silver. Normally the creditor would destroy the pertinent tablet after the loan had been remitted, 'according to the edict of the king', but on this occasion the creditor had lost the original document. So that there should be no risk of any subsequent claim for repayment against the debtor, a lump of clay was ceremonially substituted for the lost clay tablet and was symbolically broken. The tablet ends with the names of three witnesses and the date.

> Concerning the tablet for the one-third of a mina of silver which Huššutum, the daughter of Nanna-maba, and Ipqatum, the son of Aširatum, received from Nuṭuptum the daughter of Warad-ilišu, she has not surrendered the tablet to be destroyed in conformity with the edict of the king. She has stated, "The tablet is lost. Break up a lump of clay instead of my tablet!" In future, if a tablet inside an envelope ... about one-third of a mina of silver of Nuṭuptum the daughter of Ward-ilišu, should turn up it is worthless and should be destroyed. They have sworn by Šamaš, Aya, Marduk and Hammurabi.[3]

Daduša died in 1779, which provoked the subsequent tension that arose between Hammurabi and Samsi-Addu. One text refers to a war between them. No further details are given, but it caused disruption for all river transport on the Euphrates. Whatever the cause of the dispute it did not last long, and a few years later it was as though nothing had ever upset their friendship. In a letter from Išme-Dagan to his brother, he uses a picturesque metaphor, 'we have formed one single finger', to show that the relationship between the two dynasties had always been cordial and united in purpose, and that there was absolutely no need for any obstacle to be placed against developing it further.

> The house of Babylon and our house have formed one single finger. Our house finds no fault with the house of Babylon.[4]

When Samsi-Addu and Hammurabi decided to conclude an alliance with the new king of Ešnunna, Ibal-pi-El II, this resulted in the three sovereigns embarking on an operation against one of their close rivals, the king of Malgium. In 1777, the three kings set out on their campaign, and details of their movements are noted in a group of letters from Mari. The troops of the kingdom of Upper Mesopotamia came down the Tigris to link up with those from Ešnunna at Mankisum. From there the coalition army as a whole invaded the lands of Malgium, destroying various cities as they advanced to besiege Malgium itself. The king of Malgium, in the face of such overwhelming might from these adversaries, decided to buy them off. He paid 15 talents of silver as an indemnity and the three kings shared this among themselves as they departed. Such a large amount of silver would have weighed about 450 kilograms.[5] The victory must have been of considerable importance to Hammurabi, but even so he chose a completely different event, the consecration of a statue of the goddess Eštar, as the name for Year 17.

In the winter of 1777–1776 Samsi-Addu sent messengers to a distant island named Tilmun, which is to be identified with Bahrain in the Arabian Gulf. It was an event of considerable symbolic significance. He had already achieved fame for having advanced his troops westwards to Lebanon as far as the Mediterranean coast; for having crossed Tur Abdin in the north; and for having reached the Zagros in the east. But he had not sent any expedition to the remote south. Having adopted the traditional royal title for this period, 'the king of the four shores', he now became the embodiment of that title by sending this embassy to the Gulf and symbolically occupying the fourth point of the compass. From the various letters and administrative texts referring to the messengers Samsi-Addu sent to Tilmun, we learn that they were provided with gifts for the local potentate of this famous land. His ambassadors stayed some time at their destination, and when they came back, in the autumn of 1776, they brought with them messengers from Tilmun, who brought costly gifts from their land for the king. To undertake such travel must have required expert guidance from the nomadic Suti tribesmen, who would have been well acquainted with all the desert tracks. In the following spring Samsi-Addu sent messengers back to Tilmun, but that was shortly before his death in the summer of 1775.

Išme-Dagan was already king of Ekallatum, the successor of Samsi-Addu, and he renewed the alliances which had united his father with the principal sovereigns of the region, in particular with Ibi-pi-El II of Ešnunna and Hammurabi of Babylon. He chose Hulalum to send to Hammurabi as his representative, a man who had served as secretary to Samsi-Addu and one of the most high-ranking officials in the kingdom. Because of the various troubles in the area at this time, some very careful security measures had to be designed and adopted before despatching this ambassador to Babylon. The ambassador whom Samsi-Addu had sent to Tilmun just a few months before he died came back at a critical time, for the area to the south of Mari was in revolt and there was some cause for concern for the safety of the men from Tilmun as well as for the goods they were transporting in their caravan. They were kept safe by one of the Suti nomad chiefs. Because it was necessary for Yasmah-Addu to safeguard the ambassador to Babylon, he simultaneously wrote two letters: one was addressed to Hulalum and the other to Hammurabi himself, in which he gave instructions.

> May you not be concerned in your heart about anything! I am now sending Zikriya and Imgurrum to you who have to escort this caravan to you in Babylon. The caravan should stay with you until your brother writes to you to say that it should leave. Your brother Išme-Dagan is well and all is well in the town of Ekallatum. I myself am well and all is well in the town of Mari.[6]

Although revolts had sporadically arisen in various parts of his kingdom in the later years of the reign of Samsi-Addu, with the help of his son he had always been able to suppress them. But when he died, the situation became much more serious. The kingdoms that he had annexed all felt that this was the moment to reclaim their independence. Pretenders for the thrones, most of whom had been sent into exile, started making their way back to their capital cities. One well-documented instance is the return of Zimri-Lim to Mari. With the help of the king of Aleppo, he advanced down the Euphrates valley and took Tuttul, before regaining his capital Mari a few months later. Yasmah-Addu was immediately forced to quit. And there are other examples. Kurda, Andarig and Qaṭṭara south of Jebel Sinjar, Ašnakkum, Ilan-ṣura and many others in the Habur triangle, ancient kingdoms in the region which had submitted to Samsi-Addu, all began to assert their independence. As the kingdom of Upper Mespotamia began to crumble away, Ibal-pi-El II, the king of Ešnunna, changed sides. When he revoked his loyalty to Išme-Dagan, Hammurabi realised he was also under threat. His response was to mobilise 6,000 troops in an effort to save Išme-Dagan, which provoked Ibal-pi-El II to write to Zimri-Lim proposing an alliance for them to act together as a coalition to overcome the threat posed by these troops.

> Go out and conquer these troops, and do not let them escape or let them regroup, for they plan to save Išme-Dagan.[7]

For a while Išme-Dagan was able to maintain the small kingdom of Ekallatum, restricted to a stretch of territory along the middle Tigris, but he was later obliged to take refuge in Babylon.

Chapter 2

From the Death of Samsi-Addu to the Victory over Elam (1775–1764)

The historical information that can be retrieved from the kingdom of Babylon for the period 1775–1764 is no more than it was for the earlier years, and the year names of Hammurabi refer to hardly any political or military events. But we do have a mass of information from the archives of the palace of Mari, from which occasionally we can trace the progress of events month by month. Very few texts from this period have been excavated from other sites in Northern Mesopotamia, but the documents from Mari dated in the reign of Zimri-Lim include tablets from some of the principal capital cities of the Near East. They comprise letters from foreign sovereigns and reports from the royal officials of Mari while occupied on missions abroad, in particular in Babylonia. Because these administrative texts and correspondence can be dated precisely, we are able to construct a detailed chronological framework and recreate the intricate web of events surrounding some of the events referred to.

Redrawing of the Political Map after the Death of Samsi-Addu

Samsi-Addu died in 1775, the fourth year of Ibal-pi-El II of Ešnunna. Hammurabi had occupied the throne of Babylon for 18 years, and Rim-Sin the throne of Larsa for 47 years. It might seem reasonable to suppose that, once Samsi-Addu had disappeared from the scene, Hammurabi might be afforded an opportunity for his imperial aspirations. But in the years immediately following his death, notwithstanding what has often been written elsewhere, there was no profound transformation of the political scene in Babylonia.

This is perfectly understandable, for Hammurabi was his ally, and in all the enterprises he had undertaken, which until that time had been directed primarily towards the south, Samsi-Addu had never bothered him. After their coordinated attack upon Rapiqum and, later, Malgium, they even shared the fruits of their spoil.

Fig. 9 The statue of 'Baal of thunder', found at Ugarit, is now in the Louvre. The God of the Storm is here shown battling with the God of the Sea, symbolically represented by waves under his feet. The mythical narrative is recorded in Ugaritic on tablets dating from the thirteenth century. But now, thanks to the Mari archives, we know that it was documented at Aleppo five centuries earlier. The weapons with which the God of the Storm was supposed to have overcome the God of the Sea were sent from Aleppo to Zimri-Lim as a sign of support.

But since the new king of Mari, Zimri-Lim, had been one of the architects of the downfall of Hammurabi's ally Samsi-Addu, new relationships between Mari and Babylon can hardly have begun on the best of terms. One more important question which again arose concerned the matter of who owned the region of Suhum, between Hanat and Rapiqum. The king of Ešnunna considered the territory to be his by right and in a letter to Zimri-Lim he proposed that the terms of an agreement made between his father and Mari should be revived. That would have fixed the frontier between the two states about 90 kilometres downstream from Mari. But Zimri-Lim gave priority to maintaining his friendly relations with the powers of Western Syria and did not accept that proposal. He was particularly close to Yarim-Lim, the king of Aleppo, who had helped him to take possession of the throne of Mari and with whom he had made a treaty in proper and fitting terms. We do not know how the situation in Hit and Rapiqum in the immediate aftermath was controlled, but three years later the whole region was once more part of the kingdom of Mari.

At the end of the first year of his reign, Zimri-Lim was back in contact with Hammurabi about resolving problems for Kurda, an important kingdom to the south of Jebel Sinjar. One of the pretenders to the throne was residing in Babylon, and Zimri-Lim realised he would need the support of Hammurabi in his desire to help the pretender to fulfil his aspirations. When he first writes to Hammurabi he refers to himself as 'his son', thereby showing all the marks of deference traditionally adopted by a new king towards an older one. But subsequently he uses the term 'brother', in accordance with the diplomatic etiquette of the period, showing that he considers himself to be Hammurabi's equal.[1]

As a member of the tribe of Bene Sim'al, Zimri-Lim committed himself to an attack against the princes of the Bene Yamina, a serious ethnic conflict at the end of the first and the beginning of the second year of his reign. He was victorious. Calm was restored in the Euphrates valley and Zimri-Lim was free to start a new campaign against the towns of the Habur triangle. He had managed to capture Kahat in his first year, and he now aimed for Ašlakka. Because he had established a group of kings in the Habur triangle who acknowledged his authority, he may well have thought that there was no question that the influence of Mari was firmly established in the Habur triangle. But he was soon to be disabused of any such notion.

Ups and Downs for Ešnunna

The documentation concerning Hammurabi between 1772 and 1766 that has survived suggests that he was responding to the varying fortunes of his neighbour, the king of Ešnunna. In 1770 Ibal-pi-El II had been obliged to conclude a peace treaty after launching major campaigns towards the west and the north-west, but in the following years he became the object of major attacks spearheaded by the emperor of Elam with the support of Hammurabi and Zimri-Lim.

After the death of Samsi-Addu, it would have been obvious that Ibal-pi-El II was attempting to reform the kingdom of Upper Mesopotamia for his own advantage. In 1772 he had launched an attack against the region of the Middle Euphrates, beginning with the capture of Rapiqum, an event celebrated in the name of his Year 9. He had made troops from Mari abandon Rapiqum and retreat upstream first to Yabliya, and then a little later to Mulhan. They may well have thought they would have to evacuate that town as well and thus abandon all the lower part of Suhum. A revolt by the Bene Yamina opened up a second front in a clearly coordinated attack, but it was crushed by Zimri-Lim and he exacted from them considerable booty.

Hammurabi's decision to lend his support to the king of Mari was fraught with consequences. He would have realised that victory for Ešnunna would definitely expose him to danger, for Ibal-pi-El II would have threatened him from upstream in the valleys of the Tigris and the Euphrates. At the beginning of the winter in 1772, Babylonian envoys at Mari were participating in negotiations which led to an agreement, and the records show that an army, commanded by Mut-hadqim and four other Babylonian generals, had been sent by Hammurabi to help Zimri-Lim before the end of that winter. Two of the generals were stationed in local fortresses in the Euphrates valley above Terqa, both commanding 1,200 of their men. The king of Mari seems to have been using them primarily to stifle any whisper of fresh revolutionary activity on the part of the Bene Yamina. It is quite probable that Zimri-Lim would have correspondingly sent out some troops to Hammurabi, but there is no documented support for this idea.

The forces of Ešnunna continued to advance upstream along the Euphrates to the borders of Mari and a governor from Ešnunna was installed at Hanat. When Ibal-pi-El II opened up another front to the north-west, he wrote somewhat symbolically to Zimri-Lim that his stated aim was to conquer Šubat-Enlil. He could hardly have shown more clearly that his intention was to re-establish the kingdom of Upper Mesopotamia. In the face of another group of invading soldiers, coming upstream from Ešnunna along the Tigris and encamping first at Assur and then at Ekallatum, Išme-Dagan was obliged to leave his capital to seek refuge in Babylon. Qarni-Lim, the king of Andarig, felt he could have expected support from Zimri-Lim, but nothing came in response to his request, and once he went over to the side of Ešnunna he became an object of hostility to the surrounding powers. The troops of Ešnunna also occupied various towns of the southern piedmont of the Jebel Sinjar before crossing the mountain and

Fig. 10 The Jebel Sinjar as seen from the south. Although the mountain is not particularly high, rising to about 1,200 metres, it presents a significant barrier to communication.

settling in Šubat-Enlil. Šubat-Enlil capitulated and several other kings in the region submitted. Ibal-pi-El II had achieved his aim, but the war had not been completely won since there were two kings to the south of Jebel Sinjar who remained hostile to him.

Zimri-Lim left Mari at the beginning of the spring of 1771 and used Ašlakka as the base for his operations. He stayed there for more than two months, assembling a strong army to attack Andarig. Shortly afterwards, Ešnunna left Šubat-Enlil and advanced towards Andarig. A letter to Zimri-Lim tells him that Ešnunna had suffered from aggressive activity in the eastern part of the kingdom, which would explain this sudden withdrawal. Zimri-Lim began to lay a successful siege to Andarig in the autumn of 1771. But the king of Mari hurriedly left the Jebel Sinjar region and headed back to his capital, a move which brought bitter disappointment to his allies, who assumed he had concluded a secret deal with Ešnunna and with Qarni-Lim. In fact Zimri-Lim had been distracted by the activities of the Bene Yamina, who had been persistently attacking the western part of the kingdom of Mari. Almost as soon as he had gained his victory at Andarig they started their raids in the Euphrates valley. By the end of 1771 things had become much calmer on all fronts, but when Ešnunna withdrew from the area of the Jebel Sinjar the way was open for some accounts to be settled, and they were settled rather violently. Bunu-Eštar from Kurda wholeheartedly and vindictively took the side of the Babylonian army. They had been in his territory for more than a year, and he wanted to help them gain extra booty before they returned home. The commanders of the Babylonian troops formulated a direct request to Zimri-Lim, addressed as 'our lord', for permission to leave him and go back to Hammurabi, also referred to as 'our lord'.

> And may our lord (Zimri-Lim) send back the valiant army which our lord (Hammurabi) sent to you and which has been there for more than a year, so that our lord (Hammurabi) may be honoured. Furthermore may our lord (Hammurabi) hear about these three great enterprises you have undertaken and may he rejoice.[2]

The forces of Ešnunna also retired from Suhum, and then tension increased between Mari and Babylon on the question of where on the Euphrates to fix the frontier between their two kingdoms. Zimri-Lim sent two negotiators to Babylon to sort out the matter and from Babylon they wrote to him in a most colourful way about how Hammurabi reacted in the discussions. Their letter begins with a preamble emphasising the importance of the historical relationship between Babylon and Mari and continues:

> We have arrived at Great Sippar. Yanṣib-Addu, the servant of my lord, has delivered a message from my lord to Hammurabi. Hammurabi did not stop listening when Yanṣib-Addu was delivering the message from my lord … He did not open his mouth for the whole time when he was delivering the message. He remained very attentive until he had come to the end of his message. When the message was over he began to speak to us with these words: 'Has this house ever had the smallest dispute with the house of Mari? And is there any element of contention between the town of Mari and Babylon? The towns of Mari and Babylon have always been one house and one finger;[3] they could not be separated. Then as now Zimri-Lim has sent me full reports and has written to me frankly, though formerly his father and grandfather did not send complete reports to this house. Ever since the day that Zimri-Lim turned to me and began to send me letters there has never been any complaint on my part and no aggression towards him. I have given him all goods that were possible and he knows all the goods that I have given him in his heart of hearts.'[4]

The letter continues with the reply of Zimri-Lim's envoy to Hammurabi:

> You have no dispute with my master, and my master has no dispute with you. You have given all possible goods to my master and my master has given all possible goods to you. He has honoured you and has made you famous. Among those sovereigns allied to you, you have been a spokesman

and you have repeatedly passed on compliments to the emperor of Elam. Among these sovereigns no-one has regarded and honoured you more than my master. It has been at your request that he has put into irons the messengers from Ešnunna and sent them to you. And furthermore you have written to him a second time to send you troops and my master has chosen the best troops to send to you. In actual fact it is not once, nor five times, but on innumerable occasions that I have been telling you this. I have never stopped. If, despite the repeated letters from my master you are never going to accept these messages from my master, and even if my master should go out of your heart, then mark me well. You should carefully consider my master and see that my master is gaining the upper hand over you in his generosity. From the beginning I have not been failing to repeat it to you. Even so have you not examined in detail what my master has proposed? Now is the time, in response to the goodness that my master has shown for you and the way in which he has honoured you, to give my master satisfaction and turn your attention to the subject of the towns which the emperor of Elam your father has given to him, so that all may proceed without any recrimination.[5]

From this document we can see how the envoy of Zimri-Lim leads up to the gist of the matter. He suggests that in view of the goods that had been exchanged between the two kings, Hammurabi is in fact in debt to Zimri-Lim. So he asks the king of Babylon to accept the mediation which the king of Elam had offered and that he should bring some satisfaction to the king of Mari. But this was not related only to things in general. The end of the dialogue shows how Hammurabi has Zimri-Lim's territorial claims properly formulated by his envoy. Yanṣib-Addu continues his report as follows:

That is what I said to him, and he replied to me, 'Amongst all the allied kings there has been none who has treated me as well or has honoured me so much as Zimri-Lim. In recognition of the goods that he has given me I will give him satisfaction and an eternal alliance shall be concluded between us. But on the other hand formulate clearly the matters so that I can give you my answer.' I said to him, 'It is for you to formulate the matter clearly.' He replied, 'I will do. State the names of the towns about which I am to concern myself.' I said, 'Hit, Harbe and Yabliya.' He said to me, 'Do not mention Hit. It should remain as before, when Samsi-Addu took Rapiqum from Ešnunna and he allowed me to have it. From that time my garrisons have been stationed there and they are stationed there even now. Just as at that time when the garrisons of Samsi-Addu used to be stationed there, so now the garrisons of Zimri-Lim are stationed there. Just as my garrisons and his garrisons were stationed there together, these garrisons are stationed there together. Let eternal peace reign between us.'[6]

Hammurabi here refuses to conclude an alliance if Zimri-Lim persists with his claim to Hit. It was at this town that the ordeal of the River was enacted, so it clearly had some considerable religious status. It also had an economic importance as the area was a rich natural source for bitumen. What Hammurabi was proposing was a compromise resembling the position at Rapiqum in the time of Samsi-Addu. The town would be shared, with troops from Babylon living together with troops from Mari. However, these negotiations came to nothing, and five years later the problem of Hit was to arise yet again. But Hammurabi's intransigence about Hit put some pressure on Zimri-Lim to make peace with his former enemies.

Firstly he concluded a treaty with the new set of chiefs of the Bene Yamina, who concluded in their assembly that

> From this day forwards let us conclude a permanent peace. May there be no more grief and fear between the Bene Sim'al and the Bene Yamin! May they let their flocks graze in peace![7]

In the summer of 1770 all the kings of the Bene Yamina came to Mari. A ransom was paid and those of their tribesmen who had been imprisoned were returned to their families and any land that had been confiscated was returned to the previous owners.

The negotiations he began with Ešnunna turned out to be much more important than those with Babylon, which had come to nothing. A diplomat was sent by Zimri-Lim bringing with him 'his gods', probably divine statues or symbols, so that an oath could be formally sworn with Ibal-pi-El II. This was a way of concluding an alliance without both parties being present in the same place (it will be discussed further in Chapter 7). Then the diplomat returned to Mari with messengers from the king of Ešnunna who brought his gods with them. However, the process of ratifying the peace with Ešnunna raised serious opposition expressed in a remarkable form of religious sentiment by the prophets of Mari. They wanted to put the king on his guard against any offers made by this deceitful man of Ešnunna. For a long time, Zimri-Lim hesitated, but he finally accepted the treaty as proposed by Ibal-pi-El II. The text of which has been partly preserved, and in it the king of Mari addresses the king of Ešnunna as 'father', thereby recognising his superiority. The renouncing of any further territorial ambitions in the area of Suhum as well as the Jebel Sinjar amounts to a concession by Ešnunna. Babylon and Mari occupied the gap created by the withdrawal of Ešnunna from Suhum. Hammurabi took control of Rapiqum and Zimri-Lim recovered Yabliya, Harbe and Hit.

This introduced a relative balance of power among the kingdoms of the Near East (1769–1766) and for a period a much calmer atmosphere prevailed.

Groups of second-rate powers had kings as their tutelary heads according to a letter from a close associate of Zimri-Lim, Itur-Asdu, to some of his vassals.

> There is no king who by himself can be said to be really strong. There are ten or fifteen kings following Hammurabi, the master of Babylon, similarly for Rim-Sin, the master of Larsa, similarly for Ibal-pi-El, the master of Ešnunna, similarly for Amud-pi-El, the master of Qaṭna. Twenty kings are following Yarim-Lim, the master of Yamhad.[8]

This observation paints a picture in which the Near East is divided into six zones of influence: the three in the east were Babylon, Larsa and Ešnunna, and in the west were Qaṭna and Aleppo. The power of Aleppo at that time was considered to be stronger than that of Babylon. But the letter goes on to show that Mari, located in the centre, was considered to be the sixth of these important kingdoms. Of course the tutelary emperor of Elam towered even higher, but there was no occasion to refer to him in this letter. Its primary purpose was to mobilise the allies of Zimri-Lim so that they could meet at Mari for the traditional feast of Eštar. The reference to 'ten or fifteen kings following Hammurabi' seems to be a circumstantial detail without any recapitulation and it would be difficult to identify them.

The relationship between Zimri-Lim and Hammurabi had now begun to turn sour, and the kings who were aware of this tried to exploit the situation. One such ruler was the new king of Kurda, who was also named Hammurabi and who was not altogether happy with the privileged relationship which Zimri-Lim was cultivating with his two principal neighbours. He decided to request military assistance from Hammurabi of Babylon, whom he referred to as his 'father', through the intermediation of Išme-Dagan, his 'brother', who had had to take refuge with Hammurabi. The king of Kurda was proposing an alliance with Hammurabi of Babylon because Zimri-Lim was becoming friendly towards the enemies of Kurda. This diplomatic intrigue implies that he knew the relationships between Mari and Babylon were not consistently positive. In fact in that same year (1769) Zimri-Lim tried once again to negotiate with Hammurabi on the subject of Hit, but he was not successful.

We do not know exactly why, but the emperor of Elam decided to move against Ešnunna and he claimed support from his Mesopotamian allies. Hammurabi needed no coaxing. When discussing the territorial reorganisation of 1770 and the mediation of the emperor of Elam, we have already noted how the envoy of Zimri-Lim represented him as the 'father' of Hammurabi and of a number of other kings. Zimri-Lim did become involved with the coalition forces, despite the treaty he had concluded with Ibal-pi-El II. The town of Ešnunna was besieged and fell in the spring of 1765. The emperor of Elam moved there and took control of the army of Ešnunna, who had to work alongside the soldiers of Elam. In order to disable Ešnunna as a power base, some territories had to be reassigned. Hammurabi profited by regaining control of Mankisum and Upi. These towns on the banks of the Tigris had been conquered by his grandfather, Apil-Sin, long ago but had then been annexed by Ešnunna. Išme-Dagan, who had been in exile for several years, was similarly able to regain his kingdom of Ekallatum.

Elam on the Offensive in Mesopotamia (1765–1764)

The capture of Ešnunna was just the first scene of a series of actions which were going to prove decisive for the ambitions of Hammurabi. Even though he must have played a part in bringing about the downfall of the city and had lent his support to the Elamites, he still felt threatened by them. They must have been encouraged by their first success at Ešnunna for they then began what was in effect a double-edged advance: on the one hand invading Babylonia and on the other initiating a campaign towards the north-west. Their aim was to capture Šubat-Enlil, just as Ibal-pi-El II had wanted to do a few years earlier.

That Mankisum and Upi came into the possession of Hammurabi after the downfall of Ešnunna seems not to have been to the liking of the emperor of Elam. The terms of his ultimatum are unmistakably threatening:

> Do not the towns of Ešnunna that you are occupying belong to me? Evacuate them and submit to my yoke. If you do not I shall pillage your country up and down. The army will set out from Mankisum and cross the river at this point. I shall be at the head of my troops and I shall cross the river and invade your country.[9]

The army of Elam laid siege to Mankisum because Hammurabi refused to submit, and once the town had fallen into their hands they progressed downstream along the Tigris and laid siege to Upi. To protect himself Hammurabi sent envoys to Larsa with the intention of negotiating an alliance with them. He decreed a general mobilisation of troops in Babylon, and while Upi was being besieged he was impatiently expecting troops to arrive from Rim-Sin of Larsa. But the envoys were slow to return. An impression of the crisis is given in a letter from Yarim-Addu, who was the principal ambassador for Mari at the court of Hammurabi.

> The troops of the enemy have set up camp in the town of Upi and are staying there. The conscripted troops of Hammurabi oppose them face to face. They are ready for combat, observing one another. Today, when I am sending this present tablet to my master, Hammurabi has just issued a decree for a general mobilisation in the country. He has required merchants and

every man to participate, going so far as to free slaves, which he will also use. Furthermore, to strengthen the army he has just sent important officials to Rim-Sin, and every day without fail his messengers are making their way to Maškan-šapir. But so far I do not have any news about the arrival of these troops. After this tablet I will write again to my lord a complete report about what I have learned.[10]

When the officials sent to Larsa did finally return, the contents of the message they brought from Rim-Sin were sent on to Zimri-Lim by Yarim-Addu. At first it seemed that there would be a positive outcome to the request for assistance:

Rim-Sin has written to Hammurabi in the following terms: 'My troops are assembled in my country, and let your troops be assembled also in your country. If the enemy advances against you, then my troops and my boats will join you. And similarly if the enemy advances against me, let your troops and your boats join me.' That is what Rim-Sin has written to Hammurabi. But their troops have not yet made contact with each other. I have not been able to write to my lord a complete report on this matter.[11]

A later report is more sceptical about whether the king of Larsa did intend to send troops:

This is the message that they have brought back: 'I have been considering what you have repeatedly been writing concerning troops, but the enemy plans to move off against some other country. Because of this I have not sent my troops to you, though they are ready. If the enemy plans to advance against you my troops will come to your help. And if the enemy decides to advance against me, let your troops come to my help.' That is what Rim-Sin has written to Hammurabi.[12]

It is obvious that the references in both these documents are to the same message from Rim-Sin to Hammurabi. It was first thought that the king of Larsa was sympathetic to the idea of a reciprocal defensive alliance. But it then seemed that in fact Rim-Sin was turning a deaf ear to Hammurabi's request and did not wish to make any practical contribution to any alliance. He does not send any troops on the pretext that the Elamites will turn their attention to another country. Why Rim-Sin should be unwilling to join an anti-Elamite coalition is never stated explicitly in any extant document, but we can reach the obvious conclusion that he had some family ties with Elam since his father and his grandfather had Elamite names. No more precise details of those links are known.

By stirring up a revolt among the people of Mutiabal around the town of Kazallu the emperor of Elam opened up a second front and threatened Hammurabi from the rear. We know about this again from one of the letters of Yarim-Addu:

> Among the Babylonian troops that have been taken prisoner in the last month there is a chief of a section, belonging to the Mutiabal, who said to the emperor of Elam, 'The whole of Mutiabal has been waiting for this day. Send me back to my country and I will make the Mutiabal revolt in your favour.' That is what this man has stated to the emperor of Elam, and he has been sent to Babylon. When he arrived in Babylon he was interviewed by the king but he kept his intentions secret from the king. Then he arose and went off to Kazallu, where he explained the message that the king of Elam had sent to him. The people of Kazallu paid attention to it, have questioned what they should do and have written to the emperor of Elam.[13]

Hammurabi must have got wind of the affair since he made a proposal to the inhabitants of Kazallu that they should come and take refuge in Babylon with all their possessions. A few accepted but others preferred to take sides with the Elamites. That was their undoing, for Hammurabi came and quickly crushed the revolt. Only a few escaped and found refuge in the north of the kingdom of Larsa. Later Hammurabi sent a message to Rim-Sin, requesting their extradition which was agreed.

Meanwhile, the Babylonian troops had been obliged to evacuate Upi:

> The enemy forces have entered Upi. They have left behind a garrison and the Elamite forces have gone away and reached Ešnunna.[14]

We suppose that a joint force of soldiers from Elam and Ešnunna captured Upi, and that when the soldiers from Elam went on to rejoin their sovereign at Ešnunna, men from Ešnunna were left behind as garrison troops.

The next target selected by the emperor of Elam was Babylon. He sent messengers giving orders to the kings of Upper Mesopotamia:

> Stop quarrelling among yourselves! Come, I am going to lay siege to Babylon.[15]

The Elamites, as they made their way from Upi to Babylon, had to take Hiritum, and the seriousness of the situation confronting Hammurabi could be disguised no longer. He puts his trust in Šamaš that he would be able to overcome the 40,000 strong enemy forces with his more meagre supply of soldiers. Some damage to the tablet means that the number given for his troops is illegible.

> Hammurabi is disturbed that the enemy – Šamaš test them! – is so numerous. However he knows that under orders from the god a force of [x] thousand men can face a powerful enemy and fight a force of 40,000 men.[16]

A second Elamite army advancing up the valley of the Tigris took Ekallatum and then turned north-westwards to invade the Habur triangle. In Šubat-Enlil an Elamite noble was installed and from there he attempted to govern the whole region in

Fig. 11 A view of the island of ʿAna (ancient Hanat) in 1985, at the time when it was being submerged by the Euphrates as the Haditha Dam was constructed. Rescue excavations were undertaken in the years before this happened but they never managed to reach the levels contemporary with Hammurabi.

the name of the emperor. A link between the capture of Ešnunna and the campaign against Šubat-Enlil does not seem to have been forged by chance, for these are landmarks on one of the grandest Near Eastern trade routes of the period. The 'tin route' stretched from the valley of the Diyala to the heart of Anatolia, and in all probability the Elamites intended to control it for profit. There was another group of soldiers from Elam and from Ešnunna stationed to the east of Šubat-Enlil. It was led by Atamrum, who took Andarig before moving on to lay siege to Razama.

Mari was far away from the scene of these events. In the spring of 1766 Zimri-Lim was even further away, for he had left with his whole army to go to support his father-in-law Yarim-Lim, the king of Aleppo. The message sent to tell Zimri-Lim about the Elamite invasion had to be forwarded on to Ugarit, on the Mediterranean coast. The governor of Mari, who had stayed in the capital, had the duty of relaying the messages from the king of Ilan-ṣura, as well as from the king of Babylon, who was pressing him to intervene in the situation.

> Speak to Bahdi-Lim, thus says Hammurabi: 'There are tablets that I have sent to Zimri-Lim. This message is urgent. Have the tablets taken to Zimri-Lim. Write to me with any news you have about the enemy.'[17]

When the king of Mari did receive the news he rushed back to his capital and then on to liberate Razama. Atamrum was thrown into confusion and wrote to the emperor of Elam asking for reinforcements. He suggested an attack on Suhum so that Zimri-Lim would be obliged to retrace his steps. But he gained nothing, no doubt because the operations in Babylonia were in full swing. Now as things had turned out Hammurabi and Zimri-Lim found themselves *de facto* opponents of the same enemy. External events had bought them together without their having wished it. They realised that it was in their best common interest to coordinate their actions. Troops were exchanged even before they had concluded a formal agreement. Just when the Elamites had captured Upi someone called Sakirum from Mari arrived in Babylon with 600 soldiers, and in return Babylonian troops were sent to Zimri-Lim.

The kings of Mari and Babylon solemnly agreed not to conclude any independent peace treaty with the sovereign of Elam, but only after long and complicated discussions about their differences on who had the right to the territory of Hit. It is an alliance that has special interest for the historian, since we have details of the preliminary negotiations as well as the procedure and the text of the agreement. When Hammurabi addresses the ambassador from Mari he raises his hand to Šamaš as a sign of his alliance with Zimri-Lim. He also refers to two types of flour, *mashatum* and *saskum*, which will have had a specific significance of solemnity for the ritual associated with his oath.

> Come, and while I stand upright I raise my hand for him to the god Šamaš. You make me swear before Šamaš with *mashatum* and *saskum*. I will write, and in the same way that I take an oath your master must also take an oath.[18]

The central emphasis of the oath taken by Hammurabi prohibited any separate peace treaty with Siwapalarhuhpak, the emperor of Elam.

> From this day forward and for my whole life I am at war with Siwapalarhuhpak. I will not have servants of mine on the road as messengers along with servants of his and I will not send them to him. I will not make peace with Siwapalarhuhpak without the knowledge of Zimri-Lim, the king of Mari and of the territory of the Bedouin. If I have it in mind to make peace with Siwapalarhuhpak I swear that I will deliberate with Zimri-Lim, the king of Mari and of the territory of the Bedouin, about not making peace. I swear that any peace we make with Siwapalarhuhpak will be concluded together. It is with the best intentions and with complete sincerity that I am formulating this oath with my gods, Šamaš and Addu, which is sworn for Zimri-Lim, the king of Mari and of the territory of the Bedouin, and that I am approaching him.[19]

Despite the solemnity of the language there seem to have been some afterthoughts by each of the contracting parties. A letter from Ibal-pi-El, written only a little while after the alliance had been concluded, shows Hammurabi still with doubts about whether Zimri-Lim would mobilise against him.

> Hammurabi has said this: 'This is what I have heard being said, "Zimri-Lim proposes to go up to Ida-Maraṣ but in fact it is against this place that he proposes to come."'[20]

Some oracular questions posed by one of his diviners show that Zimri-Lim feared for the safety of the troops he had sent from Mari to Babylon to support the struggle against Elam. He thought that perhaps Hammurabi would submit them to a deathly fate.

> About the army of my lord which he has sent to Hammurabi, will not Hammurabi capture this army? Will he not kill it or have it killed? Will he not retain the soldiers as prisoners at will or by force? They went out from the great gate of Mari in good condition. But will they come back again through the great gate of Mari in good condition?[21]

In the autumn of 1765 the alliance was concluded, but it stretched beyond Babylon and Mari, for Yarim-Lim, the king of Aleppo, was also party to it. The *sukkal* of Elam had always enjoyed unquestioned supremacy and it seems he could not have envisaged this resistance he now faced. Zimri-Lim made the whole population take an oath of loyalty, for he was so fearful for the safety of the very heart of his kingdom. Hammurabi may well have acted likewise, though there is no documented evidence for the idea.

For several months the situation further north in the Habur triangle had been growing very much worse and it was reported that 'the Elamite army has swallowed the whole of Subartum'. Some sovereigns in the region supported the Elamites while others opposed them, and they seized the opportunity to settle a number of conflicts among themselves, often violently. South of the Jebel Sinjar a similarly tense situation had arisen. Hammurabi of Kurda had been constrained to recognise the superiority of Atamrum but was suspected of attempting to make friendly overtures to Babylon and Mari. A letter sent to Zimri-Lim states that the *sukkal*, after reminding him that he has been 'taken as a son', i.e. taken as a vassal, intimidated him with orders to stop any such correspondence.

> Speak to my lord, thus says Aqba-Ahum your servant: 'I am sending here to my lord a copy of a tablet which the emperor of the Elamites has sent to Hammurabi [the king of Kurda]. The emperor spoke to Hammurabi thus: "Atamrum, a servant of mine, has accepted you as a vassal [literally, 'taken you as a son'].

> Now all the time I am hearing it said that you are constantly having letters taken to Babylon and Mari. Do not have any more letters sent to Babylon and Mari! If you do send any more letters to Babylon and Mari I shall come down on you like a thunderstorm." This is the message which the emperor of the Elamites has sent to Hammurabi. I have personally listened to this message.'[22]

Išme-Dagan was denounced by the kings of the region and taken off to the emperor at Ešnunna for having remained faithful to Hammurabi of Babylon. He was tortured there and could be released only after a considerable ransom had been paid for him to return to Babylon. From there, Išme-Dagan managed to have his shattered health restored enough to enable him to return to his capital, Ekallatum.

In the end the wind turned against the Elamite invaders. This was largely because of cohesive actions adopted by the Amorite kingdoms and also because Atamrum suddenly went over to the other side. In 1764, after the harvest, Zimri-Lim agreed to send some supplementary troops to Babylonia. Because of his alliance with the kingdoms of Syria, troops were also sent from Zalmaqum in the Balih valley and even from Aleppo. By attempting to bring a degree of reconciliation between Qaṭna and Aleppo, Hammurabi hoped that the king of Qaṭna would send him troops to fight against Elam. But he does not appear to have been successful in this enterprise.

The Elamite siege of Hiritum proved fruitless and they had to abandon it. The emperor of Elam marched back up the Tigris at the head of his 30,000 men towards Mankisum, attacking Šitullum further upstream. But then he was faced with an anti-Elamite coalition Zimri-Lim had successfully put together in Upper Mesopotamia so he was unable to advance any further north. As their last act to mark the end of their adventure, the Elamite army ravaged the territory of Ešnunna before returning to Susa. The name of Hammurabi Year 30 celebrates their withdrawal. The phraseology used emphasises that the one single cause for reversing the situation presented by the might of the armies assembled by Elam was the divine help of Marduk. There is no mention of the aid for Hammurabi that his allies had provided.

> King Hammurabi, the mighty one, beloved of Marduk, thanks to the sublime power of the great gods, has overcome the army of Elam, who had recruited large numbers behind the frontier with Marhaši: Subartum, Gutium, Ešnunna and Malgium. He consolidated the foundations of Sumer and Akkad.

By contrast one of the generals of Zimri-Lim writes in a letter, not without some flattery, how the Babylonians have recognised that it was the aid that the king of Mari had provided which proved decisive.

Fig. 12 A view of the palace in the lower town of Šubat-Enlil (Tell Leilan). The archives that were found here in the course of excavations in 1985 and 1987 can be dated for the most part to the 25 years following the death of Hammurabi. They are particularly important for providing information about the history of Syria for several decades after the archives of Mari become silent.

> Seeing that my lord has organised all that and has saved the king of Babylon and his country, now Hammurabi and his country proclaim the pre-eminence of my lord from earth to heaven.[23]

These two citations are a particularly good illustration of how the different socio-linguistic contexts of two different kingdoms produce different rhetorical styles. In the one the king is presented against the background of the gods, while in the other it is the relationship between a courtier and his king that is portrayed.

The final overthrow of Ešnunna by the Elamites proves to be the decisive factor enabling Hammurabi to expand the kingdom of Babylon as he did in the last third of his reign. In previous centuries the Diyala region had enjoyed such prosperity and power that it curbed any ambitions for expansion that Babylonia may have had. On the other hand, perhaps Zimri-Lim did not make the best choice, for helping the king of Babylon to be victorious would lead to the destruction of Mari, whereas an Elamite victory would probably have put an end to Hammurabi once and for all.

The throne of Ešnunna now lay vacant and Hammurabi, the great victor over Elam, would have liked to occupy it. A letter from Ibal-pi-El, one of the generals at Mari, shows that he had Zimri-Lim's agreement.

> I have read the copy of the letter to Hammurabi which my lord has had sent to me. Concerning his opinion about the land of Ešnunna my lord has written to Hammurabi in these terms: 'If the people of Ešnunna give you their agreement then you yourself should assume the kingship of Ešnunna. But if they do not give you their agreement let one of the princes you have with you be installed in power.'[24]

Another document confirms that a faction favourable to Hammurabi existed at Ešnunna. This letter suggests that members of the royal family of Ešnunna had taken refuge with Hammurabi. But the inhabitants of Ešnunna decided otherwise, and preferred Ṣilli-Sin as their new king. He had been a simple officer in the army and was someone with lower-class roots. Therefore, as Hammurabi re-established diplomatic relations with Elam it was natural that tension between Babylon and Ešnunna would escalate. Ṣilli-Sin sent messengers to Išme-Dagan and to Hammurabi of Kurda asking them not to provide any auxiliary troops if their ally in Babylon should request them to do so. He wrote also to Zimri-Lim asking him to do likewise. But the king of Mari did not need such advice, for he was expecting to get back the troops that he had sent off almost a year previously. These were the troops Hammurabi wished to retain, for he was afraid that there would be another conflict with Ešnunna if Ṣilli-Sin refused to accept the territorial compromises which he had asked for.

In fact the diplomatic ploys Hammurabi of Babylon was adopting discouraged the new king of Ešnunna. Hammurabi concluded an alliance with Atamrum, whom he recognised as king of Andarig, and then immediately afterwards declared his proposals to the messengers of Atamrum, Hammurabi of Kurda and Išme-Dagan.

> The ruler of Ešnunna is holding fast to his previous proposals. If he will abandon Mankisum, Upi, Šaduni and the banks of the Tigris for some distance [literally 'three double-leagues'] upstream of Upi, my territory, which my grandfather Apil-Sin instituted, I will be glad to make peace with him. However, if I am obliged to abandon Mankisum he should reimburse me for the costs I have incurred in confronting the emperor of Elam in view of holding on to Mankisum, and then he will get Mankisum. As for me, I shall keep possession of Upi, Šaduni and the banks of the Tigris for the same distance upstream of Upi.[25]

Hammurabi was adopting a logical position. He had committed himself to a costly war against Elam for the sake of conserving Mankisum and Upi, and he did not want to abandon those towns that had belonged to the kingdom of Babylon in times past without receiving something in compensation. Contradictory information emerged concerning news of the alliance. After having first sent an optimistic message, Yarim-Addu subsequently had to report that Ṣilli-Sin had refused to accept the proposals made by Hammurabi. No treaty was ratified until a year later.

Chapter 3

The Great Conquests (1764–1759)

A new page in the history of the reign of Hammurabi was opened after his victory over Elam. The war he had been waging was essentially of a defensive nature, but in the years that followed various territories were annexed. The first was Larsa, then Mari and Malgium. But this chain of events developed somewhat haphazardly, suggesting that Hammurabi had not given great forethought to formulating a plan for these conquests.

The Annexation of Larsa (1763)

The only Mesopotamian sovereign who failed to join the struggle against the Elamites was Rim-Sin of Larsa. Apparently the victory of Hammurabi and his allies did not overawe him, as time after time he made forays into Babylonian territory. That is the version of events that Hammurabi described to Zimri-Lim in order to justify his request for military support from the king of Mari so as to further his plans to mount an attack against the kingdom of Larsa. This was the first of the confrontations during the last third of his reign that were to result in the king of Babylon substantially extending his territory.

The reasons for the conflict, according to a letter from Yarim-Addu, were that on several occasions detachments of troops from Larsa had been raiding Babylonian territory, ravaging the land and taking captive the inhabitants. Hammurabi refers to Rim-Sin in a letter as 'the man of Larsa' and that he was a constant threat to his country.

> Now the man of Larsa has disturbed my country through his pillage. Since the great gods have removed the grip of the Elamite from this land, I have

> shown several favours to the man of Larsa but he has not repaid me with any single help.¹

At first, Hammurabi limited his anger by breaking off all diplomatic contact, but now he felt he must attack, but not before securing a guarantee for success from the gods. He did not assemble his troops without approaching the gods, uttering a formal prayer requesting an oracle to confirm their authority for him to proceed:

> Now I have made my utterance to Šamaš and Marduk and they have always answered 'Yes'. I have not embarked on this attack without divine approval.²

Tactically the Babylonians and their allies would first have to take the town of Maškan-šapir, which was a secure barrier against any assault on the kingdom from the north. Only after that could they proceed to lay siege to the town of Larsa. When Hammurabi addressed his troops as he sent them against Maškan-šapir, he reiterated that they were marching against a town of betrayers 'who have disobeyed their oath by Šamaš and Marduk'. Such terms show further that he treated the expedition as a holy war in which the support of divine powers was assured. Even so, Hammurabi told them that they must show mercy to the enemy. This suggested that he hoped that, when they first caught sight of the Babylonian troops, the inhabitants of Maškan-šapir would submit without a fight. The same letter states that Sin-muballiṭ, the brother of Rim-Sin, three generals and a force of several thousand soldiers were installed at Maškan-šapir, but they were unable to resist for long and the siege was expected to end quite quickly.

> Three or four days from now the town of Maškan-šapir will be conquered.³

We have no evidence from Mari about the precise date when Maškan-šapir and the northern part of the kingdom of Rim-Sin were taken. Texts from Nippur show that there the year names of Hammurabi were used from the fourth month of his Year 30, and texts from Isin use his year names from the middle of the fifth month. This tends to confirm that once Maškan-šapir was overthrown, a large part of the kingdom of Larsa passed into the hands of the Babylonians. The overthrow of Maškan-šapir and of the principal temple of the town, the Emeslam devoted to the god Nergal, is one of the events commemorated in the Prologue of the Code. Hammurabi there presents it as being accomplished without resorting to violence and states that it was an act of clemency on his part.

> Champion of the kings, unrivalled in combat, I am the one who granted life to the town of Maškan-šapir, the one who provides for the prosperity of E-meslam.⁴

Fig. 13 The façade of the temple of Šamaš at Larsa. The monotony of brick has been relieved by a pattern of half-columns, some of which are shaped spirally.

Following the overthrow of the town, the inhabitants of the region rallied to the side of Hammurabi the victor and enlisted in his army. This notably brusque transfer of loyalty can be explained by traditional hostility between Maškan-šapir and Larsa. The town had been annexed by Nur-Adad of Larsa (1865–1850) and then there was the revolt during the reign of Warad-Sin (1834–1823).

It was now time for the troops of Hammurabi, side by side (the text reads literally that they 'lay down on the couch beside the army of Hammurabi') with those of Yamutbal to advance and lay siege to Larsa.

> He had just conquered Maškan-šapir when the whole country of Yamutbal cried out to Hammurabi, 'Long may my lord live!' Then the army of Yamutbal worked side by side with the army of Hammurabi. Hammurabi went at the head of these forces and laid siege to Larsa.[5]

From a royal inscription of Gungunnum (1932–1906) many years earlier we know that Larsa was surrounded by strong, defensive walls. They seem to have been regularly maintained by his successors as they were still an obstacle for Hammurabi as he made his attack. The siege lasted almost six months. It was not just the troops of the now 'freed' Yamutbal that assisted the Babylonian army. Hammurabi had demanded extra men from his allies, and so in addition he had 1,000 soldiers sent by the king of Malgium and several thousand under the command of a general named Zimri-Addu, sent by Zimri-Lim of Mari. Some letters from officers to Mari described a few details of the siege. One speaks of towers and battering rams and another mentions earthworks, that is to say ramps, used by Hammurabi to advance.

From these letters we learn of some other incidents which took place during the long siege. It appears that the king of Qaṭna, in the west of Syria, had sent messengers to Rim-Sin who were seized by the Babylonians. It is possible that they had been involved with a request to provide some military assistance. There was also a report to Zimri-Lim speaking of the joy of Hammurabi when he heard of the death of the *sukkal* of Elam. This report was nevertheless an exaggeration because although the sovereign had become seriously ill, he was not dead.

The siege may well have lasted longer than the king of Babylon had expected. A letter delivered to Hammurabi by the representatives of Zimri-Lim asked for some of his soldiers to be returned because the king of Mari had great need of them to fulfil his own military duties. But Hammurabi was reluctant to let them go before the siege was over.

> We ask Hammurabi about the day when they will come, and he never fails to reply to us with words like this, 'Yes, today, yes, immediately, I will send a large army to your lord and your lord will be able to achieve his goal.' That is how he never fails to answer us. And we say this, 'Even before you have overcome Larsa and you are able to send a large army to your brother [i.e. Zimri-Lim], before that moment our lord [i.e. Hammurabi] must send his brother a force of two hundred or even of a thousand men, not an extraordinary number but enough for the allies to hear the announcement, "The Babylonian troops have arrived".' With great difficulty our discussions have made him agree to a force of a thousand men, but under these terms: 'Five days from now I shall know what is happening at this town. If the town resists I shall send to your lord a force of a thousand men. But if the town is taken I shall send a force of …' That is what Hammurabi has replied to us.[6]

Once it had exhausted its reserves of grain, Larsa was at last forced to give in, and the news was sent to Zimri-Lim in a letter. However, the letter portrays the event in such a lyrical style that we are unable to learn any precise details about the fall of the town.

> I had noticed, as I had done before, the keen spirit of the Bedouin, but on no other occasion have I ever noticed their spirit so keen as this. Today the god of my lord went in front of the armies of my lord. The lance of the wicked enemy has been broken. The town of Larsa has been taken. There have been no losses, nothing needs replacing. The armies of my lord have survived well. My lord need have no worry. We are doing fine. May my lord rejoice.[7]

A letter from someone else is more specific.

> Once the Babylonian troops had entered Larsa they took possession of the fortified area.[8] In the morning all the men went in. As for Rim-Sin, he was allowed to go out alive.[9]

Hammurabi recalls this victory in the name for his Year 31.

> Hammurabi the king, with the assistance of the gods An and Enlil, went at the head of his troops and, thanks to the supreme power that the great gods had granted to him, he took possession of the territory of Emutbalum and its king Rim-Sin.

Few details are known about events immediately following the capture of Larsa, but those who participated in the attack would naturally have expected to get something for themselves after their efforts. A letter of Yarim-Addu to the secretary to Zimri-Lim, addressed as 'father', gives details of his acquisitions.

> Furthermore, on the matter of a subject about which I am late, may my father not be angry with me! It has now been possible to purchase in Babylon a cook. My father will be delighted to see him. But so far I have not been able to find a brewer for sale. Since the downfall of Larsa I shall be able to get anything my father wants.[10]

Such expectations were followed by disenchantment. Zimri-Addu wrote that 'the whole land of Larsa lies prostrate' and 'they are knocked out by fear'. Now that relationships with Susa had been interrupted, this general who had been commissioned by the king of Mari to buy lapis lazuli, could not find anyone who would grant him credit or anyone to sell it to him.

From the documents at our disposal we know much more about the first half of Rim-Sin's reign than we do the last, which means that finding the factors that led to his downfall is a particularly difficult task. Some of the hypotheses that have been formulated are more probable than others. He will have made strenuous efforts to secure his victory over Isin, which of course would have weakened his military resources. But it would be astonishing to find that during the course of the following thirty years he was never able to replenish those resources. His advanced age may also have worked against him and perhaps he made some wrong decisions. This fails to take account of the fact that his brother and at least one of his sons served with him at the end of his reign, and they would have played an important role in decision making. His downfall could well have been a result of the severe shortage of water in his territory, which had an enormous impact on agricultural productivity.

Evidence for this comes from the record of a commercial expedition in 1781 from Larsa to Ešnunna to buy a large quantity of cereals. The boats loaded with grain had serious difficulties in passing through the canals as the local authorities put up much resistance in opening the canals for them. This may also be the background to Hammurabi's decision after his victory that one of his first tasks would be the restoration of defects in the irrigation system in the south. He commemorates this achievement in the first part of the name for Year 33, however nothing was truly solved as his successor encountered the same problems at the beginning of his reign.

> The king Hammurabi excavated the canal called 'Hammurabi brings abundant supplies for the people whom the gods An and Enlil loved so much'. He provided a perpetual source of prosperity for Nippur, Eridu, Ur, Larsa, Uruk and Isin.[11]

Though there is no textual support for the idea, it would be plausible to suppose that in the time of tension preceding his victory Hammurabi managed to achieve a spontaneous interruption of the water supply, and then repaired the damage which he himself had caused when he had gained possession of the town. A more likely hypothesis is that some structural defect in the irrigation system caused the food shortage that is known to have persisted in 1781. Little by little this weakened the economy of the southern kingdom.

Hammurabi occupied Larsa, where he became known as 'the king of Sumer and Akkad', and Rim-Sin with his courtiers and all his possessions was taken to Babylon. He adopted a new epithet into his royal title, 'the king who made the four regions live together in peace'. He also had a statue of himself inscribed bilingually, in Sumerian and Akkadian, with the words of a hymn recording the favourable oracles he had received from the gods. In the Code Hammurabi is described as 'the one who spared Larsa', implying that although he dismantled the fortifications he did not actually destroy the town.

At first Hammurabi instituted a personal union between Babylon and Larsa. One way in which this becomes apparent is the system adopted for reckoning the sequence of years. The Babylonian formulas had been introduced at Nippur and Isin after the conquest of these cities. But after the fall of the rest of the kingdom, Hammurabi used his conquest of Larsa as the new base for the date formulas. He also proclaimed a *mišarum*, just like any other new sovereign on the throne, but it was limited in scope to the ancient kingdom of Larsa. However, this transpired to be a short-lived façade, with steps quickly taken towards annexation. The townsfolk could hardly be under any illusions when the ramparts of Larsa were demolished soon after it was conquered, and very soon he imposed the Babylonian year name formulas.

The new organisation of the ancient kingdom of Larsa, also known as Emutbalum, in many respects maintained previous practices. The Lower Region to the south, centred on Larsa, was distinguished from the Upper Region to the north, centred on Maškan-šapir. Our principal information for events in the southern region comes from a collection of letters Hammurabi sent to Sin-idinnam. Until then he had been the king's private secretary, now given authority over all the governors of that region. The suggestion that Hammurabi proceeded to confiscate private property from individual landowners is hardly likely since the lands he was now administering were the same lands that had belonged to the royal domain of Rim-Sin. Since he maintained the rights of those who had previously enjoyed beneficial tenancies there was clearly no serious disruption to the way affairs were managed. The continuity of previous practices is confirmed in part of a letter from an official of Hammurabi to the person in charge of rights to land in the Larsa region.[12]

> Concerning the field for the support of Damqi-ilišu and the field of Niggi-na-kiag ... these men have been in possession of the land for twenty years before my lord conquered Larsa.[13] Make a decision on the matter and punish those who have contested their right, and give back to them the grain and the land.[14]

One letter sent by Hammurabi to Sin-idinnam suggests that the provisions of Babylonian law were imposed in the conquered territory. Hammurabi gives orders to Sin-idinnam to pass judgment on some deserters 'according to the laws which now apply in Emutbalum'.[15] These deserters seem to have fled from Larsa in the war and to have taken refuge in Babylonia. Hammurabi insisted that they be judged according to the Babylonian laws, which were now applicable in what had been the kingdom of Larsa.

Disruption

When Hammurabi annexed the kingdom of Larsa he disrupted the general balance of power that had been maintained for several years in the region. Now he could claim that Babylon was the greatest power in the region and he was not shy of demonstrating the power he had obtained. His victory over Larsa led him immediately to conclude several alliances. One that is most noteworthy is his treaty with Ešnunna, where negotiations had been dragging on for nearly a year. At first, when hostilities had just started between Larsa and Babylon, Ṣilli-Sin refused to negotiate with him. It can hardly have been coincidental that the treaty was agreed immediately after the capture of Larsa.

While Larsa was being besieged Išme-Dagan, the king of Ekallatum, took the opportunity to stir up trouble in the region of the Jebel Sinjar and prejudice the position of the king of Mari. He had tried without success to obtain troops from Hammurabi, so then he turned to Ṣilli-Sin of Ešnunna for help. An alliance was concluded between the two of them and he received the requested troops. Zimri-Lim learned that Hammurabi was intolerant of what had developed, thinking that he had been betrayed, that he had invoked the anger of the gods against Išme-Dagan, 'the enemy of my lord', and that he would 'reconsider his attitude to him'.

> When Hammurabi had given his instructions, he put an end to his mourning and did not cease to invoke the god against the enemy of my lord. This is what he said: 'This is not the time but in two months I shall make him reconsider his actions and make him sit in the dust' ... On the other hand I have heard it said that he has said: 'Because he (Išme-Dagan) has entered into an alliance with the man of Ešnunna, I shall reconsider my attitude to him.' May my lord know that![16]

Atamrum, the king of Andarig, found himself threatened by Išme-Dagan. Zimri-Lim was obliged to lead a campaign to relieve his ally, but Išme-Dagan found himself in an abandoned position when Hammurabi and Ešnunna concluded their alliance. Once again Išme-Dagan was obliged to leave his capital, Ekallatum, and he seems to have been in Sippar, not far from Hammurabi, when messengers announced the death of Atamrum in the spring of 1762. Because Atamrum died without leaving any obvious descendant capable of succeeding him, the king of Babylon took control, dividing the kingdom into two to have a better oversight. This Babylonian intervention was marked with the dispatch of an army of 20,000 men. They were sent without much forethought and the arrival of such a massive force set up a panic in the region south of Jebel Sinjar. At Mari there was concern that Hammurabi should not profit from Zimri-Lim laying siege to Ašlakka, which had rebelled, and thus come to besiege the capital of the Middle Euphrates. This concern is evident from a report about a consultation with an oracle, which is dated to the beginning of Year 1762.[17]

It was in this year that a conflict between Babylon and Ešnunna erupted. This makes it clear that the peace treaty they concluded just after the capture of Larsa did not last long. Because no troops from Mari were fighting beside the Babylonians in this conflict this war is less well known than the earlier conflict between Babylon and Larsa. Not only did Zimri-Lim fail to send troops to help Hammurabi, but he actually sent gifts to Ṣilli-Sin as a sign of his support for Ešnunna, thereby showing his opposition to the king of Babylon in this affair. Zimri-Lim must have been angry that Hammurabi had refused to send him the troops he requested during the siege of Larsa. When he saw the king of Babylon entering the region south of Jebel Sinjar, it was a threat to his survival. That is most likely why he decided to change his attitude.

Fig. 14 The slowly flowing River Balih, a tributary of the Euphrates, played an essential role in the environment, not only for the transhumance of sheep and cattle farmers but also for the settled population of the region.

A decisive move in the conflict between Ešnunna and Babylon will have been the capture of Mankisum on the Tigris. The question of the rightful ownership of this town had earlier raised the hackles of Ṣilli-Sin against Hammurabi. The name of Year 32 commemorates the victory of Hammurabi over the army of Ešnunna and its allies, but we have no further details about the battle.

> The year when … he conquered the armies of Ešnunna, of Šubartum and of Gutium and when he annexed the country of Mankisum along the banks of the Tigris as far as the land of Šubartum.

A shorter variant of the year name mentions only Mankisum.

> The year when Hammurabi took Mankisum.

After Ešnunna was defeated the status of the kingdom is not known. At present we know the names of only two of the years of the reign of Ṣilli-Sin, and these correspond to Hammurabi Years 30 and 31 (1763 and 1762). Hammurabi captured Ešnunna in Year 31, so it could well be that the reign of Ṣilli-Sin came to an end.

Fig. 15 The statue of the goddess found shattered in the palace of Mari. She holds a vase-fountain from which floods of little fish would spurt as a traditional sign of fertility. It is now in the Aleppo Museum in Syria.

Not long afterwards the reign of Zimri-Lim also came to an end, commemorated by two different year names of Hammurabi. These state that Mari was defeated in Year 32 and destroyed during Year 34. The first phase is commemorated by the name for Year 33, which begins by mentioning the excavation of a canal to provide water for the towns of Sumer and then continues:

> He (Hammurabi) was victorious in fighting the armies of Mari and Malgium. He subdued Mari and the surrounding area as well as several towns in the land of Šubartum, including Ekallatum, all of Burundum and the land of Zalmaqum, from the banks of the Tigris to the Euphrates, and he made them live together peacefully under his jurisdiction.

There is no mention of the Babylonian attack in the Mari documents. This may be because Zimri-Lim did not return to his palace before his army was defeated, in which case the last set of letters he received would not have been deposited in the archives.

This campaign can be seen as a continuation of the preceding one. The Babylonian troops were pursuing their advance towards the north-west and Ekallatum is now mentioned explicitly. But this creates a problem. We know that at the beginning of the year 1762 Išme-Dagan had been obliged to leave his capital, and he again became a refugee in Babylonia. It could be that Hammurabi reinstalled him on the throne of Ekallatum, and that would concur with the record of the Assyrian king list, which credits him with a reign of 40 years.

The name for Year 33 gives no indication of how these victories were achieved. The Babylonians may have mounted a double-pronged attack, as the men of Ešnunna had done 12 years earlier. One set of troops would have followed the Tigris upstream and then moved westwards to the region of Zalmaqum, high in the valley of the Balih, while a second set went up the Euphrates until they reached Mari. Another equally likely possibility is that a single force marched up the Tigris as far as Zalmaqum. Then they came down the Balih as far as Tuttul and then down the Euphrates, conquering Mari on the way. In his campaign along the Euphrates, Hammurabi aimed for more than the conquest of Mari. In the Prologue to the Code he includes the epithet 'the foremost of kings, the one who has subdued the kingdom of the Euphrates under the "sign" of the god Dagan, his creator, who has shown his anger against the people of Mari and Tuttul'. Here Hammurabi is claiming to have reached the confluence of the Balih and the Euphrates. The victory over Malgium is more poorly documented than that over Mari. This seems to be the third time Malgium had conflicted with Hammurabi. He claims to have destroyed it in the name for Year 10 (1784), and seven years later he won another victory there, helped by Samsi-Addu and Ešnunna.

The two years following the defeat of Mari correspond to the names for Years 34 and 35. For Year 34, work of an unspecified nature on the temple at Babylon is commemorated, but Mari is mentioned in the name for Year 35.

> On the order of the gods An and Enlil Hammurabi, the king, destroyed the great wall of Mari and the wall of Malgium.

The words 'great wall' translate literally the Sumerian expression $bad_3.gal$, and this could be understood to mean either the destruction of the town of Mari as a whole, including its walls, or a special term for the royal palace. It is clear from the archaeological excavations, which always excited the excavator, André Parrot, that the palace had been systematically destroyed. All that remained for us to enjoy were the architectural outlines and, to a lesser extent, some of the painted decoration. The building that came to light had been left almost completely empty aside from the archives, and it is obvious that it had been carefully stripped before being destroyed. Some interesting cake-moulds were found still in place, but these would have had no value in antiquity. The statue of the goddess holding a vase-fountain, as well as those of King Iddin-ilum and King Ištup-ilum, had all been mutilated and left worthless. Another proof of the looting that must have taken place has turned up in 'Nebuchanezzar's Museum' in Babylon, in the form of two stone statues of sovereigns of Mari from the twenty-first century. These must have been ransacked by the Babylonians and brought home as booty after the sacking of Mari.

The amazing number of archives concerned with daily life has made Mari famous. The documents comprise not just the administrative archives, but those of the separate records for the harem. Room 115 housed many thousands of letters which appear to have been stored in seven chests, all sealed and labelled. A part of these archives seems to have been removed, for almost all the letters sent to Zimri-Lim from Babylon and Aleppo are missing. The labels are dated to Year 32 (Month 7) of Hammurabi. The destruction of Mari will have taken place in Year 34, since it is commemorated in the name for Year 35. We have no information about what was happening in Mari for at least seventeen months, between the date on that label and whatever month it was in Year 34 when the destruction took place.

The destruction of the city was carried out systematically. In one of Hammurabi's inscriptions he commemorates the destruction of Mari with these words:

> When he took Mari and the towns in that area he destroyed the walls and changed the landscape into tells and ruins. [18]

This is why, paradoxically, the palace has been discovered in a relatively good condition. When the upper storey was smashed it tumbled down onto the rooms on the ground floor, and some of them that were excavated still stood as high as four metres. It can be presumed that the reference to taking Mari and the destruction of the walls allude to the same facts as in the names of Years 33 and 35, and the rest of the sentence emphasises that the kingdom had been completely annihilated. it is still unknown why Hammurabi elected to wait over a year after he had overcome Mari and the surrounding area before destroying it completely. From Year 34 onwards he used 'the king of all the Amorite land' as his royal title.

Malgium curiously suffered a fate similar to that of Mari. Not only did the king of Malgium maintain diplomatic relations with Hammurabi at the time when he was angry with Rim-Sin, but he concluded a formal treaty with the king of Babylon after Hammurabi had sent him 'help of two talents of silver and seventy gur of grain'. A force of a thousand men sent by Ipiq-Eštar had been helping in the assault against the kingdom of Larsa ever since it was instigated, but this act of loyalty had not been properly recognised by Hammurabi, for in effect he was attacking Malgium. After all, it did occupy a strategically important position on the Tigris and was able to threaten anyone who took up a position in the regions further south. Therefore, it is not surprising that once he had conquered Maškan-šapir and Larsa, Hammurabi should wish to secure the provision of water for the territories he had recently annexed by gaining a victory over Malgium. In the name for Year 34, Hammurabi states that he had gained his first victory (i.e. in his 33rd year) and two years later, in the name for Year 35, he records that he destroyed the walls of Malgium. Like the retelling of his achievements against Mari, a less explicit and rhapsodic version of his achievements in Malgium is given in the Prologue to the Code:

> The clever one, the organiser, the one who has mastered the whole field of wisdom, the one who protects the people of Malgium against being annihilated, the one who set plentifulness around their establishments, who has decreed that pure food-offerings shall always be made to the gods Enki and Damkina who praise his sovereignty.

It appears that an important section of the population of the conquered kingdom was deported to the kingdom of Babylon, for some of them appear in documents from the region of Kiš-Dilbat-Marad, from the fourth year of Samsu-iluna onwards. In one letter, which sadly provides little context to the phrase, we read of fields in the area 'belonging to 5,000 men of Malgium'. It can be assumed that these men are exiles, some of whom have managed to become integrated into Babylonian society.

The fact that Hammurabi did not mount an attack against Der, whose king decided not to take part in the attack against Larsa, is something of a paradox. On the one hand Der had such power that it could have avoided attracting the desire of the king of Babylon to take it under his wing, and on the other hand it was situated to the east and therefore did not represent such a potential threat as Malgium.

Chapter 4

The End of the Reign (1758–1750)

The resounding victories of the previous decade are conspicuous by their absence from the last nine years of Hammurabi's reign. While this may have had something to do with the king's advanced age, it would have been difficult even for someone younger to extend his kingdom further, since the logistical opportunities available at the time were limited. The destruction of the palace of Mari meant that our most important source for information on the political history of the Near East dried up. We have the archives found at Qaṭṭara (Tell al-Rimah) for a few of the years, but they are mainly concerned with local affairs. In rooms VI and XIV of the palace, the archives of a woman named Iltani were found, consisting of about 150 letters and 50 administrative documents. They cover a period of six years which correspond to Hammurabi Years 33–39 (1760–1754). Iltani was the sister of Asqur-Addu, the king of Karana, who seems to have disappeared in the confusion which arose when the Babylonians advanced into that region. Her husband, Haqba-Hammu, had been a highly placed official under Asqur-Addu. He represented himself on his seal as a diviner and styles himself 'the servant of Hammurabi'. From this we conclude that the king of Babylon appointed him to take charge of the country on his behalf, until he occupied the throne of Karana in his own right for three years. His position enabled Iltani to live on in the palace in the royal domain of Qaṭṭara. The reasons behind the destruction of the site are not known.

Information about the events of the last ten years of the reign of Hammurabi is far more meagre than what we had for the previous period. Some of the year names occur only in an abbreviated form whereas the complete formulations would provide more detail. Another problem arises from the fact that some

Fig. 16 Modern Tell Afar, at the eastern end of Jebel Sinjar, now dominated by a fort from the Ottoman period, is perhaps the site of ancient Karana.

scribes do not always use the official formulations. While the variant texts are interesting in themselves it is impossible always to place the events they refer to in a correct chronological sequence. The historical documentation we have for the last part of the reign of Hammurabi is no better than what we had for the beginning of his reign, but there are some administrative and family archives which throw light on the economic and social history of the period. These will be discussed later, in Parts II and III.

The Events

We know nothing about what happened to Hammurabi in Year 35 (1758) but work on the temple at Kiš was commemorated for Year 36. Year 37 is marked by renewed military campaigning. He went north and north-eastwards and notes specifically his victory over 'the army of the Guti, of the Turukku, of Kakmum and of the country of Šubartum'. Afterwards there were a relatively large number of deportees and this would explain the appearance of Hurrian names in the region of Dilbat in the following decades. A victory over 'all the enemies in the land of Šubartum' is commemorated for Year 39, so he was obliged to reinforce his authority there two years later.

The year names for the very end of Hammurabi's reign refer to the construction of a large wall beside the Tigris and the fortification of Rapiqum on the Euphrates for Year 42. In the following year he has a fortification erected at Sippar. It has been thought that these were defensive measures against some military threat, but it is hard to think of an enemy daring to threaten him at the height of his power. What is much more likely is that this work was undertaken because of the threat of flooding, a danger intimated by the massive flood that destroyed Ešnunna in 1756, referred to in the name for Year 38. That disaster was probably caused by the Diyala's change of course. The inhabitants would have had to abandon their city and perhaps take refuge in Babylon. Although there is nothing in the archives to tell us more and no trace of their presence has been found, a clue may be found in the way that Hammurabi describes himself in the Prologue to the Code.

> I am the pious prince, who makes Tišpak rejoice, the one who provides pure offerings for the god Ninazu, the one who has saved his people from distress, the one who secures their foundations amidst Babylon peacefully.

A tablet for Year 43 contains a composite year name in which the shorter formulation for Hammurabi Year 43 is followed by the name of Samsu-iluna. From this we know that he died sometime before Day 10, Month 5, Year 43, the actual date on the tablet. We also have a letter of Samsu-iluna recording that Hammurabi had succumbed to sickness.

The Kingdom of Babylon at the Death of Hammurabi

From the day that Hammurabi inherited the relatively modest kingdom of Babylon from his father, he had transformed it beyond anyone's expectation over a period of 43 years. At the time of his death the Near East was dominated by two power centres: Aleppo in the west and Babylon in the east. Traditionally the new picture of Babylonia has been painted following the topographical outline of 26 towns presented in the Prologue to the Code, summarising the state of affairs at the end of Hammurabi's reign. But a more careful examination has shown that this outline was written not simply from a geographical viewpoint but that it is partly theological, for the list of towns fits neatly into four groups. The first group of seven comprises Nippur, Eridu and Babylon followed by Ur, Sippar, Larsa and Uruk. The first three towns were particularly associated with the major 'political' deities Enlil, Ea and Marduk, and the others were dedicated to major astral deities Sin at Ur, Šamaš at Sippar and Larsa, and An and Eštar at Uruk. Drawing a circle on the map of central Babylonia would link the towns in the second group, beginning with Isin, going northwards to Kiš and Kutha, westwards to Borsippa, southwards to Dilbat, and finally back again to the region of Isin, to Keš.

Travelling upstream from the lower reaches of the Tigris would trace a path through the towns of the third group, beginning with Lagaš-Girsu and then on to Zabala, Karkar, Adab, Maškan-Šapir as far as Malgium. The towns in the fourth group were all conquered by Hammurabi towards the end of his reign, Mari and Tuttul, Ešnunna and Agade and finally Aššur and Nineveh. This new study of the reasons behind the sequence of names is interesting in itself, but we would also like to know why there is no mention of a number of obviously important towns. Kazallu, for example, might have been omitted if it had lost all its importance, but since we now know that the townsfolk there had revolted against Hammurabi just a little while earlier, he probably preferred to pass over the name of this town in silence.

The modern definition of an empire requires it to fulfil three conditions: to have an ethno-linguistic diversity; to occupy an extensive territory; and to be governed by an administration with strong personnel and centralised power. At the end of his reign the kingdom of Hammurabi can be considered to fulfil these criteria, even though it has not been the custom to speak of it as an empire. It is difficult to formulate a general opinion about the matter. We may ask what was the goal of Hammurabi, but cannot be certain that he had one. He may have taken the empire of Agade or that of Ur III as the examples he aimed to emulate. He was certainly able to take control in the west of Mari and Tuttul, but he did not attempt to integrate Susa in the east. The empire of Hammurabi was different from that of Agade and Ur III even when he reached the height of his power. His empire was probably based on taking advantage of a series of lucky opportunities rather than a process of deliberate political planning. But he is also to be remembered for synthesising the ideology of the Sumero-Akkadian world of the third millennium he inherited with the tribal links characteristic of his Amorite background, a task which he accomplished most successfully.

Part 2

Politics

The events that occurred in the reign of Hammurabi outlined in the first part of this book included chronological and geographical descriptions which are absolutely indispensable for a historian. But it was only a skeletal outline, which will be fleshed out in parts two and three of this book. By restoring some measure of life to Hammurabi's half-century of power, we can more clearly appreciate many of the differences between life in that ancient world and the world of today. It will also help to show how we have become the ultimate inheritors of his legacy. Of course we shall have to broach the subject of 'politics', in the way that that word is generally understood, but first we shall look more closely at the way the sovereign fulfilled the privileged position he was acknowledged to hold in respect of his relationship to the gods. The gods had guaranteed him their support and in return he was required to obey their commands. On the human front Hammurabi relied on the personnel of the royal court, his entourage, for without their practical support it would have been impossible for him to govern his kingdom as it grew from year to year. They were directly affected by the diplomatic and military decisions he took in order to extend the boundaries of Babylonia, and these matters will be discussed in Chapter 7.

Chapter 5

The King and the Gods

In general, when writing an historical account, the scholar is first concerned with institutional and political matters and with describing social and economic infrastructures before tackling questions about religion. But religion formed such an integral part of the life of the ancient Babylonians that it is encountered in every theme a historian plans to develop. So in this book you will find no chapter devoted specifically to religion. Even a cursory examination of the relationship between the king and the gods shows that he was the intermediary *par excellence* between the divine world and his subjects. In the ideology of the time he was seen to have a pastoral role and the people are referred to as 'the Shepherd's flock', a metaphor which can be traced back to the third millennium. The power of the monarch was legitimated through a reciprocal arrangement with the gods. Provided the sovereign submitted to their decisions and maintained the upkeep of their temples, they sanctioned his authority as king.

The Theology of Royal Authority

Almost all political entities in the time of Hammurabi centred on a monarchy which assumed a divine right to power, though then as now, this concept can cover different situations. Some idea of how royal power was thought to have been endowed can be gained from reading the traditional titles ascribed to the king. In these statements the king not only boasts of a royal lineage, but that he could also claim to have been chosen to rule by the gods. How he sought to be accepted by his new subjects after his accession or after the annexation of a conquered realm is a subject for further examination. The official ideology of state records also confirms the important role played by the gods, and this stimulates questions about what kinds of political influence the clergy and the temple exerted.

In the case of Hammurabi, his royal titles and epithets can be studied diachronically, clearly synchronising the changes with the changing political situation. The basic title, 'King of Babylon', defines his relationship with his capital city, and it is enhanced by the phrase 'powerful king'. But different phraseology is introduced as the political situation changed in the course of time. After he had expanded his kingdom by conquering Larsa he becomes 'King of Sumer and Akkad', and after the fall of Mari 'King of all the Amorite lands'.[1] Other epithets, such as 'accomplished king', 'competent king', 'mighty king and hero' and 'one whose works are matchless', emphasise the personal qualities of the sovereign. His claim to universal domination is expressed in the traditional title 'king of the four boundaries', and when it is stated that 'he brought peace to the four banks' he is being credited with having imposed his order on the entire universe. The aim of the king is to establish peace, and this peace is guaranteed by the total annihilation of his adversaries. Ceremonial hymns express his royal virtues in a lyrical style.

> Hammurabi, the king, the mighty warrior, the destroyer of enemies, a flood in battles, ravaging the enemy's land, bringing battles to an end, terminating disputes, annihilating warriors like figures of clay.[2]

Some inscriptions, such as the text imprinted on bricks at Larsa, comprise no more than a title with an epithet commemorating one particular royal enterprise.

> Hammurabi, the powerful king, the king of Babylon, the king of the four boundaries, the builder of the Ebabbar, temple of the god Šamaš at Larsa.[3]

The Babylonians considered that the legitimacy of royal power derived from the king's membership of a dynasty. However, although it seems to indicate some inconsistency in thought, legitimacy depended on the fact that he was seen to have been elected to office by the gods. In his commemorative inscriptions Hammurabi is described as the 'son of Sin-muballiṭ, king of Babylon' or as 'descendant of Sumu-la-El, the powerful heir of Sin-muballiṭ, the eternal seed of royalty', a formula which links him both with his ancestors and his own posterity. These allusions to his own royal lineage and the identification of his ancestors may be compared with the names in the dynastic lists. There it is Sumu-abum who is named as the founder of the dynasty to which Hammurabi belonged, so it is somewhat surprising to find no mention of him in Hammurabi's royal epithets. The explanation is that Sumu-abum was a very important nomadic chief of the Amorites but who never actually took up residence in Babylon. Because the prestige he enjoyed during his lifetime was never erased from popular memory, he was later placed officially at the head of the line of kings of Babylon. But because his contemporary, Sumu-la-El (1880–1845), had been responsible for the construction of the great wall of Babylon and the royal palace, he should be considered by us, as he was by Hammurabi, as the founder of the dynasty. Hammurabi named a fortress he had built as *Dur-Sin-muballiṭ-abim-walidiya*, 'Fortress of Sin-muballiṭ, the father who begot me'. In this way he cherishes the memory of his father and concludes the commemorative inscription for the building with the words:

> I made the name of Sin-muballiṭ, the father who begot me, pre-eminent at the four boundaries.[4]

Whenever a king planned to restore a ruined ancient building, a search would be conducted for the original foundation inscription, for in a restored edifice it was customary for the name of the restorer to be placed beside that of the king who had first built it. When he restored the temple at Kiš for the god Zababa, Hammurabi followed that practice and was thus able to commemorate his great-great-grandfather Sumu-la-El, the founder of his dynasty.

> Hammurabi, the strong king, the king of Sumer and Akkad, renovated the Emeteursag, the temple of the god Zababa at Kiš, which Sumu-la-El his forefather had built and which had fallen into ruins.[5]

On several occasions in diplomatic life, Hammurabi made historical references connecting himself with his predecessors to establish a political advantage. He recounted what had happened in the time of his grandfather, Apil-Sin, when he was negotiating with the king of Ešnunna about marking the boundary between their kingdoms, and in discussions with an envoy from Zimri-Lim of Mari he alluded to the kings of Babylon 'since the time of Sumu-la-El and my father, Sin-muballiṭ.[7]

The ritual known as *kispum*, a ritual concerned with the care of the deceased members of one's family, also emphasises the importance attached to the royal lineage. The principal text of this ritual is dated to the reign of Ammi-ṣaduqa (1646–1626). The names of distant ancestors followed by the names of the king's immediate predecessors on the throne of Babylon are listed on the tablet. The king summons them all together, with 'every person from east and west who has no-one to prepare food-offerings for him or to utter his name'. The text is concluded by an invitation to 'Come, eat this, drink this and bless Ammi-ṣaduqa, son of Ammi-ditana, king of Babylon!' It was a well-established ritual and was certainly practised in the reign of Hammurabi.

The kings of the Amorite period laid a special emphasis on their tribal affiliations and most traced their lineage to tribes which had been sedentary for only a few generations. Many political feuds can be seen to stem from persistent tribal rivalries, and by contrast many alliances can be seen to be based on elements of tribal solidarity. The dynasty of Babylon was linked to the tribe of the Bene Yamina, the Benjaminites.[8] In fact in the *kispum* ritual, the ancestors of the kings of Babylon correspond to those recorded on the Assyrian King List. That common tradition may help to explain the close bonds between Hammurabi and Samsi-Addu and his son Išme-Dagan. When Hammurabi mounted his attack against Rim-Sin of Larsa, he did not hesitate in a time of crisis to allude to tribal affinity when referring to the lineage of his principal ally, Zimri-Lim, the king of Mari.

> Apart from the great gods, there is no-one else who has come to my aid except King Zimri-Lim of the Bene Sim'al tribe.[9]

The long involved opening sentence of the Prologue to the Code of Hammurabi is distinctly theological in tone, and royal power is shown to be justified on theological grounds. This suggests that lineage by itself was not sufficient to legitimise the authority of the king.

> When the august god Anu, king of the Anunnaku deities, and the god Enlil, lord of heaven and earth, who determines the destinies of the land, allotted supreme power over all peoples to the god Marduk, the firstborn son of the god Ea, exalted him among the Igigu deities, named the city of Babylon with its august name and made it supreme within the regions of the world and established for him within it eternal kingship, whose foundations are as fixed as heaven and earth, at that time the gods Anu and Enlil, for the enhancement of the wellbeing of the people, named me by name, Hammurabi, the pious prince, who venerates the gods, to make justice prevail in the land, to abolish the wicked and the evil, to prevent the strong from oppressing the weak, to rise like the sun-god Šamaš over all humankind, to illuminate the land.[10]

It could hardly be stated more clearly than here that it is the chief gods of the Mesopotamian pantheon, An and Enlil, who have given all power to Marduk,[11] and that it was they who had made his city of Babylon the centre of the universe and chosen Hammurabi as its king. In this way, the fortunes of the tutelary god of a city are indissolubly linked with the sovereign of that city. This was no new concept. It can be seen also in the text of the prologue to the Code of Lipit-Eštar, where Nin-Isina is mentioned at the same place as Marduk, the city of Isin instead of Babylon, and King Lipit-Eštar instead of Hammurabi. So whether we are talking about Isin or Babylon, Nin-Isina or Marduk, Lipit-Eštar or Hammurabi, the legitimation of hegemony depends on divine favour.

The King and the Gods   79

****

As soon as the people heard that their sovereign had died the whole country would go into mourning and the air would resound with lamentation. In Babylon the sovereign was likely buried reasonably soon after his death and his body placed in a kind of crypt underneath the royal palace, as was the practice elsewhere. A stream of foreign visitors would then arrive, all bearing gifts to show the esteem with which they held the deceased, which they would deposit in his tomb. We do not have a description of the ceremonial mourning for Sin-muballiṭ and Hammurabi, but it seems reasonable to infer that these ceremonies were similar to those we know about for their predecessors and successors.

Fig. 17 The figurine of a man in an attitude of prayer said to have come from Larsa. He intercedes with the god Amurru on behalf of Hammurabi, the king of Babylon.

Once the burial ceremonies were complete the successor to the throne would prepare for the ceremonies surrounding his ascent to the throne. There would be a month of mourning during which he allowed his hair and his beard to grow and he abstained from washing. The end of mourning was announced by brandishing a golden torch, the symbol of Šamaš, and in the name of that god he would promulgate an act of grace, known as a *mîšarum*. There will have been some traditional ceremonies to be performed to mark his ascent to the throne, but the only documentation for these concerns Assyrian kings and comes from the second half of the second millennium. The new king wore a special head-dress, usually described as a crown. The traditional terminology, that he had 'acceded to the throne of his paternal house', has been taken to suggest that the ceremony was performed within the confines of the palace. The scene depicted in a painting from the palace at Mari, which has come to be known as 'the investiture', shows the king dressed in formal apparel and facing the goddess Eštar. The goddess holds a rod and a ring, her symbols of power, and reaches out to touch him. It may well depict the ceremony of a new king ascending to the throne.

Once a new king had taken office it was traditional for him to show generosity to his people by instituting certain measures for their comfort and so increase his popularity. Similarly, when later he overcame foreign powers and annexed their territory, he had to demonstrate that they had now become his people and that he was going to accept responsibility for them. When Hammurabi defeated Rim-Sin and annexed Larsa he presented himself to the local population as a new king, and showed his magnanimity to those he had conquered by proclaiming a *mîšarum*, an 'act of grace'. The people signified their allegiance by shouting 'Long life for my lord!'. Several objects have been found with a laudatory inscription which had been dedicated to the sovereign. One of the most famous is now preserved in the Louvre and has been called 'the suppliant of Larsa', a male figurine, with hands and face overlaid with gold. The man kneels on his right knee and has his right hand raised to his mouth. On the base, as though to set the figurine in context, a relief carving shows someone adopting the same posture facing a deity sitting on a throne. The inscription records that the man is interceding with his god Amurru on behalf of Hammurabi.

> Lu-Nanna ... the son of Sin-le'i has made this statuette of a suppliant in copper, with its face overlaid with gold, for his god Amurru, for the life of Hammurabi, king of Babylon, and for his own life, and he has dedicated it to him as his servant.[12]

It was once thought that the figurine represented Hammurabi himself, but the inscription disproves this. At the time of purchase, the Louvre was informed that the figurine came from the ancient kingdom of Larsa, in which case such an individual intercession for Hammurabi would imply that there was a measure of popular support for the new victorious king. Another example of an individual's political allegiance expressed through religious observance can be seen in the record of a man dedicating one of his daughters as a *nadîtum*, a kind of nun, to the temple of Šamaš at Sippar after Hammurabi conquered the town of Rapiqum in 1783.

****

Seeing that the king of Babylon ruled by divine right it is appropriate to question the role played by the clergy in the administration. This involves making a closer examination of the functions of the temple personnel, for it is all too easy to treat such a question anachronistically, particularly insofar as concerns the term 'clergy'. The role of diviners, who were not attached to the temples, will be discussed elsewhere.[13]

The best examples we have of religious personnel interfering in political affairs concern the activities of the 'prophets', for which most of our evidence comes from documents from Mari. It has long been thought that prophesying was a characteristic feature of religious behaviour in the west and was not to be associated with Babylonia. There the comparable function would have been performed by the professional diviners. Such separation of east from west relied on inadequate documentation, but now we know that prophets were also active in ancient Babylonia. Similarly, we now know that hepatoscopy, the pronouncement of an oracle based on the interpretation of the anatomy of the liver of a carefully selected sheep, a practice attested widely and for a long in Babylonia, was also practised in the kingdoms of Qaṭna and Aleppo in the west. At the time of the invasion of Elam, the political opposition of a prophet at Babylon is recorded in very great detail. In a letter sent to Zimri-Lim, the king of Mari, the utterances of an *âpilum* of Marduk, a prophet of that god, is colourfully recounted.

> The prophet of Marduk has been standing at the gate of the palace and not stopped shouting, 'Išme-Dagan shall not go out from the hand of Marduk! She binds the sheaf and he will be his booty.' That is what he has not stopped shouting at the gate of the palace, but no-one has said anything to him. Immediately afterwards he stood at the gate of Išme-Dagan and did not stop shouting in the midst of a crowd from the whole country, 'You went to the emperor of Elam to establish peaceable relations, but to establish that peace you took away treasures belonging to Marduk and to the town of Babylon for the emperor of Elam. There is nothing left in my granaries and storehouses. You are not repaying me for the favour that I have shown you.

> Will you leave for Ekallatum? Someone who has wasted away treasures that belong to me can not claim any increase from me'.[14]

The way the text is constructed is not without interest. In the beginning, the *âpilum* of Marduk had looked for an opportunity to speak to Hammurabi himself but he was not allowed to enter the palace. Normally it would have been the guards who would have controlled the admission of messengers from the gate to the palace, but if there were some difficulty, one of the higher officials would intervene. That is why at the same moment we see the minister Erra-nada and the secretary Sin-idinnam leaving the palace to explain to messengers from Elam that they are not being allowed to have an audience with the king. The person responsible for keeping the *âpilum* of Marduk at a distance belonged to the inner circle of the advisers of Hammurabi. What would also be interesting to know is if access was denied to the prophet because of a general instruction from the sovereign to his officials. What is more likely is that it was dependent on the nature of the message that the messenger had to relay. Far from concealing the purpose of his mission, the prophet let everyone know what he was about to say. Once he had been sent away from the gate to the palace he turned to the residence of Išme-Dagan, who was in poor health since he had taken refuge in Babylon. He addressed him in the name of Marduk and declaimed that when he came to return to his own land he need not expect help from Babylon.

If we also possessed the letters that were sent to Hammurabi as well as those he sent, there is little doubt that we should have evidence that prophetic activity was just as commonplace at his court as it was at the court of Zimri-Lim, his contemporary at Mari. The prophecies uttered against Hammurabi at the time when he turned against his former ally are particularly interesting. The *âpilum* of the god Dagan makes his support for Zimri-Lim clear.

> O Babylon, will you not stop acting thus? I shall catch you in a net with a cutlass, but I am going to endow Zimri-Lim richly, with the houses of the seven conspirators and their treasures.[15]

Towards the end of his reign Zimri-Lim was increasingly concerned about Hammurabi, and in a letter to the queen Šibtu he asks her to question the prophets about Hammurabi.

> It is now the time to find out about Hammurabi of Babylon. 'Will this man die? Will he speak truthfully with us? Will he mount a hostile expedition against us? Will he take the opportunity of laying siege to us while I am away in the upper country? What is the situation?' Find out what you can about this man. Follow one set of questions with a second set and write to me what you have found out once you have done your questioning.[16]

Her reply must have been an encouragement for Zimri-Lim.

> Concerning Babylon: after having arranged for 'the signs' to drink I put my questions. This man is making many plans against this land but he will not succeed. My lord will see what the god will do to this individual, for you will capture him and control him. His time is near. He will not live. My lord should know this.[17]

The queen carried out the instructions she had been given, first giving something to drink to the prophets, designated as 'the signs'. We do not know what they were given to drink, but whatever was given was presumably designed to give them the inspiration to make their prophetic utterances in the name of the god. Despite the encouraging tone of her response, subsequent events meant that things did not work out as she had been told they would.

It has often been understood that the clergy of Nippur played an important role in legitimising the power of the sovereign. At the beginning of the second millennium, Nippur had never been the seat of any royal dynasty. The city god there was Ninurta. But the main temple in the city, the Ekur, was the sanctuary of Enlil, one of the principal deities of the whole pantheon. The aims of the kings of Isin, of Larsa and also of Babylon had been to possess Nippur, for a ruler could assume the prestigious title 'King of Sumer and Akkad' only through recognition by the priests there. The official year-names on administrative tablets from Nippur document the frequent changes of loyalty. However, there is still no evidence for supposing political interference by the clergy of Nippur. What can be said is that the town enjoyed a special status and was protected from any attempted violent destruction. This must have been an incentive for siting so many historic monuments there in the courtyard of the temple of Enlil, particularly from the Agade and the Ur III periods. They were used as exemplars from which to teach scribes how to make accurate copies of ancient inscriptions.

Many complex questions arise about the divine nature of kingship and we do not know enough to decide whether or not the king was regarded as a god incarnate during his life. In the Amorite period the idea has to be seen as a survival of the third millennium and one restricted to the ancient territories of Sumer and the lands which came to be dominated by them. We do know that the cuneiform sign normally prefixed to the name of a god can also be prefixed to the name of a king, but the name of Hammurabi does not have it until after his capture of Larsa. One inscription does begin with the words 'Hammurabi, the god of his land', but as the sentence continues it seems the expression does not mean all that it seems to mean at first sight.

Hammurabi, the god of his land, the one whom the god An has covered with the aura of royalty, whose great destiny has been fixed by the god Enlil, the obedient one who fervently prays to the great gods.[18]

Decisions of the King

The king would consult his diviners to secure an opinion from the gods before making any decisions about diplomatic matters or military expeditions. No alliance would have been concluded and no troops enlisted for a campaign without such a consultation taking place. Furthermore, he would pay careful attention to the reports he received about any auspicious sign that had occurred in his kingdom, for these would certainly be an indication of what the gods wanted to happen. Moreover, the king had to observe his duties as prescribed in the religious calendar. All this shows that he wished to demonstrate his obedience to the divine will.

When negotiations were being conducted between Hammurabi and Zimri-Lim about who should take possession of the town of Hit, a diviner sent a very detailed report to the king of Mari. He was especially careful in his divinatory techniques to ensure that the answer from the gods was correct. After sacrificing

Fig. 18 One of the inscribed clay models of a liver from the Louvre. Thirty or so of them have been found in the Mari excavations but how they were used is not altogether clear. Objects like this are valuable supplements to the information from literature about the importance of hepatoscopy in the period of the Amorites in revealing the will of the gods.

a sheep and stating the question to be answered, he examined the sheep's liver. This produced a negative answer to the question he had posed. In order to verify that this was the correct answer he sacrificed another sheep and reformulated his question, but this time with a negated verb. The answer he now received was positive. By following such a convoluted procedure, he satisfied himself that the gods were consistent in their opinion. In accordance with the result of the consultation, Zimri-Lim sent his messengers to Hammurabi and put pressure on him to give up his claim to Hit.

> I have dealt with two sheep with the following results. I asked, 'If Zimri-Lim cedes Hit to the king of Babylon, will Zimri-Lim be safe, will his country be in good shape and will it be expanded?' The omens I obtained were not favourable. Again I posed questions to the oracles thus, 'If Zimri-Lim does not cede Hit to the king of Babylon, will Zimri-Lim be safe, will his country be in good shape and will it be expanded?' I consulted the oracle about not ceding, and the omen I received was favourable.[19]

Amorite kings adopted a systematic process for consulting oracles when conducting their military campaigns. For Hammurabi we have evidence from the Mari archives, but a later document excavated at Nimrud, a principal city of the Assyrians and known by them as Kalhu, tells us more. It belongs to the series of tablets known as *tâmîtu* 'questions'. These consist of lists of questions formulated by diviners to Šamaš and Adad. These were the gods who specialised in divination matters when a sheep was sacrificed. The tablet was found in the library of the temple of Nabu and can be dated to the seventh century, but some of the questions are said to have been formulated during a campaign by Hammurabi against the town of Kazallu. The historical information in the *tâmîtu* text can be assumed to be reliable even though there is no mention in year names or commemorative inscriptions of Hammurabi of this campaign. Other questions were posed during Hammurabi's campaigns to the east of the Tigris. From this text we learn more about the Babylonian army and in particular about the attitude required to be adopted by the army chief.

It was normal for the king to be accompanied by his diviners on his military campaigns and they would keep him informed orally of the results of their consultations with the gods. Their reports would not have been put into writing, and this is confirmed by records from Mari referring to divination as it was practised within the royal circle. We have messages from the generals despatched by Zimri-Lim to head the troops provided to help Hammurabi in his military ambitions, and from the diviners who were sent to accompany them.

Diviners from Mari and from Babylon could work together in close collaboration and no questions would be raised about manipulating results.

There is no suggestion that there was ever any suspicion, even a veiled suspicion, about the technique of divination.[20] But it could happen that the interpretation of omens was sometimes open to question and such doubts should not be overlooked. A somewhat complicated situation arose during the confrontation with Elam described in a letter written from Babylonia by two diviners from Mari to Zimri-Lim. Even though it was the diviners from Mari who were the first to draw conclusions from the omens they had examined, they would have preferred the diviners of Hammurabi to be the first to announce them.

> The next day Inib-Šamaš took the omens for the towns of Šitullum and Assur, and I took them for Šubat-Enlil and the land beside the Euphrates. The omens that we had taken we brought to Hammurabi. The diviners, his servants, said nothing and, keeping his face turned towards us, he said: 'Speak!' This is how we responded to him. 'Your servants, the diviners, our older brothers, must speak.' They rose and said, 'Rather it should be you to speak'. But since they did not want to, we spoke thus. 'So far as concerns the towns, all of the towns for which we have taken omens, the enemy will not come and capture the town of Šubat-Enlil. But this town of Šubat-Enlil will be captured by Zimri-Lim.'[21]

There is another letter in which the diviners from Zimri-Lim show some surprise with their Babylonian colleagues after they had conducted their examination of omens according to their own techniques.

When Hammurabi sent out his troops to mount an attack on Maškan-šapir he underlines the fact that he had been guaranteed support from the gods.

> Now I have expressed my concerns to Šamaš and Marduk and their constant response has been 'Yes'. I have not mounted this attack without the gods.[22]

The king might also choose to make a tour of the temples himself to seek the approval of the gods before deciding to set out on a military campaign. He could expect to receive a unanimous positive response and to be told to set out on the campaign without further delay. This is shown in a hymn which contains the text of an oracle which was originally part of an inscription on a royal statue. Whilst we have copies of the inscription on clay tablets, the original statue has not been found.

> Enlil has granted you supremacy. Who do you wait for?
> Sin has granted you supremacy. Who do you wait for?
> Ninurta has granted you a powerful weapon. Who do you wait for?
> Eštar has granted you the conflict and the battle. Who do you wait for?
> Šamaš and Adad are your protectors. Who do you wait for?
> Zababa and Erra are your supports. Who do you wait for?

Marduk and Amurrum [xxx]. Who do you wait for?
Depart![23]

It was not always the king who took the initiative in consulting the gods. We read that sometimes an ominous occurrence was reported to him, and this needed to be referred to his diviners for an interpretation. In the first millennium huge compendia were compiled for such portents. From the Old Babylonian period there are a few preliminary versions of these tablets, referred to as 'forerunners'. Some idea of these instances can be obtained from surviving archival documents, especially from the letters. Various phenomena regarded as supernatural were referred to, such as abnormal births occurring in the flocks and lunar and solar eclipses, but some of the events would hardly appear portentous today, such as the emergence of ants in the palace courtyard. When a governor wrote simply to announce that he had heard thunder, he was fulfilling his obligation as a servant of the king, for he knew that it was to him that the gods would address their message.

Fig. 19 The head of a god in clay. A deity depicted anthropomorphically is often given the traditional emblem of a horned tiara.

The days of the month and the months of the year which were auspicious or inauspicious for carrying out specific tasks, such as concluding a treaty, are listed in calendars. Although the treaties that we possess date only from the first millennium we can show that some of the prohibitions and prescriptions date back further. Perhaps the clearest example is the treaty Hammurabi and Zimri-Lim made against Elam. Here the king of Babylon explains to the king of Mari that because the moon-god Sin had been invoked among the other gods to guarantee the treaty he could not take an oath, for there seems to have been an ancient hemerological tradition in Babylon that that was an inauspicious day.

> He has not made a solemn commitment on the 25th, saying, 'If Sin had not been named on the tablet for a solemn commitment I would have willingly accepted the 25th. But now, given that Sin has been named, I shall make no solemn commitment on the 25th'.[24]

The preliminary rituals were in fact conducted on the 27th and Hammurabi concluded the treaty on the 28th.

****

One of the traditional duties of the sovereign which showed his respect for the gods was to construct and to maintain their temples, and there are a number of inscriptions in which Hammurabi is recognised as 'the one who renovates the sanctuaries of the great gods'. In one dedicatory inscription, when Babylon set out to conquer Larsa, he expresses his gratefulness for the support of the goddess Inanna, principal goddess of the town of Zabala, then part of Larsa.

> After the goddess Inanna had given him favourable omens to govern the country of Sumer and Akkad and had entrusted him with the leash,[25] he has built for the goddess Inanna, well-loved by him, in Zabala, the city where she is sovereign, the temple that she loves, the Ezikalama.[26]

Old Babylonian sovereigns took over the prerogatives which the kings of Ur had exercised over provisions for the temples. It is worth remembering that a chief administrator of a temple on his personal seal could style himself as 'the servant of the king'.

Some of the official names for the years of the rulers in this period clearly show generosity towards the temples in providing them with statues and furniture. As for Hammurabi, a statue was made for the goddess Šala (Year 29), a throne was made for Nanna of Babylon (Year 3), for Zarpanitum (Year 12) and for Adad of Babylon (Year 20), a podium was made for Nin-pirig (Year 6), another for Enlil of Babylon (Year 18), and another for Šamaš, Adad and Šerda

(Year 26). Red gold and gemstones were presented as an offering to Tašmetum (Year 41), and a similar offering to Eštar of Babylon (Year 14) is described in great detail.

> Hammurabi the king made a throne for the goddess Eštar of Babylon on a raised podium which was decorated with gold, silver, precious stones and lapis lazuli. It was decorated like a flash of light to be used on her cart.[27]

****

The prosperity of the country depended on the king. With the rainfall so poor, royal support was given for the maintenance and expansion of a carefully developed system of canals, designed to irrigate the soil that the people depended upon. Without it the economy would have been crippled. In an inscription found at Sippar, Hammurabi praises the goddess Aya through naming a new canal after her, Aya-hegal, 'plenitude of Aya'. The fortified walls of a city were also to be constructed and kept in good repair by the king, for the protection they offered could be seen as a symbol of his care for the people. Hammurabi, in the name for Year 25, commemorates constructing a wall at Sippar, confirmed by several inscribed cones excavated from the walls there. In case the construction itself was not enough to defend the city, he gave a name to the wall intended to endow it with supernatural resistance against attack, 'By the decree of Šamaš, may Hammurabi have no rival'.[28]

Chapter 6

The Government of the Kingdom

In the course of expanding his territory, Hammurabi developed his methods of administration and we know some specific details about the ways in which he governed his kingdom. The relevant documentation comes in the main from his later years, after the annexation of Larsa (1763), where we find references to his 'important servants', more senior officials who were assisting him. For most of the time Hammurabi was resident in his royal palace in the capital but we know that there were occasions when he stayed elsewhere. There were governors in the provinces who were responsible for maintaining his authority locally. Even so, in various ways he was able to maintain direct contact with his people. The role played by the royal family in politics is something which certainly needs to be examined.

The Royal Household

Ancient Mesopotamian society revolved around the concept of the *bītum*. This word was more significant than the basic English equivalent 'house', for it meant more than just a building. The *bītum* included all the people living in the house, all the family members and their dependents, and possibly even their deceased ancestors. Family graves have been excavated beneath many homes, which implies a desire to maintain continuity between the dead and the living. When the word moves from a domestic context to a political one, it asserts the prevalent idea of a patrimonial state. The state of Ešnunna is referred to by the nomad chief Ibal-pi-El, in a letter to Zimri-Lim denouncing the king, as a 'house full of deceit':

> This house has been behaving in all respects like Samsi-Addu in not ceasing to fix its frontiers. It has taken Ekallatum, it has set up its camp against Qaṭṭara and Allahad and it will annex the town it takes. This house is full of deceit.[1]

But in the correspondence of the Amorite period, *bītum* is mostly used to underline a unity perceived to exist between two kingdoms. In a letter to Sin-muballiṭ Anam of Uruk writes that Uruk and Babylon constitute 'one house'. The same idea occurs in another letter reporting the discussions the envoys of Rim-Sin had had with the king of Ešnunna, where it is said 'Larsa and Ešnunna are one single house'. In similar vein Hammurabi writes to the envoys of Zimri-Lim:

> Has this house ever had the least dispute with the town of Mari and is there any matter of contention between the towns of Mari and Babylon? The towns of Mari and Babylon have always been one house and one finger.[2]

When there was an actual affiliation arising from the intermarriage of two royal families *bītum*, comes to indicate a dynasty, but it is too much to infer that such a union existed whenever two powers are said to form 'one house'.

One sovereign writing to another may refer to himself as 'the father' and to the addressee as 'the son', or perhaps to himself and the addressee as 'brothers', and this marks a further expansion of the concept of household unity. Similarly a subject of the king, including any high palace official, will be referred to as *wardum* ('a servant'). This is intended to emphasise obedience and loyalty and should not be taken as evidence that all the men in the royal household were slaves.

****

At present we know nothing about Hammurabi's wives. We do have a record of the names of three of the wives of Rim-Sin of Larsa and, rather unusually, we have personal inscriptions for two of them. One is for Simat-Eštar, who commemorates the construction of a temple to the goddess Nin-egal, apparently with reference to the consecration of a chapel in the palace. The other was inscribed on a diorite vase dedicated by Rim-Sin-Šala-baštašu to the goddess Inanna. She dedicated it on behalf of her husband and her daughter, who was suffering from an ophthalmic disorder. The third wife's name is Beltani, which appears on a cylinder seal. We do know the names of the fathers of these three queens but none of them appears to have been a king.

Royal marriages were generally an occasion for different royal families to establish a formal relationship together or to strengthen relationships that existed already and the Mari archives provide an especially rich set of details on this subject. A short time after Yasmah-Addu married a princess from Qaṭna, his father-in-law Išhi-Addu wrote to him.

> I have given into your arms my flesh and my offspring. May the deity allow that she who is your servant and she whom I have given you should find favour in your eyes! I have given into your arms my flesh and my offspring. The house here has become your house and the house of Mari has become my house.³

An Amorite king would have had two principal wives and both of these queens had the right to the title *bêltum*. He would also have had a number of secondary wives. The status of a queen was one which was most desirable, for one of her prerogatives was giving and receiving presents in her own name. This was the practice of Queen Šibtu at Mari and of her mother, the queen of Aleppo. Some of the daughters of Zimri-Lim who were married off to vassals of their father became disillusioned when they arrived at their husbands' palaces, for they found that they could not enjoy the preeminent position they had hoped for. There

Fig. 20 Music played an extremely important role in the life of the palace and also in the life of the temples. This depiction of a harpist on baked clay is now in the Louvre.

would have been several hundred women in an Amorite royal palace, including numerous musicians with various skills (some of whom were royal concubines) and a large number of domestic servants allocated to do all sorts of work. There was a special area in the inner parts of the palace reserved for the women, usually referred to as the harem. It was guarded on the outside by men, and on the inside by women. In times of conflict the victor would often seek to take possession of the harem for, since it fell to the king's wives to maintain the continuity of his dynasty, he sought to put an end to his enemy's royal lineage.

With regards to Hammurabi's sisters, the information we have is sparse. We can safely assume that he and his contemporary kings will have had siblings, but identifying his sisters to some extent depends on our understanding of the phrase *marat šarrim* (literally 'the daughter of the king'). It used to be thought that this phrase referred to a girl whose father was the reigning sovereign, but it is now understood more generally to indicate any woman with royal blood, including the sovereign's sisters and aunts as well as his daughters. So a less specific translation, such as 'princess', is to be preferred. A king would frequently appoint his sisters to fulfil important duties within the religious personnel, as by having them installed as priestesses or nuns he aimed to foster a good relationship with the gods. Iltani, the only sister of Hammurabi whose name is known, was appointed to serve in the temple of Šamaš at Sippar as a *nadîtum*. Once a girl had been consecrated in the temple she was known as 'the wife' of a god, and this title suggested that her appointment might have been regarded as analogous to being offered in marriage to a foreign court. A king could give away one of his sisters in marriage to a neighbouring potentate to secure some political advantage. Zimri-Lim seems to have been particularly active in arranging such marriages, and at the beginning of his reign he gave away his sisters in marriage before he gave away his daughters. It can be assumed that Hammurabi behaved in a similar way, but in fact the only attested instance is the gift of one of his daughters as a wife for Ṣilli-Sin of Ešnunna. This was probably arranged when the treaty between the two countries was concluded.

One of the best known examples of a king's sister serving as the 'high priestess' of a deity is the sister of Rim-Sin, king of Larsa, who served as the high priestess of Nanna-Sin at Ur and who had a long inscription composed in her name. Some of the names of the regnal years of the kings of Isin and Larsa state that before they were enthroned as priestesses, the girls had been designated by divination to show that the gods had chosen them at birth. The high priestesses of Nanna at Ur are well documented and representations of some of them have been found in the chapel within the building where they lived. Elsewhere, Samsi-Addu installed one of his daughters as the high priestess of Dagan at Terqa. At the convent at Sippar, where his aunt had already been installed, Hammurabi gave one of his daughters as a *nadîtum*. The same act of devotion could also be demanded from a foreign sovereign. Zimri-Lim, king of Mari, was approached by an *âpilum*, a prophet-like figure, on behalf of the god Šamaš, requesting that he send one of his daughters to Sippar as a *nadîtum*. The letters which Amat-Šamaš, a daughter of the king of Karana, sent from Sippar to her sister, Queen Iltani, and which were discovered in the excavations at Tell Rimah, give further information on this topic.

The relationship between a king and his brothers could sometimes lead to tensions and the attitude he adopted towards them was often ambiguous. Normally he would entrust them with senior positions of responsibility. He would naturally have a measure of confidence in their abilities and their loyalty, so it is not surprising to find them playing a significant role in the administration of government. When the Babylonians mounted their famous attack on Maškan-šapir, it was the brother of Rim-Sin who took control of the army in its defence. We also have evidence that he was influential in diplomatic discussions and military matters some time earlier. Rim-Sin's devolving of various aspects of his authority to members of the royal household is most likely what allowed him to reach the ripe old age he did. Some evidence from the records of the great kings of Eastern and Central Mesopotamia, and even more from the records of the tiny kingdoms in the North, show that the king assigned military duties to his brothers. But there were times when a king's

Fig. 21 The relative luxury of life in Amorite palaces can be seen from the splendid bathroom at Mari.

brothers posed a personal threat to his occupation of the throne. This could lead to fratricide, and a letter describing what Asqur-Addu did soon after he arrived in Karana in 1764 expresses disapproval of such an act.

> Also he has executed his brother, who had come up from Ešnunna, as well as three of his very young brothers who had been accompanying him.[4]

****

Because of his many concubines an Amorite king had very many children, but the royal line of succession was maintained by the children he fathered by only one of his queens. They would often be given names that were reminiscent of their ancestors, demonstrating concern about succession in the royal house. It can hardly be by chance that two of the sons of Hammurabi were called Sumu-ditana and Mutu-Numaha and that Ditanu and Namhu (i.e. Numaha) were the names of two of his dynastic ancestors. Similarly Zimri-Lim named three of his sons, Yagid-Lim, Hadni-Addu and Yahdun-Lim, after famous ancestors. He also obliged his subjects in Mari to swear an oath of loyalty to him and also to his first-born son. Emphasis is laid on the continuity of the royal lineage by referring to his father and also to his successors.

> I swear by my gods that I will not transgress this oath which I have sworn by my gods to my lord Zimri-Lim, the son of Yahdun-Lim, the king of Mari and of the lands of the Bedouin. I swear that I will not sin against my lord Zimri-Lim. I swear to repeat every aggressive word I hear from the mouth of the Bedouin in the steppe or settled communities suggesting 'Zimri-Lim and his successors will not govern us any more.'[5]

The usurper who murdered the king of Andarig, Qarni-Lim, focused on eliminating his sons also and thereby to remove any chance of them inheriting power.

We know a little about the children of the king when they are very young from some administrative documents, which note gifts sent to the women of the harem after they had given birth. Such glad occasions are sometimes referred to in letters and there was a general desire to participate in the celebrations. Conversely, there was a great sense of grief when a child of the royal household died. We know of the careful precautions taken by the advisers of Zimri-Lim when they had to prepare him to hear the news that a princess had died at an extremely young age. There were nurses living outside the palace who looked after the royal children, but once the babies had been weaned they were brought back into the palace to be trained. When they reached the age of what we would call adolescence, they did not necessarily have to continue to live beside their

Fig. 22 This tablet, one of the largest found in the archives of the palace of Mari, measuring 23 x 16.5 cm, has five columns on each side. It lists more than 500 persons in the harem of King Zimri-Lim to whom rations of oil were dispensed.

father in the palace in the capital city. Two sons of Hammurabi of Babylon were sent away to be exposed to life in another country. Sumu-ditana was sent to Mari, though the presence of workmen in his retinue suggests that this was not a short visit for a particular occassion. Presumably Hammurabi was satisfied with how things had gone for Sumu-ditana, for later he decided to send his younger brother Mutu-Numaha. Unfortunately the letter about this is damaged and two lines, apparently discussing whether they can both live there together, are missing.

> Hammurabi has sent his son Mutu-Numaha to my lord. Furthermore he has written to my lord as follows: 'Earlier I sent you my older son and he is living with you. Just now I am going to send his brother to you ... about not living together ... allow him to come. If not, send this child to Yamhad or to Qatna, whichever place you find convenient.' That is what Hammurabi wrote to my lord.[6]

We do not know if such an 'introduction to life abroad' was a normal experience for young princes, but the letter provides a remarkable glimpse into the personal relationships that could be found between two different court circles in this period in the Near East. It should not necessarily be thought of as a cultural or idyllic experience, for Hammurabi sent his son just at the time when Zimri-Lim had sent a large number of soldiers to Hammurabi. It could be that the royal princes were regarded in Mari as pledged hostages.

The Palace Circle

Those who held office within the palace circle were all known as 'grand servants', an expression which apparently covers the fact that no formal description of their ministerial duties had been given. While they were all assigned particular tasks, whenever the occasion demanded they could be called away to fulfil functions far removed from their primary sphere of competence. Bureaucracy dominated by administrative hierarchy was a characteristic of the Ur III period, but in the Amorite period what had become more important to the high-ranking officials were personal relationships and their closeness to the king.

The prime position was held by the *šukkallum*, often translated as 'vizier' in an effort to use an English word with an oriental flavour; some very basic questions about his office are still obscure. More than one person may have held this title at any one time. Some letters sent from Babylon by ambassadors of Zimri-Lim, king of Mari, imply that in Babylon under Hammurabi two officials bore this title. Erra-nada is referred to as *šukkallum* and Sin-bel-aplim as *šukkal ubâri*, 'the minister for foreigners', who was especially responsible for keeping an eye on the foreigners resident in Babylonia. He was sent by Hammurabi to Maškan-šapir, where he functioned as a kind of plenipotentiary ambassador and arranged for troops to be sent by the kingdom of Larsa against Elam.

The financial administrator was known as the *šandabakkum*. He supervised the royal domains to ensure that the kingdom had sufficient provisions. In Babylon it was likely Lu-Ninurta who held that title, for he sent numerous letters to Šamaš-hazir, the superintendent of the royal domain at Larsa, which are very similar to those written by Hammurabi himself. We gain a fine insight into the functions of this office from Mari documents from the time of Zimri-Lim, when Yasim-sumu was the *šandabakkum*. High officials such as these as well as the king himself would have at their disposal a *ṭupšar sakkakkim*, 'the scribe of the secret', and they fulfilled the role of private secretaries. The Mari documents give the names of two successive secretaries of Hammurabi, Sin-iddinam and Marduk-naṣir. Šu-nuhra-alu is well known as the private secretary of Zimri-Lim. He was required to read all the routine correspondence sent to the king by his ministers from the provinces and during the course of expeditions abroad, as well as to draft responses for the king.

Of the other dignitaries in the royal entourage we know some titles, but have little evidence of the associated duties. Similarly, we know of duties performed but not of the specific figures responsible for them. For example there were apparently two 'chief barbers' who in lists of witnesses dating back to the reign of Samsu-iluna occur above the *šukkallum*, but identifying them depends on circumstantial evidence. The king would have to trust his barber, for he would hardly allow someone in whom he did not have complete confidence to approach him brandishing a razor. So when we read in letters that Zimri-Lim, the king of Mari, was very close indeed in the court to Dariš-libur we may reasonably infer that he could well have been a 'chief barber'. We can also infer that Ṭab-eli-matim, one of the 'grand servants' of Hammurabi of Babylon, held the same title, although the title he held is not stated.

We also know the names and titles of other high officials who welcomed the 300 troops sent from Mari to reinforce the troops of Babylon at the start of the assault against Elam.

> Apil-ilišu, the son of Damiq-ilišu; Marduk-qarrad, head of the cellar; Šamaš-ili, head of the cooks; and Marduk-naṣir, the scribe.[7]

But it could well be that the titles assigned to the royal courtiers are only remotely connected with the function they actually performed. The literal meaning of the archaic English title 'Lord Chamberlain' would be similarly misleading. There were of course many other lower-ranking officials, such as bodyguards and domestic servants, surrounding the king. Some of them, such as those who carried the parasols, were deaf, which was a way of ensuring that those who were never far away from the royal personage would always be discreet in what they passed on.

****

The term used to denote the king's Council can be literally translated as 'the secret'. Apparently the number of members was not fixed and whenever he felt it necessary the king could admit anyone he wished to. At the time of the war against Elam, three high officials from Išme-Dagan, the king of Ekallatum, set about currying the favour of Hammurabi. They were admitted to his Council and permitted to listen to confidential reports from two diviners from Mari, Hali-Haldun and Inib-Šamaš, although some Babylonian members were not admitted to this Council. The event is recorded in a letter which Ibal-pi-El sends to the king of Mari, and at the end he warns that trouble will follow.

The servants of Išme-Dagan, Išar-Lim, Mutu-Hadqim and Rim-Addu, have evicted the counsellors of the land and they themselves have become the counsellors in the Council of Hammurabi. He holds to their opinion. Hali-Haldun and Inib-Šamaš once or twice consulted oracles but when they reported their findings Išar-Lim, Mutu-Hadqim and Rim-Addu did not take themselves away. They were present and they heard the results of the oracles every time. Apart from the secret report of the diviners what other secret is there? Although his own servants heard nothing about the secret reports of the diviners, they heard them. These men and Išme-Dagan are going to start a quarrel between Hammurabi and my lord.[8]

There are also other letters written to the king of Mari which mention debates that took place in the Council, where Hammurabi always had the last word. On one occasion the king of Mari complained about leaking confidential proposals he himself had made with those close to him leading up to the reunion. In some kingdoms where the sovereign used the elders as intermediaries, his subjects seem to have had an influence on his decisions. On several occasions at Kurda, when taking important diplomatic decisions the kings took account of what was said by the elders.

****

The names of some people surrounding the king are Sumerian while others were given Akkadian names. The names will almost certainly have been carefully chosen because of the significance of their meaning. Because of these meanings, it has been suggested that some members of the king's entourage as well as of the temple personnel were given new names when they formally assumed the duties to which they had been appointed, but since many such appointments were hereditary they could have been given those names at birth. Similar patterns can be seen in theophoric names, such as Sin-muballiṭ, 'The god Sin is the one who lets live', and basilophoric names, such as Hammurabi-muballiṭ, 'King Hammurabi is the one who lets live'. The king is explicitly eulogised in a name such as Rim-Sin-namsipani-dug, 'The shepherding of Rim Sin is good', and implicitly in the shortened form Namsipani-dug. Šu-iliya, the king of Isin, is invoked in the name Šu-iliya-hamatil, 'May Šu-iliya live for me', and so it can be assumed that a king is similarly invoked in a shortened form of the name, Hamatil. A variant form of this name occurs in Mari and in Ešnunna as Ušareš-hetil, 'May he live eternally'. Some of the names of office holders include a distinctively royal attribute, such as Ṭabat-šarrussu, 'His royalty is good'. Similar attributes occur in names expressing vows, such as the Akkadian names Šumšu-liter, 'May his fame increase' and Balassu-lirik, which is also found in its Sumerian form Tilani-hesud, 'May his life be long'. Names such as Rim-Sin-Nergal-lamassašu, 'Rim-

Sin, Nergal is his protective deity' and Rim-Sin-Enlil-kurgalani, 'Rim-Sin, Enlil is his great mountain' express the closeness of the relationship between god and king. The name Kanšassum-matum, 'The land has been made submissive to him' is an example of a programmatic name, those that refer to royal achievements and given to some *nadîtu*-women. At first sight it seems curious that some nurses of the royal children had names such as Abi-liter, 'May my father increase'; Abi-bašti, 'My father is my pride'; Abi-nuri, 'My father is my light' and Abu-lu-dari, 'May my father live long'. But it could be that by including *abî*, 'my father', in the name ensured that as soon as the child was able to utter the name of his or her nurse he or she would unwittingly be ascribing praise to his or her father or formulating a vow for his welfare.

****

The Royal Residences

The natural centre for the power of the king was the *ekallum*, 'the palace'. This word not only refers specifically to the building in which the king resided but also to places under royal authority. So in Babylonia, *ekallum* was used in much the same way as 'crown' is used in England, and expressions such as 'fields of the palace' or 'flocks of the palace' signify crown property. His palace in the capital city was the normal place in which the sovereign resided, although there may have been more than one palace in the capital. There were also palaces in the provinces where he could also spend time.

Excavations have been conducted at palaces and temples discovered in major urban centres such as Isin, Larsa, Uruk, Ešnunna, Mari, Šubat-Enlil and Qatna. Babylon and Aleppo are two major centres where the palace is still to be located. Mesopotamian archaeologists have often been criticised for concentrating their efforts on these centres, but as a result of their efforts we have learned much about the royal palaces of the Amorite period, though admittedly our knowledge is not nearly as complete as we might have hoped. The excavation of the palace of Nur-Adad at Larsa proved to be particularly interesting, even though no written documents were found to help us reconstruct the history of events there. What seems to have happened is that it was abandoned before it was actually occupied. There had been an earlier palace in Larsa but we know nothing about it, not even if there was a resumed occupation by Nur-Adad's successors. They may have decided in the end to build a third palace. Because what was found was just what was in the mind of the original builders, without all the subsequent accretions that are normally found in palaces which have been occupied from one generation to another, the architectural features of the palace of Nur-Adad are unique. At Isin, archives were found in part of one building and from these it

Fig. 23 The sacred area of the pre-Sargonic palace at Mari. Several centuries later, in the reign of Zimri-Lim, the chapel consecrated to Belet-ekallim, 'the Lady of the Palace', was sited on the same spot.

has been concluded that it is a part of the palace of Enlil-bani (1862–1839). The palace at Uruk was built around 1865 by Sin-kašid and has been almost totally destroyed by erosion. All that remains are ruined foundations. It is extremely hard to trace the passages from one room to another and so any interpretation of this evidence is necessarily delicate. Other palaces of the Old Babylonian period that have been partially excavated include the 'old palace' of Assur and the palaces of Ešnunna, Šušarra, Qaṭṭara and Šubat-Enlil. Some of the smaller palace buildings have been completely excavated at Alalah (Level VII) and more recently at Tuttul in the palace of Yasmah-Addu. Of the palaces unearthed at Ebla only the Western Palace, which seems to have been the residence of the crown prince, produced any archives from our period. The more famous archives from Ebla are dated to the twenty-fourth century.

At Ešnunna, a sacred area was found within the palace which is not altogether easy to explain. The area is known as the audience chamber and any attempt to understand its precise function must take into account that there was found within it a chapel consecrated to Tišpak, including a stele on which the name

Fig. 24 A mural painting from 'Palm Tree Court' (Court 106) in the palace of Mari depicting a procession in preparation for a sacrifice. People are processing in two registers, with the sacrificial bull in the lower register, behind a much taller figure, who is probably the king. It is dated as being in the time of Yasmah-Addu.

of the god was inscribed. When such a chapel was first found at Mari, it was thought to be an exceptional feature. The palace had been constructed on top of a building that the excavator described as the 'pre-Sargonic palace'. But it is now suggested that that building had been very much or even primarily used for sacred ceremonies, which can be taken as a partial explanation for the presence of the chapel. In the Old Babylonian period at Mari, the religious tradition survived on a smaller scale in the form of a chapel for the goddess Belet-ekallim. For several days each month the queens were required to absent themselves from the palace to prevent it becoming ritually impure. This requirement may well have been occasioned by the presence of a sacred area within the palace. There could be a reference to the sacred area in a letter from Yarim-Lim, the king of Aleppo. The king had given his daughter in marriage to Zimri-Lim and was being informed about the place where she was now living.

I have often heard it said that the gods are powerful in the palace.[9]

By far the best-known palace in the Old Babylonian world is the palace of Mari. It is remarkable how well the artifacts and the texts that have been excavated complement one another to recreate a clear picture of what was happening within the palace walls. For example, some painted fragments which were found in storerooms on the ground floor led the archaeologists to conclude that the royal apartments must have been above, on the first floor on the eastern side of Court 131. That idea was confirmed when a letter from Zimri-Lim to his mother was recently re-interpreted to show that that courtyard was in fact used to stable the horses offered as gifts to the king.

> Say to Addu-duri, thus speaks your lord: I never stop hearing about the white horses that come from Qatna. They are of fine quality. Well then, on the day on which you get to know about this tablet of mine, you should make a stable in the courtyard of the painted building, beside the gate for the guards, so that there is some shade to protect from the heat of the day. You should spread out some reeds. Let the horses rest there. Let them be brought grain. Furthermore, do not show negligence concerning these orders of mine. The stable for the horses must be made in front of my apartments.[10]

Recent work at Mari has revealed a small palace in Section A of the dig. It had been constructed in the twenty-first century and was occupied by Yasmah-Addu during the first years of his installation there while major construction works were being undertaken in the main palace. At the beginning of the reign of Zimri-Lim it had been assigned to Aqsudum the diviner, the husband of a daughter of Yahdun-Lim. Later documents show that this building came to serve as the residence of Queen Šibtu. Two tomb chambers were found but they had been raided in antiquity, so we cannot know who was buried in them.

When Hammurabi was not residing in the palace in Babylon he was most likely to be found at Sippar, and we hope that one day it will be possible to excavate the palace of Great Sippar at Tell ed-Der. The king also had palaces at Borsippa and at Kiš. That town was only 25 kilometres from Babylon but a document from Mari, dated to 1765, says that he had not made a journey there for at least ten years. If this observation is correct it suggests that the king did not make systematic tours of the principal cities in his kingdom at regular intervals. When Hammurabi started to besiege Larsa he selected the small town of Dildaba as his headquarters. But in one text about that event his soldiers are said to have arrived at 'his palace', which suggests that *ekallum* could refer to any building where the king chose to stay. The town of Larsa with its palace was duly taken and became part of the kingdom of Babylonia. The palaces at Isin and Uruk, which also seem to have been preserved, were similarly integrated. Two bronze knobs bearing the inscription 'palace of Hammurabi' were found when archaeological soundings were made at Tell Muhammad, a site on the outskirts of Baghdad. We do not yet know the ancient name of this site but it will certainly have belonged to the territory of Ešnunna which had been annexed by Hammurabi. In all probability those knobs had been removed from a provincial palace of the king of Ešnunna which had been taken over by Hammurabi rather than being original items in a new palace he had

Fig. 25 Canals were used both for irrigating the agricultural land and for transport by boat; a photo taken in the region of El-Hibbah in the south of Iraq.

constructed. The palace at Mari was destroyed shortly after it was conquered, but this was exceptional. Normally the palaces of a conquered territory were preserved by the victor.

Dissemination of Royal Authority

To ensure that his absolute authority was communicated with his subjects efficiently, an Amorite monarch adopted practical measures. In every important town in Babylonia he appointed a *šâpirum* (governor) as his principal intermediary. In Ešnunna, Mari and Upper Mesopotamia this official bore the title *šâpiṭum*, often translated as 'judge', documentary evidence shows that the person bearing this title was the one to whom the sovereign had delegated supreme authority over the local community. We know that the kingdom of Mari under Zimri-Lim was divided into four main districts, Mari, Terqa, Saggaratum and Qaṭṭunan, with the region of Suhum given a separate status. But for Babylon under Hammurabi we do not know how many regions there were, let alone their names. After Larsa had been conquered there was some reorganisation of the local administration, and such reorganisation was probably the standard procedure after annexing foreign territory. Every smaller region was linked to one of two larger regions (*lîtum*), the Upper Region,

Fig. 26 Excavations at Tell Harmal were begun in 1948 by Iraqi archaeologists to reveal the ancient small town of Šaduppum. The site has been the subject of much restoration work. This photograph shows in the background the plans of the 'temple of the lions', dedicated to Bel-gašer the local god, with the splendid house of the governor in the foreground.

presumably with Maškan-šapir at its centre, and the Lower Region, centred on Larsa. Sin-iddinam had been appointed to take charge of the Lower Region, as becomes clear in a letter from Hammurabi addressed to him.

> When you see this tablet of mine write to all the governors of the Lower Region who are under your authority that they should send to Babylon from the stocks for which they are responsible oxen and sheep, which constitute their due contribution.[11]

Another letter suggests that the Babylonians held the governor of Larsa responsible for maintaining the dykes, though the official bearing the title *šâpir nârim* ('governor of the river') would have had responsibility for the water courses.

> The dyke of the Tigris as far as the sea and the dykes of the territory he governs have been entrusted to Nabium-malik. Nabium-malik shall be responsible to the palace for the fields for which income is due and for those of the *rêdûm*-soldiers, the *bâ'irum*-soldiers and the people known as *nâši biltim*, and if ever a breach should occur and crops should be damaged, for anyone who may suffer loss.[12]

Just after he became king, Samsu-iluna, in connection with the *mîšarum*, that he had promulgated, sent a general letter to all his governors requiring them to return to the capital city accompanied by the elders of the different localities under their control. This illustrates perfectly how governors were the main channel for communicating the decisions of the king to his subjects. Decisions about any matters raised by a town's municipal authorities could also be taken by the governors, as shown by a letter sent to the governor of Kiš during the reign of the father of Hammurabi:

> If that is the desire of my chief, you should call together the town and the elders and then make a decision of the matter.[13]

In the reign of Zimri-Lim the governors of the kingdom of Mari were involved in several different kinds of problems. In the course of their general administration they would have had to investigate crimes, mete out justice and regulate matters affecting the cult. From their letters they often seem to have lacked initiative. Zimri-Lim appointed a former governor of Mari to be the governor of Nahur, and once he had moved far away from the capital, this man had more scope to show his initiative. In solving crimes and administering justice throughout the kingdom of Babylonia the leaders of the community, the elders (the heads of the most influential families) and the *rabiânum* ('mayor') played an important role. Their responsibility is alluded to in a sentence in the Code.

> The community and the mayor of the territory within whose boundaries the act of brigandry has been committed must compensate him for the loss that he has suffered.[14]

The part they played in keeping order in their community is also referred to in letters and reports of judicial decisions. One letter states that

> The murderer of my brother has been handed over to the mayor and the elders of the town.[15]

From this statement it should not be assumed that the mayor had the right to condemn someone to death, but he was responsible for the prison in the town and those who were detained there. A father who alleged that his son had been bewitched by his wife and his mother-in-law also brought his complaint before the leaders of his community.

> I have gone to find the mayor and the elders of the town and I have explained this problem to them.[16]

Fig. 27 The impression of 'Seal I' of Mukanišum, the steward of the king of Mari. The inscription reads: 'Mukanišum, son of Habdi-bahati, servant of Zimri-Lim'.

Fig. 28 A haematite cylinder-seal representing the king as 'the warrior with a mace'; see D. Collon, *Cylinder Seals III. Isin-Larsa and Old Babylonian Period*, (London, 1986), pl. I, no. 388.

They attempted to make a reconciliation but when the attempt was rejected he went to find the judges, and they urged the mayor and the elders to bring the son, the wife and the mother-in-law before them. A letter addressed to 'our fathers, the judges of Nippur' written by the mayor and the elders of Isin is another example of local community leaders liaising with the judges.

The official appointed to make public announcements about important information to the king's subjects was the *nâgiru* ('herald'). He functioned like a town crier, traversing his local streets to draw attention to events such as the loss of someone's seal, to which great importance was attached. Other occasions requiring his services included summoning those required for a military expedition; for conscription to work on government building projects and announcing the arrival of merchandise; the organisation of expiatory rituals after the outbreak of an epidemic. According to the Code, the services of the herald would also be required when a slave went missing.

> If someone has given shelter in his house to an escaped male or female slave belonging to the palace or to an individual, and if he has not brought him out at the cry of the herald, the master of the house shall be put to death.[17]

The Image of the King: The King and his People

It would be wrong to conclude this chapter without drawing attention to the ceremonial occasions when the king appeared in public. When Zimri-Lim was required to achieve some measure of reconciliation by meeting the kings of the Benjaminite states, he clearly wished to impress his audience with all his finery, and very precise details of how to fix his headgear are recorded. It seems to have been essential for a king to conduct a review of his troops as a prelude to their going out to fight, and whenever his loyal subjects were conscripted as soldiers he would meet them in person before they marched into battle. Among the several more or less complete versions of royal addresses to troops preparing for battle that have been found, we have the speech of Hammurabi to his soldiers before they mounted their assault on Maškan-šapir. When Zimri-Lim assembled his whole army to dispatch an auxiliary force to the king of Yamhad someone from his inner circle advised him to come out in person and encourage his soldiers. Even though the oracles were not altogether favourable to the proposal that he should join them on the expedition, he was still encouraged to bid them farewell.

> May my lord go away in accordance with his oracles. If the god has responded 'Yes' to my lord concerning his movements may my lord come here. And if the oracles are bad may my lord come here, may he see his

servants and may he bid farewell to his servants. When my lord takes up position in the assembly of his servants and his servants see him, the heart of the infantrymen will live. And similarly, if my lord will take up position at the head of the field the hearts of the troops shall be as bright as the sun.[18]

Apart from the records of his public appearances, we also have a few images of the king which can be dated to the Amorite period. Examples are found of sculptures, both in the round and low-relief, of paintings and of engraved images on cylinder seals. They follow a standard pattern of craftsmanship. It is sometimes possible, as in some of the details mentioned in year-names, to link an Akkadian or Sumerian term in a text with an element in iconography, but there are still a number of words which cannot be linked in this way with any measure of certainty. Most often the king is represented as a warrior and on many cylinder-seals he is described as 'the warrior with a mace'. On a stele in the Louvre, though his face is now lost, Samsi-Addu is shown overcoming his foes. He stands erect, in profile, stamping on the enemy with his left foot and striking his brow with an axe. The king of Ešnunna is depicted on the Daduša stele from Tell Asmar, and in the lower register nine heads from his decapitated foes can be seen. A particularly bloodthirsty example from Mari is a seal of the steward Mukannišum, showing the king victorious in battle.[19] The king hoists his enemy with his left hand and strikes him with a curved club which he brandishes in his right hand. Two goddesses are looking on and the one behind him joins him in trampling over a pile of corpses. The name Mukannišum means 'one who causes to submit', referring back to the king whom he served, and the violent scene can be interpreted as an iconographic reminder of what that name implies. In the great painting decorating the rooms on the first floor of the palace at Mari the king is depicted as a hunter, a pursuit that is analogous to battle.

Such aggressive representations of the king are in stark contrast to those where he stands face to face with a deity, where his posture illustrates his piety and corresponds to statements in texts where he is said to be prayerful. Such statues may perhaps be alluded to in several year-names where it is stated that they were brought into a temple. In the lunette of the Louvre stele on which the Code was inscribed Hammurabi is depicted in such a posture. He stands in front of Šamaš, almost certainly a statue from the temple in Sippar, with his right arm raised as he receives the insignia of power. Two similar scenes come from Mari. One is the centrepiece of the famous painting of 'the investiture' and the other is on the seal of Samsi-Addu. Sometimes the king carries an offering in his arms, the iconographic equivalent to a text stating that the king had a young child on his breast. Acts of administering justice may also be taken as embodying piety. The name for Hammurabi Year 22 refers to a statue representing 'the king of justice' in the entrance to the Esagil. The statue has never been found but the phrase occurs again in the epilogue to the Code. Other year names state that his grandson Abi-ešuh was 'clothed in justice' or that he carried the 'sceptre of justice'.

Of the few statues in the round that have survived hardly any were found within their original archaeological context. In the twelfth century BC raiders took away some statues of the kings of Ešnunna to Susa as booty. Year names suggest that most of them were destined to be placed in temples, and in 1970 in the temple of Šamaš in Larsa a statue of a king of Larsa was discovered, uninscribed and headless. Some show the king standing still and others show him on the march. The figure of Išme-Dagan of Isin presents him as a sprinting champion, following in the style of the representation of Šulgi, king of Ur, and comparable to the later image of Ammi-ṣaduqa posed as a runner. A statue of Zimri-Lim which was offered to the god Addu of Aleppo forms the subject of a set of Mari letters. There was some discussion about how the statue should be displayed in the temple, with the king of Mari insisting that it be placed on the knees of the god. Sovereigns would also have statues made of their royal predecessors who had died and have them placed in temples to make offerings to them. The key to understanding why they did this is found in an inscription of Sin-iddinam, king of Larsa (1849–1843). He had had a statue made of his father, Nur-Adad (1865–1850), had it placed in the courtyard of Ebabbar, and devoted it 'to his own life'. It becomes clear from the invocation Sin-iddinam addressed to the statue that he wished to have someone to intercede for him with the god.

> Statue of the just shepherd, take up your position every day in the sanctuary of Ebabbar, so that the days of my life may be prolonged.[20]

It is impossible now to use evidence from sculpture to draw with any certainty an image to show what Hammurabi actually looked like. The way in which he is represented at the top of the stele of the Code bears no sign of any individualising trait. It has been suggested that a stone head of a man in the Louvre may represent Hammurabi in his later years but, to say the least, this idea must be treated with caution. The statue dedicated by Lu-Nanna and the votary plaque of Itur-Asdu do not represent Hammurabi himself, but the individuals who are interceding for him.[21]

Chapter 7

War and Peace as Means of Conquest

Although perhaps imprecisely, the term 'international relations' has been used for a long time in studies concerned with the second half of the second millennium BC in particular. The texts that have made it possible for the subject to become a primary focus of research include those discovered in the palace of Pharaoh Amenophis IV at El Amarnah in Egypt, the archives of the Hittite kings at Boghazköy in Anatolia and those discovered at Ugarit (Ras Shamra) in Syria. But now our knowledge in this subject is even more extensive and detailed for the period of the eighteenth century. Material from the archives at Mari, even though the publications are far from complete, is particularly informative, and it can also be supplemented with material from other sites, such as Shemshara, Tell Rimah and Tell Leilan. The pictures we can paint now against a background of kings vying for leadership with one another is much more complete than it was thirty years ago. This fuller picture is particularly relevant when it comes to examining the middle part of the reign of Hammurabi, for we now know so much more about the general framework of his decisions about engaging in battle and of his efforts at diplomacy.

War

It is all too easy today to adopt an anachronistic attitude and to forget that going to war was a matter that brought with it a great sense of pride in a certain section of the ancient society with which we are concerned. Literary texts abound with allusions to the warrior as the embodiment of an ideal, and even in an ordinary letter from a nomad chief to one of his colleagues that ideal can be found. A victory in battle was taken as a confirmation of a blessing from the gods. The conqueror was assured of prosperity at least for a short time after his victory. All this is radically different from the values we hold today in Western society, and we have to realise that it is a relatively recent phenomenon for a country to be debating the reasons why going to war may not be justified by law, reasons which have been pushed to their limit in recent years. We now have enough material to understand some of the reasons why a king engaged in warfare: some details of the resources he had at his disposal in the way of an army and weaponry as well as details of strategy, both for the conduct of a pitched battle and for besieging the enemy.

Before undertaking any military campaign, we know that the king of Babylon would seek to assure himself of the support of the gods. But the texts that document these consultations do not state that he had received a command from the gods to go out and conquer a foreign territory. Thus it is not really possible to suggest that Hammurabi went into battle under the impression that he was engaged in some kind of 'holy war' to expand his empire. In later times the god Assur was to make it the primary duty of the king of Assyria to extend his political frontiers, but for Hammurabi it was different. In his deliberations he seems rather to be a king who was constrained to do battle for other reasons. If any reasons are given to justify starting a war it is worth looking behind the scenes to see whether these reasons correspond to reality.

An interesting exchange of correspondence between Hammurabi and Zimri-Lim concerns the question of who was going to possess the town of Hit. At a time when the Elamites had invaded Babylonian territory, Hammurabi found himself in urgent need of the support of Mari, and the ownership of this town was a crucial element on which the alliance depended. Hammurabi did not wish to give it up, and he justifies his position to an envoy of Zimri-Lim:

> The strength of your country consists of donkeys and chariots, but the strength of mine consists of boats. The reason I really want to have this town is the bitumen and the naphta. Why else would I desire it? I will agree for Zimri-Lim to have anything in exchange for Hit when writes to me.[1]

Here Hammurabi refers explicitly to items of military significance and it is likely that the control of the availability of basic materials for warfare played some part in the resolution of conflicts. Today nations are concerned with access to natural products such as oil and they had similar needs, such as the access to tin, as mentioned earlier. In Babylonia the most efficient means of transporting goods was by boat, but to caulk them properly they needed access to bitumen. Hammurabi probably demanded that Zimri-Lim abandon the town of Hit because it was famous for its rich wells of bitumen. Access to bitumen

Fig. 29 One of the sites for bitumen near Hit, on the Middle Euphrates. The possession of this town was of crucial importance in negotiations between Zimri-Lim of Mari and Hammurabi of Babylon.

was not as important for Zimri-Lim as it was for Hammurabi because essential communications in the kingdom of Mari were conducted by land.

****

An ordinary soldier in the Babylonian army was called either *rêdûm* or *bâ'irum*. Because the literal meaning of *rêdûm* is 'follower', it has been suggested that his initial duty was to escort dignitaries for their protection, a function today sometimes fulfilled by a policeman, and was then employed as a regular foot soldier in the army. The literal meaning of *bâ'irum* is 'fisherman', and this certainly suggests that he patrolled in a boat when fulfilling his military duties, especially important in the extensive marshlands of Southern Iraq. Of course, this would also afford him ample opportunities to catch fish.

The standard terminology for the higher ranks in the Amorite armies are conventionally translated as lieutenant, section commander and general. The precise duties of *šâpir rêdê* are still unclear but he seems to occupy the highest military rank. A general at Mari, Ibal-pi-El, writes that he is in overall command of a corps of 1,000 men, being immediately responsible for ten section commanders who were individually responsible for two lieutenants. A simple calculation shows that a lieutenant was probably in charge of 50 men. Within that context it could be assumed that the Babylonian army operated similarly, but we have a letter giving different numbers.

> Our colleagues, the Babylonians, appoint a general for 200 or 300 men in a corps.[2]

Very precise numbers are given for the actual manpower Zimri-Lim employed in his army. The accounts for bronze for the year 1772 show that 4,217 men were involved. When he assembled the army six years later to undertake a campaign to reinforce Yamhad he had 4,293 men, of whom 4,145 actually marched out and 148 were placed in a secured garrison position. He had enlisted these troops from three of the districts in the centre of his kingdom, Mari, Terqa and Saggaratum. Zimri-Lim also had troops provided by the nomad chiefs who had placed themselves at his disposal. These numbers are relatively modest when compared with the numbers of troops enlisted in Central and Southern Mesopotamia. When Elam took control of the kingdom of Ešnunna they supplemented their own force of 10,000 men with 20,000 men from Ešnunna. A general who had been sent out on reconnaissance to 'the land of the Guti', in the Zagros mountains, claims to have encountered an army of 9,000 Elamites and 3,000 Gutians, and accordingly he wrote to his king, probably the sovereign of Der, requisitioning a corps of 5,000 men.

Although such information has not yet been found for the army of Hammurabi, the questions he addressed to Šamaš and Adad before setting out on a campaign shed some light on the nature of his troops. What we have is a copy of the original text, made 1,000 years or so later than the original, and it shows features of modernisation that make it difficult to restore the Old Babylonian terminology exactly.

> The troops of the palace, the troops of the palace-gate, the troops of the chariots, the troops on foot, the élite troops, the troops of the steppe, the troops of the assembly (?), the troops from Sutu, the support of the nation, troops under the command of Marduk, as many as Hammurabi, the king of Babylon, makes ready, organises and sends out.[3]

Infantrymen or foot soldiers formed the core of an army's strength. The principal weapon of every *rêdûm* was his lance. This became a symbol for the whole army and the word took on metaphorical nuances. Various types of bow were also used as attacking weapons. For defence they only had shields and helmets.

The established system for payment for most soldiers was with an *ilkum*. The king had granted them the possession of a plot of land to which was attached an obligation to perform military service. Someone granted an *ilkum* was allowed to keep all that he produced from that land in return for making himself available for specified duties, whether military or civil. The Code stipulates that someone failing to meet the obligations would incur severe punishment.

> If a *rêdûm* or a *bâ'irum* who has received an order from the king to take part in a royal expedition has not gone there or has hired a mercenary and sent him instead, that *rêdûm* or *bâ'irum* shall be put to death and the informant shall take his house.[4]

According to a recent interpretation of another clause in the Code, severe punishment was not reserved for lower ranks but applied equally to officers.

> If a section commander or a lieutenant has taken into his command troops holding a different loyalty or has accepted a mercenary as a replacement on a royal expedition and included him, that section commander or lieutenant shall be put to death.[5]

An Amorite army of the period would normally include some mercenaries who had been taken on directly by the king. Letters from Mari indicate that there were occasions when different sovereigns competed with one another to attract into their forces the Guti, stalwart mountaineers from the Zagros. Other contingents of foreign troops found in the major armies would have been sent by an ally of the king. On two occasions Zimri-Lim supplied troops to support Hammurabi, against Elam and against Larsa. The status of such foreign troops presented some difficulties about where to house them. They were billeted in quarters outside the city, as allowing them to move into the capital would have posed a risk. When foreign troops arrived in support Hammurabi would go out from his palace and welcome them. The 1,000 Bedouin soldiers who came from Mari were taken into a garden where they were given a meal. When they had paraded in front of the king, they were offered presents as a sign of welcome. Since we know of other letters referring to similar events, such as the welcome afforded to the troops from Yamhad who had come to support Hammurabi in his struggle against Elam, it can be assumed that it was obligatory for him as king to go and formally welcome the allied troops in person.

Soldiers who had distinguished themselves in action were also given gifts at the end of an expedition according to their rank and their achievements.

> Hammurabi gave to every one of our soldiers who had captured the prisoners a silver ring weighing two shekels and a garment. To Kibsi-Addu who led them in the march he gave a pelisse made of sheep's wool and a silver ring weighing eight shekels. To my lord's 650 conscripted men Hammurabi gave 2 shekels of silver for ten men.[6]

Regulating the integration of foreign troops necessitated a separate command structure to be maintained, as happened when troops came from Mari to assist Hammurabi to resist the invasion from Elam and were used to lay siege to Larsa. When contingents from Babylon were sent to the aid of Mari, first in 1771 against Ešnunna, and later in 1765, against Elam, the procedure was probably similar.

The Elamites' assault against Babylon created an extremely dangerous situation and the king resorted to a general conscription. In fact the measures he adopted went beyond the scope of a normal conscription. The decision to liberate slaves was exceptional. The service of the merchants would have been especially valuable since they were used to travelling through the territories with which their own homeland was now at war.

> On the day on which I am having this present tablet dispatched to my lord, Hammurabi has just decreed a general conscription in his land. He has requisitioned the merchants as a troop and everyone else, going so far as to liberate the slaves, to have them at his disposal.[7]

At Mari the census, an event known as *têbibtum*, was a part of political life. On the basis of etymology it has been suggested that the word indicates some sort of religious purification. However, it likely had no religious connotations at all and is to be understood simply as a civil census, which had the specific aim of establishing what part the men of each locality would play when it came to mobilisation.[8] The first known census was conducted in 1776, in the reign of Yasmah-Addu, and another was conducted in 1770, in the reign of Zimri-Lim. On both occasions they occurred at the end of a period of war. Monitoring what manpower was available was obviously necessary when it came to recruiting troops to fight against Elam. One archived document of that time records that when Benjaminites arrived in Der, a town close to Mari, the number of persons present was recorded and set against the number of those who were theoretically available for mobilisation. The shortfall was noted.

As yet we have no record of Babylon conducting any such census. What we do have is a large tablet from Larsa, dated in Hammurabi Year 31. The name of the month is missing, but it is safe to assume that it was written within a few months of the town being conquered by the Babylonians. It lists the names of 360 men in 20 different sections and also seems to have military significance.

One of the most important commodities for maintaining a stock of arms in good order was bronze. It was used for renewing the tips of lances and every sovereign was concerned that stocks should be available. Zimri-Lim spent a considerable sum on replenishing the stocks of bronze in the palace of Mari in preparation for war, and on one occasion Samsi-Addu resorted to having the bronze removed from the tomb of Yahdun-Lim, the illustrious former king of Mari.

Chariots seem to have played a secondary role in Amorite military tactics, for they were used primarily to convey high-ranking persons. It has often been said that the horse did not enter the stage of the Near East until the middle of the second millennium, but recently published documents now show the role it played from the eighteenth century onwards was certainly not negligible. It was first ridden and only later used to draw chariots, after the techniques of training and harnessing had been correctly worked out.

Providing enough supplies of food for the soldiers involved complicated logistics which were not always solved, and this led to complaints from the troops. After Hammurabi had sent some Babylonian troops as reinforcements to the king of Mari, his officers wrote later setting out their grievances.

> Concerning our maintenance rations, about which we have written to our lord, and our lord wrote to us, 'I have myself questioned the men whom I had assigned to you for your maintenance rations and they have done the accounts. There is not one single man in the troop who has not received his maintenance ration.' That is what my lord wrote to us. At the moment our administrators are at Mari and Mut-Hadqim is staying with them. May our lord make enquiries. May what is missing be given to the soldiers who have not received their rations.
> Besides this, why has our lord promised us our ration of oil? It is now four months since any ration of oil was given to us. May our lord give orders for us to be provided with what he has promised us.[9]

The nature of the rations that were provided also could lead to complaints. Because it is not easy to keep a milled cereal, fresh rations would be delivered as grain. But on occasion, soldiers were sometimes supplied with flour so that they could prepare their food instantly, and their allowance of sesame was delivered not as seed but as the extracted oil to be used for the care of their bodies. At the siege of Larsa, the troops from Mari were transporting soil to build the siege ramp for an assault on the town walls. When they were told there was no oil but only sesame seed they refused to accept it, and a letter of complaint was sent by a general of Mari to Hammurabi.

> This is what the king has said to us. 'Since you are not able to receive sesame I am going to write for oil for the troops to be brought from Babylon.' That was what the king replied to us, but there is no oil for the troops, and still they are carrying the soil. May my lord know this.[10]

Sometimes a campaign would last longer than expected and the army was obliged to spend the winter far away from their base. In these circumstances the soldiers needed to be supplied with warm clothes. This situation arose in 1771, when the forces of Ešnunna were marching into the region of the Jebel Sinjar. The king of Andarig, an ally of the sovereign of Ešnunna, showed his concern for the position these men found themselves in.

> The men of Ešnunna are spending the winter at Qaṭṭara in preparation for a march into the land of Šubat-Enlil. And Qarni-Lim has just demanded for his country 4,000 garments which are to be given to the men of Ešnunna.[11]

At the same time the Babylonian soldiers who had been sent to help Zimri-Lim sent a complaint to the king of Mari.

> May our lord have garments sent to be our clothing ration. The army is completely nude and has become morose. May 2,000 garments not appear to be too important an expense for our lord. The army is moving around in the bitter cold. May our lord speedily grant them satisfaction.[12]

****

Once there had been a formal declaration of hostilities against a foreign power the army would be sent in to mount an attack and a state of peace would change to a state of war. At the beginning of the invasion of Upper Mesopotamia, the king of Ešnunna sent a message to Zimri-Lim.

> I am going to establish my frontiers. I am on the way to Šubat-Enlil.[13]

At the same time, in the Euphrates valley a prince of Ešnunna alerted one of the Mari generals that an attack was imminent. A similar ultimatum was later sent by the *sukkal* of Elam to Hammurabi.[14] A letter sent to the king of Der by a king of Aleppo threatened a lightning attack. Even though the style of the letter has given rise to the suggestion that it is not genuine it can still be taken as signifying that such letters were the normal means for making a public declaration of war.

Soldiers would sometimes be stationed on standby in a garrison in some town or other ready to be sent on an expedition. When they went into action other garrison troops would be needed to replace them. A letter from Hammurabi to the governor of Larsa specifically requests such an internal transfer of forces.

> The general Sin-idinnam, who has been resident in Rapiqum, has left on a mission with his troops. Once you see this tablet, send one of the generals of the troops of the country in your region, who has not left on an expedition and whose troops have been left within the country, with his men to Rapiqum to reside there.[15]

In 1765 the army of Elam was able to invade the Habur triangle without any difficulty, as all the men stationed there had left to follow Zimri-Lim into the kingdom of Aleppo. We can therefore see that it was not always possible to keep the forces in balance.

Success in war in the Amorite period, as at other times, relied heavily on the collection and dissemination of intelligence. As much reliable information as possible had to be obtained about the location of one's adversary, and captives were often taken, made to talk and sent back to the enemy lines as spies. Army commanders were perfectly willing and able to spread rumours based on disinformation and to dupe the enemy by leading them to believe false stories, such as those which exaggerated the numbers of men sent to the battle-front. During a war, disseminating such crucial information was not easy, because the security situation demanded precautions against a messenger and his messages being captured. Escorts were therefore provided to accompany the messengers on their dangerous journeys and merchants, who were used to travelling abroad and whose contacts granted them a measure of immunity, were often entrusted with tablets. Fire-signals were sometimes used to announce an emergency situation from one town to another. A system of codes for particular messages seems to have been used, but this method of communication was occasionally unsuccessful.

It was not unusual to intimidate the enemy into changing his opinion, perhaps by torturing some captives and sending them back with their scars or by a public humiliation. When the king of Aleppo captured soldiers in a garrison, he had them stripped of their arms, their belts and their clothing and sent them out of the town naked. But there were also occasions when a charm offensive was adopted in an attempt to rally public opinion behind the victor. After the victory over Zalmaqum, Samsi-Addu advised his son that he should treat the people well.

The name for Hammurabi Year 27 is 'He constructed the great emblem in red gold, which is carried in front of the army, for the great gods who support him', from which it is deduced that soldiers on the march carried before them an emblem of the gods. Several letters from Mari refer to 'Eštar' being carried at the front of the army of Samsi-Addu and also at the front of the army of the king of Ešnunna. The word probably refers to banners representing the goddess who is primarily distinguished for her prowess in battle. One of the generals of Mari states that he himself marched in front of the army with a diviner at his side.

> In front of the army of my lord marches the diviner Ilšu-naṣir and there is a diviner with the Babylonian army. These 600 soldiers have taken up position in Ša-Baṣṣim. The diviners are carefully pondering over the formulation of the questions to the oracle and if they are auspicious 150 soldiers will leave and 150 will come back.[16]

****

When Zimri-Lim concluded a treaty of alliance with Ibal-pi-El II of Ešnunna, he swore an oath promising assistance 'at the scene of arms and of battle, at the fortifications and the encampment'. This suggests that in the ancient mind a military distinction was made between a pitched battle and siege warfare, which obviously demanded different tactics.

It is difficult to shed much light on the military tactics adopted by Hammurabi or his contemporaries since descriptions of actual battles are rare. The detailed official accounts of battles from the later Assyrian annals have no parallel in Old Babylonian records and there is little detail available in the letters from this period. Perhaps there was some kind of inhibition, because such information could be regarded as a military secret, about committing such details to writing. It is somewhat unusual to have the record of two individuals who wished to show Zimri-Lim that they were in some way involved in the victory at the battle of Pardu, which was in fact simply an escapade of secondary importance.

When Hammurabi had to oppose the Elamites, a contingent was sent to him from Mari under the command of Zimri-Addu. Ibal-pi-El writes to complain that the second-in-command of the operation, had been insubordinate, the letter giving us some idea of his conception of the 'art of war'.

> At this moment my lord should send a message to Zimri-Addu. Does he confirm him in his position or does he dismiss him from it? As for me, should I have to allow room to be made for the palace intrigues like today? And besides, when I wish to come into battle, should I have to justify the plan of attack which comes out of my experience? If not, this man is going to make the army adopt ideas which are seditiously aimed against me and I shall not have enough resources to ensure the necessary security. I have just now written to my lord. He is informed about it. This person is giving me great trouble. As far as I have been able to see the army has already been led to adopt seditious ideas aimed against me.[17]

Fig. 30 A general view of the ruins of Mishrife, ancient Qaṭna, showing part of the imposing glacis going round all four sides of the town.

An attack could be launched with an ambush, a raid or a pitched battle. An ambush, sometimes referred to as a trap, involved duping an army on the move so that they suffered maximum losses. An illusory alliance might be suggested as attractive to the enemy, which is the dramatic manner in which the king of the Turukku tricked Išme-Dagan in 1763.

A raid into foreign territory was designed to pillage any local materials that could be found. Babylon and Mari made such raids into Ešnunna's territory at the time of the invasion by Elam, and also Larsa sent commandos to raid Babylonian territory before war broke out between them. In such circumstances it was essential to have a speedy means of communication, so that as soon as the alarm was raised, men and beasts and grain supplies could be taken into the safety of a fortified shelter. Such *razzia* tactics were famously employed by semi-nomadic groups such as the Turukku. They would set fire to the fields of the enemy and burn their produce when they made their raids just before the harvest.

In the course of a pitched battle the various sections of the army would have certain allotted positions. References to these positions in letters include the 'front', the 'right wing' and the 'left wing', the 'tail' with the centre referred to as the 'navel'. The decision about precisely where to position the commander of the army, according to the text of an oracle from the reign of Hammurabi, was fixed after consulting the gods.

Shall Hadašu-likšud, son of Sin-nerari, who is appointed chief of the foot soldiers, take his position at the head or in the navel?[18]

It was obviously most essential for the towns of this period to be fortified with a surrounding crenellated mud-brick wall. Generally the walls were raised on top of a glacis to deter any enemy assault. The gateways had a central vault and were flanked with observation towers. Mishrife, ancient Qatna, in Central Syria is a particularly fine example of such a fortified town. The glacis is imposing in itself, but would have been even more ominous if it had not been totally denuded of any trace of walls or bricks. Several commemorative inscriptions from Central and Southern Mesopotamia record the construction of these walls, which are said to be 'as high as mountains'. They alone would have obstructed the view of the distant horizon when gazing across the plain. At such a height they would have been more dominant than existing remains which conceal and to some extent protect the splendour of the ancient towns. Some towns in Upper Mesopotamia were separated into an upper section, generally referred to as the acropolis, and a lower section, but there is no evidence for such separation in the towns of Central and Southern Mesopotamia.

In the course of a military campaign the attacker would often have to resort to siege tactics to take a town in which the enemy had taken refuge. Several accounts of a military siege are preserved, including the Elamite sieges of Upi and of Hiritum and Hammurabi's siege of Larsa, as well as the siege of Qabra in 1780. Normally it would take at least a week before a town would surrender to a siege, but Qabra was able to resist for longer than this. Išme-Dagan claimed he could take a town by siege in a single day. This suggests, even though he is careful to emphasise the exceptional skill he demonstrated in his conquests, that the fortifications must have been of little use. The king of Qatna also displayed military expertise when he took several towns one after another all along the valley of the Beqa'a in a kind of progressive march. The sovereign of a well-fortified city that found itself under siege always had the possibility of buying off those besieging his city. Samsi-Addu, Hammurabi of Babylon and Ibal-pi-El of Ešnunna were bought off by the king of Malgium with a sum of 15 talents (about 440 grams) of silver, but a few years later the king of Razama, besieged in his well-fortified capital city, chose not to buy off his adversaries.

The two armaments required to mount a successful siege were the demountable siege-tower and the battering ram. First a base would be laid for an earthen ramp across which the various sections of the tower could be transported to the highest point of the glacis. Once the tower was assembled the battering ram was suspended on it and its bronze pointed head was swung against the walls in an effort to break them down. Ladders and walkways on the tower helped the attackers to set foot on the ramparts. Whilst this was taking place, the men in the town would do all they could to interfere with the construction of the ramp and the assembly of the tower. If they could possibly set it on fire then they would see all the efforts of their attackers come to nothing. This was the bitter experience of Atamrum when he tried to take Razama. But when faced with medium-sized town walls, it was sometimes enough to get sufficient ballast for the ramp to reach right up to the top of the fortifications and then the attackers could march directly on to the ramparts. Once a town had been taken it was customary to tear down its walls. That is why there were no remains of walls found during the excavations at Larsa, for after his victory there Hammurabi razed them to the ground.

A war always had important economic consequences, particularly concerning the transfer of goods and of people. Not just the capture of an enemy town, but even a successful raid was always followed by pillaging, so that the losses of the vanquished became the gains of the victor. The established procedures for sharing out the spoils among the soldiers were strictly enforced and salutary punishments were administered if they were not respected. A small group of letters sent by the Babylonian generals to the king of Mari refer to Hammurabi sending men to reinforce to troops of Zimri-Lim in 1772. They did not want to return home without their fair share of the booty and wrote about the animals that had been pillaged.

> Further to the earlier oxen that we have had brought to our lord we have just had another 300 oxen and donkeys brought to our lord. On absolutely no account should these oxen and donkeys suffer from thirst. Let our lord give orders that they may graze and be reinvigorated there where there is pasture.[19]

In reply the king of Mari proposed to keep the oxen and give some slaves in exchange for them. To this the Babylonian generals replied and stipulated a rate of exchange.

> At this moment we have not had these oxen sent. If our lord agrees then our lord may take possession of these oxen. But if it turns out that our lord has some objection, then let him count one slave for every two oxen and have them brought to us. If these oxen are not good enough to be taken, let my lord be responsible for the custody of these oxen, by giving precise instructions to Meptum, so that he can be responsible for transporting these oxen to Babylon.[20]

After they had taken their booty, the conquering army would sometimes initiate a systematic destruction. The excavations at Tell Harmal, ancient Šaduppum, confirm the reports in letters from Mari that this happened when the Elamites were withdrawing from Ešnunna. One effect of war in Central and Southern Mesopotamia that had catastrophic economic consequences was the blocking off of rivers and canals so that the enemy was deprived of their water.

Inevitably, soldiers would be taken captive in the course of a military campaign. Prisoners of war could be sold as slaves but could then be repurchased and brought back home. The Code of Hammurabi considers the situation of a foot soldier (*rêdûm*) or a marine (*bâ'irum*):

> If a merchant repurchases a foot soldier or a marine who has been taken captive while on a royal campaign and lets him return to his town, if there is something in his house with which to repurchase him he will have to repurchase himself. If there is nothing in his estate with which to repurchase him, he shall be redeemed by the temple of the god of his town. If there is nothing in the temple of the god of his town with which to repurchase him, the palace shall repurchase him. His field, his orchard or his house will not be given for his repurchase.[21]

In one letter from Hammurabi, theoretical provisions of his Code seem to be applied in practice. However, it is also possible to assume that particular legal decisions, such as this instruction to purchase the freedom of a prisoner-of-war, formed the basis for the formulation of some of the sentences in the Code.[22]

> Sin-ana-Damru-lippalis, son of Maninum, whom the enemy has captured, give ten shekels of silver from the temple of Sin to his merchant and repurchase him.[23]

Some sentences in the Code are concerned to minimise the suffering of the families of soldiers who had been taken prisoner.

> If there is a foot soldier or a marine who has been taken from a royal fortress as prisoner, and if his field and his garden has been given to someone else when he left, and if he has performed his duty, if he returns and goes back to his town, his field and his garden shall be given back to him and he shall perform his duty.
>
> If there is a foot soldier or a marine who has been taken from a royal fortress as prisoner, if his son is capable of performing his duty his field and his garden shall be given to him and he shall perform his father's duty.
>
> If his son is small and not able to perform his father's duty a third of the field and the garden shall be given to his mother and his mother can bring him up.[24]

Obviously a soldier who had been captured could not fulfil his legal obligation to work on his land, and this then had implications about how to maintain support for his family. This subject of the welfare of the soldier's family is raised elsewhere in the Code, and the solution there proposed is to allow his wife, who had been deprived of daily sustenance, to marry another man.

> If a man has been taken prisoner and there is nothing to eat in his house, if his wife has entered the house of someone else this woman does not have to be punished.
> If a man has been taken prisoner and there is nothing to eat in his house, if before he returns his wife has entered the house of someone else and gives birth to children, if her husband subsequently comes back and returned to his town, this woman must return to her first husband. The children shall follow their respective fathers.[25]

The authorities sometimes deported members of the population once victory had been achieved, including influential members of society. In Year 36 Hammurabi decided to deport the Turukkû to Dilbat. They never returned to their homeland, and a hundred years afterwards subsequent generations of their descendants were still known to be living in Dilbat. But the most worrying demographic consequences, whether looking at the problem from a military or a civil perspective, arose when a community found its numbers depleted through death. It seems that epidemics would break out frequently once an army had been sent out on a campaign, and some of them turned out to be extremely serious.

It would be wrong to say that the army never resorted to playing a political role, for we know that they did just this when Ešnunna was conquered by Elam. On the one hand, generals took it upon themselves to contact Hammurabi and invite him to intervene, and on the other it was the army which was responsible for choosing Ṣilli-Sin and installing him as their new king. But these events were triggered by the fact that every member of the former royal family had disappeared as a result of the conflict and so they are hardly to be regarded as representing normal procedure.

Diplomatic Relations

In the normal course of events, correspondence would be regularly exchanged between one palace and another. Gifts would also be exchanged. Sometimes in the interests of consolidating international friendship, such as concluding a treaty or arranging a marriage to bond together two dynasties, special events would be arranged.

The messenger was the kingpin of successful diplomacy. Usually a group of them would be sent to conduct the business required and only rarely would one travel alone. Some of the messengers referred to in the Mari texts travelled only within the territory of the kingdom. But there were others who were privileged to be granted an audience with the king, either when Mari was the final destination or when they stopped there but were obliged to travel on further. The kings would send a companion (*âlik idî*) to stay beside them as they carried out their duty, but not just to provide extra security. He often directed the way in which they fulfilled their mission. Even with such precautions there were times when a group of messengers would find itself under attack, for instance from the Sutu, nomadic groups frequenting their route.

An incident mentioned in one of the Mari letters shows that a raid by these nomads could prove useful to a king in the furtherance of his plans. A group of messengers had been sent to Aleppo from Babylon, but on their way some of them escaped and took refuge with Samsi-Addu. The standard extradition procedures of the time required him to send the messengers back to Hammurabi, but instead he welcomed them into his court and asked to know the purpose of their journey. After the Babylonian delegation had begun to return from Aleppo to Babylon in the spring, Samsi-Addu contacted two Sutu chiefs and arranged for them to attack the caravan. By operating in this way there was no reason for Hammurabi to suspect what had really happened.

The behaviour of the guards at the palace, who would carefully vet any visitors before ushering them inside, sometimes led to letters of complaint.

> When we arrived at the gate of the palace it was early morning. The guards allowed a messenger from Kurda to go inside.[26]

An envoy of Zimri-Lim who had travelled to Babylon seemed annoyed that he was not automatically granted an audience with the king.

> Since I arrived in Babylon I have not been able to have an audience with Hammurabi so that I could explain to him what I have to say. So I have not been able to send my full report to my lord about his reply to me. At the moment it is not necessary for my lord to become annoyed.[27]

The pique felt by those not admitted inside is understandable. A letter of Yarim-Lim shows that some Elamites had no reticence in expressing their annoyance.

> These messengers have not stopped shouting at the palace gate. With their own hands they have torn their clothing and say, 'We have come with proposals for peace, so why are we not able to … or to come inside and have an audience with the king?' That and many other things is what they have said at the palace gate. But no-one replied to them and they have gone away.[28]

However some people who were excluded, such as diviners from Mari who had been asked by the general Ibal-pi-El no longer to accompany him, expressed

Fig. 31 The site of ancient Kurda is almost certainly to be located at the modern town of Beled Sinjar, lying just to the south of Jebel Sinjar.

their complaint more discreetly. They state that they have been treated like a 'section–commander' so it can be assumed that normally only the higher-ranking officers of the army would be granted access to the king and that a diviner expected to be regarded as a higher ranking officer, perhaps even a general.

> We shall no longer go into the palace with him. He despises us. We have been thrown out of the dwelling like a simple section commander.[29]

Once the messengers had arrived at their destination the king would receive them and offer them hospitality. They would be housed in specially requisitioned accommodation and, as a matter of course, be offered new clothing and silver as well as a supply of meat, grain and oil. The records suggest that not everyone received the same rations, and that more generous portions would be offered to the more prestigious members of a delegation. What is more, the level of hospitality offered to the messengers seems to have been commensurate with the esteem in which the host king held the king who had sent them. When Išme-Dagan came to Babylon he was given only a basic allowance and this led him to complain that the messengers of Zimri-Lim who were in the city at the same time had been given 'pork meat, fish, poultry and pistachio nuts'.[30] This was not the only such incident. When a delegation from Mari was in Babylon at the same time as a delegation from Yamhad (Aleppo) they were treated so differently that La'um wrote a letter to Zimri-Lim, who had sent him from Mari to Babylon, complaining about the behaviour of Sin-bel-aplim, the minister of Hammurabi responsible for foreign relations.

> We went in for the meal in the presence of Hammurabi. We went into the courtyard of the palace. Zimri-Addu, myself and Yarim-Addu, just the three of us had been given new clothing. The men of Yamhad went in with us and all of them had been given new clothing. Because they had given clothing to all the men of Yamhad but they had not done so for the secretaries, the servants of my lord, I myself spoke to Sin-bel-aplim about them. 'Why are you showing discrimination against us, as if we were the sons of a sow. We ourselves, for whom are we the servants, and for whom are the secretaries the servants? All of us are servants of [the same high-ranking king]. Why do you make a difference between the left and the right?' That is what I said forcibly to Sin-bel-aplim. I myself accosted Sin-bel-aplim, and the secretaries, the servants of my lord, became angry and went out of the palace courtyard.
>
> The problem was reported to Hammurabi and in the end they were given new clothing. Once they had been clothed Ṭab-eli-matim and Sin-bel-aplim reprimanded me with these words. 'This is what Hammurabi says. "You have not stopped causing me trouble since this morning. So do you have the responsibility of taking the decisions in my palace about clothing? I dress those whom I want, and I do not dress those whom I do not want. There will be no other occasion when I shall dress messengers for a meal."' That is what Hammurabi said. My lord has been informed.[31]

The king could send his messengers as representatives of himself, as when the king of Aleppo wrote to his son-in-law that he should not require the envoy he was sending to prostrate himself, but rather that he should treat him as if he were the king himself. This exception to the rule illustrates what would have been the normal custom. Similarly, around the time of the invasion from Elam in 1765, there were kings who judged it best if they prostrated themselves in the presence of the emissaries of the *sukkal*, but the local sovereign refused to bow, according to a letter from an envoy of Zimri-Lim at Kurda.

> They have arrived at Kurda but Hammurabi has not gone out to prostrate himself before them. The messengers from Elam have said. 'Why has Hammurabi not come out to meet us, has not prostrated himself and has not sacrificed an ox or a sheep?' [32]

Messengers will have enjoyed some degree of privileged status, but in times of tension they were not exempted from harsh treatment. The envoys of the emperor who came to Hammurabi when Elam was invading were without hesitation confined to their allotted residences and then restricted to basic rations, but as soon as the troops had left Babylonian soil they were subjected to a softer regime. There were occasions when the lives of messengers were put at risk. In 1772, during the war with Ešnunna, the king of Mari refused to allow an envoy from the king of Qaṭna to pass through to there, for he had learned that earlier a messenger had been killed. This provoked a message from Qaṭna,

> Concerning my messenger whom I have sent to the king of Ešnunna you have written to me as follows: 'I have kept him back with me because they have killed the messenger you sent earlier. So are we now going to throw this one into the fire?' That is what you have written to me. What have I done to the king of Ešnunna and how have I been at fault? What have I taken that belonged to him? In accordance with your own suggestion I have discussed with my servants and it seemed good to send him. If he has to live then let him live, but if he has to die then let him die. He will have been devoted to his country and to his brothers. It could be that another king who wishes to send his messenger to Ešnunna will learn from my example. So send one of your own messengers as an escort for my messenger to Ešnunna. In those circumstances I should easily be able to recognise your brotherly attitude and your friendship.[33]

The message to be delivered could be written out on a clay tablet, which was then sealed into a clay envelope. That envelope was intended to be broken in front of the recipient to whom it was addressed so that the messenger could read out to him precisely what was written on the tablet. Alternatively, a messenger would simply carry written accreditation and was told to convey the given message orally. When he arrived at his destination, he would be able to adjust the tone of his presentation to suit the circumstances. A messenger would usually be eager to demonstrate to his master his success in performing his allotted task once he reached home. Zimri-Lim used both systems in his correspondence with Hammurabi during the conflict with Elam. He gave his messengers one tablet addressed to the king of Babylon as well as a copy intended for Ibal-pi-El, his officer in charge of the Mari soldiers, sent as an expeditionary force to Babylon. He wished to be sure that his commander would be the first to know what he had written, for he knew the letter to Hammurabi would remain in its envelope until the delegation had been granted an audience with the king. Ibal-pi-El also received instructions concerning the formal expressions of greeting to be addressed to Hammurabi, for this was a time when they were not written down.

It seems to have been customary for any messengers who had come to address the king to be taken together into his presence. This once caused some confusion to the messengers of Išme-Dagan, who had been told by Hammurabi to say what they had to say in the presence of messengers from Zimri-Lim, but they had been asked by their master to pass on to Hammurabi some complaints about the king of Mari. They began by formulating a request to be given some troops, for Išme-Dagan was aggrieved that he himself had not received any support at all from Hammurabi, although Babylonian soldiers had been sent elsewhere.

> This is what Hammurabi replied to them. 'To whom have I given troops? Tell me! Tell me!' He came closer and repeated himself five or six times obliging them to answer. 'You have supplied troops to Atamrum.' And Hammurabi replied to them. 'What troops have I supplied to Atamrum? A force of three or four hundred men is what I sent to Atamrum.'

Hammurabi clearly suspected that the messengers were embarrassed and that they had not delivered the whole of the message with which they had been charged, so he pressed them further.

> 'Surely there is other information that you have brought with you.' They then said, 'No, we have not concealed any secret report that your servant (Išme-Dagan) wanted to send to you. Do not treat us violently. Our lord would lay down like a rug under your feet. Any other king at all that held you in respect would not write to you in such submissive terms.' When the messengers of Išme-Dagan said that Hammurabi responded as follows. 'Since you will not complete your report I want my servant who has accompanied you here to complete your report.'
> Hammurabi summoned his servant who had come with them and he said to him, 'Because they would not finish the report with which they had been charged it is your turn. You, finish their report.' The servant of Hammurabi who had come with them, after he had repeated the report that the messengers of Išme-Dagan had already delivered, continued it as follows. 'Zimri-Lim, to whom you make me write as a son, is this man not my servant? He does not sit on an elevated throne and so I have not written with elaborate words of greeting.' When he heard this Hammurabi cried out, 'What a scandal!' The messengers of Išme-Dagan denied that this was their message and said, 'We have never been charged to deliver such a message. And after we left Ili-ite, the servant of Išme-Dagan, joined us and said, "The words in this message did not refer to my lord Zimri-Lim but they referred to Atamrum."'[34]

But even in the glare of such public audiences it was possible to speak a word or two in private. The general from Ekallatum, Mut-Hadqim, is recorded as having whispered something into the ear of Hammurabi. Ibal-pi-El had his ears well tuned to catch words he was not supposed to hear, and he reported them back to the king of Mari.

It was normal for audiences with the king to held in public, but there were exceptions. In a letter from Ibal-pi-El, a general from Mari, he becomes embarrassed about something that had been written on tablets about Išar-Lim, a general of Išme-Dagan, which were confidential. Apparently Zimri-Lim had called into question his propriety, since he was party to the concerted struggle against Elam. After arriving in Babylon Ibal-pi-El was received into audience with Hammurabi, as expected, and found that two Babylonian messengers were also present. Hammurabi gave them instructions about a mission they would undertake to Zimri-Lim and Ibal-pi-El records that afterwards those Babylonian messengers, Ikun-pi-Sin and Belum-kima-ilim, were brought back with him into the presence of the king.

> The next day we went in and he gave some further instructions to Ikun-pi-Sin. After he had given these instructions, as we were leaving, we were detained and Ikun-pi-Sin, Belum-kima-ilim and I were brought back in. I thought, 'For what reason have all three people been brought back and given this special treatment? It must surely be because he wants to speak about the matter of Išar-Lim.' That was my thinking.

Ibal-pi-El then said to Sin-bel-aplim, the officer in charge of international relationships, that Hammurabi should not discuss in front of the Babylonian messengers that matter, which had been raised confidentially in tablets sent by his lord Zimri-Lim.

> 'My lord [Hammurabi] must not speak about the tablets that have been sent by my lord [Zimri-Lim] in front of his own servants.' That is what I have said to Sin-bel-aplim, and he said to me, 'My lord will say nothing about that matter of the tablets. This concerns another matter which is secret. Once he has spoken about the secret affair together with Ikun-pi-Sin and Belum-kima-ilim, my lord will speak to you on your own about that matter in the tablets.' That is what he said to me.

Sin-bel-aplim indicates to Ibal-pi-El that he would have two successive restricted audiences with Hammurabi. At the first only Ikun-pi-Sin, Belum-kima-ilim and Ibal-pi-El, two messengers of Babylon and one from Mari, would be present with Hammurabi. But as the letter continues it seems that Sin-bel-aplim, his minister, and his private secretary also attended. What would follow would be a private audience, when he would meet the king on a one-to-one basis and this Ibal-pi-El also describes in his letter.

> We came back in and he gave instructions to Ikun-pi-Sin and Belum-kima-ilim. After he had completed these instructions I was kept back and he and I were alone. Neither his minister or his private secretary were there. He and I were alone, except for one deaf servant who was attending on him. As I drew near to him I began the discussion with these words.[35]

The tablet concludes with the report of the conversation between Hammurabi and Ibal-pi-El, but at that point it is too badly damaged to translate.

Messengers were required not only to convey messages but also to deliver presents. The exchange of gifts clearly marked a good relationship between the corresponding royal courts. It was quite normal for a king to suggest that he would obtain as a gift something to which his colleague had no access, no doubt expecting something comparable in return. Envoys sent by Zimri-Lim from Mari to the capital cities of neighbouring lands kept lists of the presents they were given to take as well as those they were given to bring back home. It was not a commercial enterprise, although etiquette seems to have required that the goods exchanged should be of similar value. Grievances could arise. In a letter to Išme-Dagan of Ekallatum from Išhi-Addu, the king of Qaṭna, he complains that the weight of tin he had been given was hardly worth the same as the horses he had sent. He was likely to have been less concerned about the discrepancy in the value of the gifts but more with the fact that the honour of the king of Qaṭna had been called into question.

One obvious occasion to send gifts was when a new king acceded to the throne. In 1764, shortly after Atamrum became king of Andarig, Hammurabi sent two envoys from Babylon with some splendid presents to mark his accession. The letter that the new king sent in reply expresses fulsome gratitude for the gifts, which he carefully itemises. It is also noteworthy that he repeatedly refers to Hammurabi as 'my father'.

> Šu-Eštar and Marduk-mušallim, the servants of my father, have come to me. They have told me the news about my father and I have carefully noted the news that my father has written to me. I have seen the gifts that these dignitaries have brought to me from my father, including the clothing, the sartorial finery, the turban and the throne. I am absolutely delighted. I have worn the clothing and the sartorial finery and I have sat on the throne which my father has had delivered to me. I do not cease to offer prayer for my father.[36]

The rest of the letter is concerned with making a treaty between the two of them, which Hammurabi had proposed when he sent the gifts to him.

Different styles of address found in letters show that an elaborate code of etiquette was established when kings corresponded with one another. This reflected the difference in their ages and in their relative power. Those who regarded one another as equal in rank and prestige used 'brother'. When 'son' was used the addressee was regarded as lower in status and the sender of the letter would expect to be addressed himself as 'father'. This is implicit in the many different royal letters that have survived, but an explicit reference to the implications of such etiquette is made by Išme-Dagan of Ekallatum. He was content that in a message sent to him by Hammurabi, the powerful king of Babylon, he should be addressed as 'son', but he was not at all happy to be treated as lower in status than Zimri-Lim of Mari, whom Hammurabi addressed as 'brother'. Hammurabi gave him this order:

> To the kings who address me as 'son' address them in your message as 'brother'. Zimri-Lim addresses me as 'brother' so you should address him as 'son'.[37]

This means that there is some ambiguity and that it is not always easy to decide whether a form of address is based on politeness or on an actual blood relationship. Occasionally we find a remark to say that a king continues the styles of address used by his predecessor. A king of lower status writing to one of higher status will sometimes address him as 'lord' and refer to himself as 'servant'.

Things become complicated for someone writing to someone he considers superior, but refers in his letter to people he considers inferior. Zimri-Lim corresponded with several local kings in the Habur triangle. It can be seen that Haya-sumu, king of Ilan-ṣura, functioned as an intermediary between the king of Mari, his 'lord', and considered himself the 'father' of the other local kings, his 'servants'.

> All the kings have assembled at Nahur in the presence of Haya-sumu and in their assembly they have made this declaration: 'There exists no other lord or father except Zimri-Lim and Haya-sumu. We shall do everything our lord Zimri-Lim asks'.[38]

Atamrum, king of Andarig, performed a similar role in the region of Jebel Sinjar. He became the protector of seven less powerful kings. One of these was Asqur-Addu of Karana, who recognised Atamrum and Zimri-Lim as 'father', while Atamrum himself recognised Zimri-Lim as 'brother'. The way in which these seven kings protested their allegiance shows that all of them, as vassals of Atamrum, recognised Zimri-Lim as their 'father'. To a degree Atamrum also recognised the superiority of the king of Mari by referring to him as an 'older brother'.

> There is no other king except our 'father' Zimri-Lim, our elder brother, who leads us as we march.[39]

Historians have often been inclined to suggest that a feudal system operated in ancient Near-Eastern societies, but the idea is flawed since they have mistakenly used 'fief' rather than 'tenancy' for the term *ilkum*. The term refers to a parcel of land granted by the king to one of his subjects under specific contractual terms which have already been discussed in detail. The system seems to have been

Fig. 32 The obverse of the surviving half of a four-column tablet from Mari recording the treaty between Ibal-pi-El II of Ešnunna and Zimri-Lim. It begins in the left column with the list of deities Zimri-Lim invokes for the king of Ešnunna.

more like manorialism or seigniorialism, typical of mediaeval society, rather than feudalism. It is appropriate to use the term 'vassal' in an international context when referring to vassal relationships between kings. A more powerful king would take a weaker one into his protection after he had made him swear an oath of loyalty. The new vassal relationship was formalised by a ceremony involving special symbolic actions. The vassal was required to 'grab the edge of the garment' of his lord, who in turn was required to 'touch the chin' of his vassal. There is no documentary evidence that the practice of gathering the vassals was actually performed in the kingdom of Babylon. Our sources come only from the kingdom of Mari, where vassals were summoned to a solemn assembly. It was an essential element of the Festival of Eštar, which took place every winter. The festival also included observing the Cult of the Ancestors, which emphasised a consolidation of the whole family, for the 'sons' of the king of Mari were all reunited around their 'father'.

Any stability in 'international relations', according to today's customary use of the term, must have been rather weak. It was common for war to break out and just as easy for a state of hostility to be brought to an end by agreeing peace. Alliances were formed with a group of friendly powers against an emerging common enemy and also individually with another king on the occasion of his accession to his throne. The big difference between then and now is that relationships were made between individual leaders rather than between one state and another. That is why, after a king had learned of the death of an ally, it was necessary for him to renew formally with the successor to that throne any previously existing arrangement. Oaths that were sworn as an essential part of such an agreement would often be confirmed by arranging a marriage between the two dynasties involved.

Sometimes both parties to an agreement would meet face to face. But negotiations could also be conducted through intermediaries, sent out as a special delegation from one party to the other in turn. A different protocol applied to each procedure. Two kings who met together would begin by stating their mutual obligations to one another. The alliance was established first by both participants enunciating the words of an oath, and then by a ritual in which an ass's foal would be sacrificed. The significance of sacrificing such an animal is never explained, but it may be relevant that in Upper Mesopotamia another animal could be selected. Several towns in that region agreed to make an alliance with Ibal-El, a Bedouin chief, but an argument ensued about how the ceremony should be concluded. The representatives from the towns proposed sacrificing a goat and a young puppy, but Ibal-El considered their proposal scandalous. He argued that the foal of an ass should be sacrificed to respect the customs of Zimri-Lim. This is the only clue for explaining the symbolism behind the ritual. A 'reverence' for Zimri-Lim had prompted the reaction of Ibal-El, from which it could be inferred that sacrificing the foal of an ass was nobler. There are also references to concluding an agreement 'through the blood', with one text specifying daubing oneself with the blood of the sacrifice, presumably the foal of an ass, and also that the participating kings drink from the cup, but what they drank is not stated.[40]

The procedure was much more protracted when the parties did not meet face to face and the treaty was arranged with intermediaries. First an outline of the terms of the agreement between them needed to be established before any oath could be sworn and a written statement of the conditions to pertain would have to be drawn up. During the negotiations between Hammurabi and Ṣilli-Sin, the king of Ešnunna, the two kings first exchanged a 'small tablet' containing the actual clauses each party proposed to the other which would form the basis of their agreement. In tablets of this kind a number of general conditions were included, such as that enemies of one should be seen as enemies of the other and friends of one as friends of the other. If any enemy were to attack one of them, the other would come to his aid. Neither party could make a peace treaty with someone else independently. The treaty between Ibal-pi-El II of Ešnunna and Zimri-Lim from Mari, formatted in four columns with only the upper half preserved, includes some more specific terms.[41] Even the price for ransoming prisoners could be fixed. Once the terms were agreed a 'large tablet' was exchanged. It was likely similar to the formal treaty documents that have been found, beginning with a list of deities, the guarantors of the solemnity of the agreement, and followed by the terms agreed. The deities could become a subject for negotiation, as well as the terms of the agreement,[42] as when Hammurabi expressed some surprise at the curses contained in a draft treaty submitted to him by Itur-Asdu in the name of Zimri-Lim.[43] The final text of an official treaty ends with a set of curses that will befall anyone who fails to respect the terms set out.

There seems to have been a sense of unilateralism in the way the process was approached, for each king sent his partner an individual list of conditions he wanted observed. In fact the preliminary list of terms may come to have no value, for some of the 'little tablets' were exchanged but never came to be ratified as formal treaties. The status of such texts is therefore very different from contracts noting the terms of an agreement between two individuals and from what is known for later periods. The tablets recording treaties from the second half of the second millennium came to exhibit a more bilateral approach, and they are authenticated with the seal impressions of both parties. From the middle of the second millennium an obligation to observe the terms of a treaty was placed not only on the contracting kings but also on their royal descendants. Once the validity of a contract extended beyond the lifespan of the contracting parties, that contract became a very precious document which had to be carefully preserved. Some treaties were copied on a bronze or even a silver plaque to ensure their durability.

When ratifying a treaty the delegation would bring with them the gods of the king they represented. After arriving at their destination, the king there would have to swear an oath in the presence of those deities. They may not have brought actual statues of the gods for the ceremony but the divine symbols. The king was then required to perform a gesture known as *lipit napištim*, which has always been translated 'touching the throat', and understood as a suggestive action underlining the seriousness of the oath that he swore. It has been recently suggested that 'touching the blood' is an alternative translation, suggesting that the oath was sanctified by the shedding of blood.[44] Whatever the translation, the gesture demonstrated that the one swearing the oath was putting his life at risk if he failed to respect the terms of the treaty to which he had subscribed. After the ceremony, the delegation would return to their king, accompanied by messengers from the local king carrying his gods, for the ceremony to be repeated in the presence of the first king.

One of the most irritating and protracted problems for Zimri-Lim and Hammurabi was the demarcation of the frontier between the Mari and Babylon along the Euphrates, and it was one they could not sort out themselves. In 1770 they chose to seek intermediation by a third party, the emperor of Elam, someone whom they both regarded as superior and whose decision they agreed to respect. But his intervention failed to produce an acceptable solution. Five years later the Elamite invasion commenced and Hammurabi proposed a different way to solve the problem.

> When the end has been achieved let the kings our brothers take their seats and let them make a judgement for us. I will agree to the decision that they reach.[45]

He indicated that he would be ready to accept the verdict of what amounted to an international tribunal, composed of kings whom both parties regarded as comparable in rank to themselves, once the invasion had been suppressed. Perhaps what he wrote should not be taken at face value, for he could just have been playing for time. No other instance of settling an international dispute by such a procedure is known.

Hammurabi was not averse to brandishing a carrot on a stick to persuade someone to enter into an alliance with him. Shortly after the victory over Elam, an envoy of Zimri-Lim reports that Hammurabi sent some 60 kilograms of silver and 21,000 litres of grain to facilitate negotiations for an alliance with the king of Malgium.

> Hammurabi has had two talents of silver and 70 gur of grain taken to Ipiq-Eštar, the king of Malgium, as aid. After that Ipiq-Eštar agreed to an alliance with Hammurabi. My lord should know it.[46]

We also know that Hammurabi could be quite explicit about conditions attached to any aid he had agreed to offer.

> When someone sends me troops, I will send troops to him when he has asked me for troops and I will satisfy his wish. But when someone does not send me any troops I shall give no troops to him when he writes to me about troops.[47]

****

At the conclusion of an alliance, a marriage was often arranged. After Hammurabi had brought his alliance with Ṣilli-Sin of Ešnunna to a successful conclusion, he gave that king one of his daughters. That is the only instance we know of in the reign of Hammurabi but it was not without precedent, for Sumu-la-El, the first king of Babylon, had given one of his daughters in marriage to Sin-kašid, king of Uruk. It also happened in other dynasties contemporaneous with Hammurabi. When the elders of a town renewed their alliance with the king of Mari, they wished to ensure it would be sustained by a dynastic marriage. Zimri-Lim became the protector of the young king who had now ascended the throne and offered to give him one of his daughters in marriage. The words in which the arrangement was made are rich in imagery and include evocative symbolic gestures. The first-born child of such marriages would become the demonstrable sign that a blood relationship now existed between the two countries.

> This house is and always will be your house. The edge of the garment of this house is linked to the fringe of your garment. Just now our lord made his servants swear an oath by the gods with the words, 'Install the one who inherits the throne!' So now that we have just installed your son as the inheritor to the throne you must place your hand on your son. We shall grasp the edge of your garment. Give a young girl, your daughter, to the young boy, your son, so that this house will be your house as it was before.[48]

From the Mari archives, we learn that during the reign of Hammurabi international relations were extended as diplomatic arrangements were established further and further afield. A town such as Qaṭna, situated quite near the modern city of Homs in Syria, interchanged information with places such as Larsa and Elam, and towns in Kurdistan, such as Qabra and Arrapha, sent messengers all the way to Palestine and Syria. However, over time many of these independent territories were slowly annexed, and the king of Babylon became responsible for reducing the amount of foreign contact.

****

In the Code of Hammurabi, war is portrayed from two opposite viewpoints. With phrases of blood-curdling violence, Eštar is invoked to curse any future king who fails to respect the laws that have been inscribed on the stele.

> May the goddess Eštar, the queen of the battle and the conflict, who draws out my weapons, who kindly protects me, who loves my kingship, curse his reign with fury in her heart and with tremendous rage, may she spoil any good relationships he has, may she break his weapons on the scenes of battle or conflict, may she encourage disorder and revolt against him, may she make his warriors fall, may she soak the soil with their blood, may she have the bodies of his soldiers piled in a heap on the plain, may she show no compassion for his army. And as for him, may she deliver him to his enemies and may she lead him in chains into his enemy's land.[49]

But Hammurabi resorted to war as a means to bring peace, according to the opening passage of the epilogue.

> I am Hammurabi, the noble king. I have not been careless or negligent towards the men whom Enlil has entrusted to me and whom Marduk gave me to pasture. I found peaceful spots for them. I removed distressing worries far away and shed over them the light. With the powerful weapon that was given to me by the gods Zababa and Eštar, with the wisdom bestowed on my by Ea, with the ability given me by Marduk, everywhere I made enemies disappear and I have put an end to conflicts. I have improved the well-being of the country, I have made dwellings for the sedentary population in green pastures. I have allowed no-one to harm them. The great gods have nominated me. I am the shepherd who leads safely and soundly, with a rod that is straight. My protective shadow is spread over my city. I have held the people of Sumer and Akkad on my breast. They have prospered because of my guardian spirit. I have kept them safe and sound. I have protected them through my wisdom.[50]

This discourse is directed at the people whom the king governs and so the accent on belligerence that is found elsewhere is stifled. He presents himself not so much as the one who overcomes the enemy as the one who brings wars to an end and fights for the security of his people. To do that he would annihilate any opponent, an achievement made possible and acceptable only with support from the gods.

Part 3

The Administrator

The extent of the kingdom of Babylonia was gradually increasing and came to a point when it must have become increasingly difficult for Hammurabi to maintain direct contact for routine administration with all the people he led. That is why, not just from ideological motives but also because of practical necessity, the need arose to formulate laws to meet the expectation of the sovereign that everyone could expect to receive a just solution to their problems. Although commentators have often been inclined to exaggerate the role played by the palace in economic affairs, there were in fact a number of ways the king could intervene to solve crises and ensure that justice was done. The Code of Hammurabi provides a number of detailed insights into Babylonian society, some of which can be complemented from documents found in local archives.

Chapter 8

Hammurabi, the Legislator and the Judge

When the king is said to be a good shepherd in Ancient Mesopotamian texts, it conveys the idea that he was someone who acted justly, one who led his people on correct tracks. His capacity for showing justice is a question of primary concern to the historian. Several rulers express royal concern for the weaker members of society, including Nur-Adad, king of Larsa (1865–1850).

> I have given my people all sorts of food to eat and an abundance of water to drink. I have battered the villains, the wicked and the evil ones among them. I have made the weak, the widow and the orphan content.[1]

Since many other Babylonian kings take up this theme in their inscriptions and also develop it further, it should not be regarded as something special for Hammurabi to have professed to do the same. Furthermore, it must be emphasised that the Babylonian kings were no 'fountains of justice' in the sense that that term was applied to some mediaeval European sovereigns.[2] For Babylonian kings the eternal source of justice was the god Šamaš, so to praise a king for his justice amounted to praising him for his religious piety.

Even so, a question arises about whether a king's frequently repeated affirmations of justice do in fact correspond to reality, for such statements could easily be standard rhetorical formulations. Some light is shed on this question from supplementary documentation which gives some insights into when and how in the normal run of affairs the king himself administered justice. There were also the occasions when he announced a *mîšarum*, that special royal judicial decree often translated as an 'edict of grace'. For Hammurabi the most famous text concerned with justice is his Code of laws, the status of which is not so easy to define.

Routine Judicial Decisions

We do not have any composite description of the various bodies involved in the administration of justice in Babylonia. Since we have nothing like the different constitutions of the cities of Ancient Greece supposedly written by Aristotle, we have to rely on more ephemeral documentation. To find out more about the role of the king in the administration of justice, which is the primary concern of this book, we are fortunate to have at our disposal a considerable amount of primary material, including correspondence from individual citizens and hundreds of letters sent from Hammurabi himself to his provincial administrators. Those letters that give most information were written to Sin-idinnam, his governor at Larsa after it was annexed, and there are also letters to Šamaš-hazir, who looked after the royal domain. Apart from these we have texts which can be described as 'judicial decisions', comprising documents issued to a successful litigant officially summarising the decision of a court. This was the written proof of his legal position which could be used against anyone contesting the matter in the future. We have about fifty such documents which can be dated to the reign of Hammurabi. There are also a number of 'contracts' which show the ways in which ordinary folk conducted straightforward commercial affairs. Although it often takes an extraordinary amount of time and patience to peruse and organise such a wealth of information from different sources, it is well worth the effort, for such primary information paints a realistic picture.

There seems to have been a standard sequence of events for solving any legal problem that arose. First the parties in dispute were required to appear before the judges and present their case. If it were possible they would produce relevant written evidence and witnesses, but otherwise they would have to testify on oath. A text, apparently from Marad, involving Ahum-waqar and Puzur-Gula, two brothers from Isin, illustrates the procedure. These men had been obliged to go away from their hometown as a result of a Babylonian military campaign.[3] A disagreement subsequently arose between them over an earlier contractual partnership they had made. But, because they had had to leave behind their personal documents and their friends and neighbours who had been the witnesses to that contract, they could not produce any clear evidence in court. Without documents or witnesses, Puzur-Gula had no proof to resist the claims made against him by Ahum-waqar. In these circumstances he was required to swear an oath by Šamaš, the god of justice, and by the goddess Gula, the tutelary deity of Isin.

Hammurabi, the Legislator and the Judge **147**

> Ahum-waqar has brought a complaint against his brother Puzur-Gula concerning a partnership. The judges have reached a decision. They have demanded from him the contract for the partnership but he has no tablet and no witnesses. Because he has not been able to produce the contract for the partnership and there are no witnesses present, they have handed over Puzur-Gula to swear an oath to his gods, Šamaš and Gula.[4]

The next stage was for the judges to make their decision, which was often done in the temple, and they would stipulate that the unsuccessful litigant give his successful opponent a document confirming his agreement to the decision, a *ṭuppi lā ragāmim* ('tablet of non-complaining'), which stated that he would never again raise the matter. Such a stipulation is contained in two other texts concerning contractual partnership disputes.[5]

Even though an unsuccessful litigant had agreed never to raise the matter again, sometimes he did in fact return to the judges and complain that he was not satisfied with the previous verdict, but there does not seem to have been any regular system of appeal and such occasions were exceptional. One of the few records of a resurgent complaint notes that the defendant was able to produce the *ṭuppi lā ragāmim* issued to him at the first trial. No retrial was deemed necessary and the plaintiff, who was clearly at fault, was severely punished. He

Fig. 33 Ur (modern Tell Muqayyar) showing the remains of the famous *ziggurat* in the background. In the foreground is the building called Dublamah, where those under trial took the oath prescribed by the judges.

was publicly humiliated by having half his hair shaved off, his nose pierced and being forced to march around the city with his arms outstretched.[6]

One document concerned with reopening a case about a contractual business partnership was particularly complex. The enterprise had required an investment of initial capital for some commercial activity in the town and also some 'silver for an expedition', for commercial activity further afield. There was also a question about the inheritance of a house and its contents. The case was reopened and the innocent party, who had received 1 mina (about 500 grams) of silver at the first hearing, now at the second hearing received an extra 10 shekels (about 80 grams, 1 mina = 60 shekels) in compensation.

> After Warad-Sin had weighed out 1 mina of silver for Šamaš-rabi and had been made to deposit a tablet of non-complaining, once again he asserted his claim and Warad-Sin weighed out 10 shekels of silver for Šamaš-rabi. In the future Šamaš-rabi and his sons should not reassert a claim against Warad-Sin for a mina of silver for the palace, for silver for an expedition and for silver for within the town, silver for the house of Rim-Šamaš, the tablets and everything belonging to the paternal house, whether it is straw or gold. He must not say, 'I forgot this'. They have sworn by Šamaš, Marduk, Hammurabi and the town of Sippar.[7]

The tablet concludes with the names of eight witnesses and is dated in the year Hammurabi 43 (1750). It seems that there was no disagreement about Warad-Sin owing silver to Šamaš-rabi. But when the matter had first been brought to trial Šamaš-rabi had neglected to list every item. Later a full account of what was owing showed that more was due, so the judges agreed to reopen his case and to award him extra compensation. But they declared in no uncertain terms that the matter was never to be brought up again.

When judges found that they could not reach a solution for a particularly difficult case, they could pass on the responsibility for doing so to the gods. According to one of the early sentences in the Code of Hammurabi an allegation that someone was practicing sorcery, even though unproved, led to the accused receiving divine judgment, specifically by being subjected to an ordeal by the god of the river.

> If someone has accused a man of sorcery but he has not been able to prove it, the one who has been accused of sorcery must go to the River-god. He must leap into the River. If the River overcomes him his accuser shall take his house. If the River acquits this man and if he emerges safe and sound, the one who has accused him of sorcery shall be put to death. The one who has leapt into the river shall take the house of his accuser.[8]

In Ancient Mesopotamia a divine ordeal always involved the god of the river, but exactly what happened in that test of physical strength is still a matter of discussion.

So far as we know not all the matters brought before the court in the capital city were judged by the king in person. The letters of Šamaš-hazir show that the person in charge of some of the trials there during the reign of Hammurabi was named Lu-Ninurta. He seems to have functioned as the king's own representative, although the title of the office to which he had been appointed is not given. It seems clear that only on special occasions would the king have judged a case himself, such when an appeal was made against a judicial decision. But since documents seldom make a clear distinction between a first hearing and an appeal, we have no evidence that any established appeal procedure actually existed.

On occasions someone discontented with a verdict would 'go to find the king'. A letter found at Sippar records someone requesting that the head of the assembly should sort out a problem by listening to the judges and to the *nadîtum*-nuns of Šamaš. If he comes up with some objection, then the writer states that he will submit his grievance to the king.[9] A dispute referred to the king would provoke one of three reactions. He could make a decision himself and issue a definitive verdict. He could alternatively refer the matter back to the local judges, but give them his opinion about the points of law that needed to be kept in mind. But there are also instances where he simply referred the matter back to the local judges without expressing any opinion, although he would usually ask to be kept informed about how the affair was concluded. From the available evidence it seems that most disputes concerned land which actually belonged to the king. In those cases it is possible to interpret his verdict as coming from the king in his capacity as the sovereign administrator of justice for the whole land or from him as the owner of the royal domain. There are also examples of the king adjudicating in arguments between private individuals about the ownership of property. It would be wrong to expect the neat distinctions we are used to in our world also to apply to theirs.

A document from Mari shows that a master was only able to punish his servant for a misdemeanour within certain limits. After the servant of a certain Hardum had run off and was later caught, he was punished harshly and his eyes were gouged out. When the master told his supervisor that he wanted to punish him even more, the supervisor wrote to 'his lord', King Zimri-Lim.

> He has come to find me and has said to me, 'I want to kill this man. Let him be impaled and let anyone passing by learn from his example!'. That is what he has said to me. I have responded to him, 'You can do nothing without my lord knowing. I am going to write to my lord and I will do everything my lord orders me to do.' That is what I have replied to him. May my lord write to me what has to be done.[10]

The 'Edict of Grace'

That the Babylonian kings had a sense of justice is shown by the regular epithet *šar kittim u mîšarim*, 'king of integrity and rectitude'. Both *kittum* and *mîšarum* can be translated as 'justice', but the different meanings of those terms should be distinguished. The maintenance of public order, such as when a borrower is required to repay his creditor according to the terms of their agreement, is covered by *kittum*, whereas *mîšarum* concerns the restoration of balance in society, such as when someone burdened with debt is given a measure of relief. This is the kind of justice embodied in the proclamation of a *mîšarum* on the occasion of a new king acceding to the throne, the royal decree for a general amnesty.[11] Later in his reign, if circumstances suggested there was need, the king could have a *mîšarum* proclaimed again. The famous text of the decree of Ammi-ṣaduqa in 1646 is probably based on a prototype dating back to the later part of the reign of Hammurabi, and references to such measures occur from time to time in archival documents.

In a *mîšarum*-edict some clauses concern internal matters for the palace itself and the administration of the royal domain, while others affect the status of property and of individuals. The first set of clauses was essentially intended to excuse the payment of any outstanding dues from agricultural workers, shepherds, knackers and suchlike entrepreneurs engaged on palace contracts. They can be seen as a simple regulation of the internal administration of the royal domain. But the king also had the power to intervene in financial agreements made between any of his individual citizens, and he could abolish debts that had been incurred as a consequence of non-commercial activity. A number of different phrases are used to describe such action, including 'he remitted the debts of his country', 'he abolished the debts' and 'he broke the tablets'. Here the king is clearly acting in his capacity as one with sovereign power, a power that stretched further than the relatively simple remission of debt. The king made provisions for those debtors who had been unable to discharge their commitments and had had to surrender members of their family into the custody of their creditors to be returned to their own households. The affairs of those who had been forced to hand over their patrimony in exchange for their debts would be investigated by a committee who could revise the terms of the sale. Sometimes the confiscated land, as a whole or in part, would be given back to its former owner, and sometimes the new owner would be obliged to make a payment for the whole or a part of what he had acquired, corresponding to the amount of debt that had precipitated the confiscation. What happened to a 4 sar (about 144 m^2) plot of ground which came under the terms of the *mîšarum*-decree issued by Samsu-iluna immediately after the death of Hammurabi is a good illustration of the effects of a *mîšarum*-edict.

Concerning the 4 sar of uncultivated land bordering on the one side the house of Ea-naṣir, on the other the street Sin-gamil, on the front the house of Amurrum-šemi and on the back the house of Watar-piša, which Amurrum-šemi bought from Watar-piša for 5 shekels of silver during the reign of Hammurabi, and he has built on it: now during the reign of Samsu-iluna Watar-piša, in accordance with the edict of the king, has laid claim to the land which has been built on and he has said, 'In accordance with the edict of the king give me uncultivated land in replacement for the uncultivated land which we sold to you and on which you have built. Alternatively give us silver to replace the uncultivated land.' In agreement [he has paid x shekels] of silver [... which] before [...]. Again Amurrum-šemi has paid Watar-piša. In the future Watar-piša and his heirs, however many he has, shall not contest this agreement. They have sworn by the name of the king.[12]

The document concludes with the names of nine witnesses and is dated to 1750 (Hammurabi Year 43, sixteenth day of the seventh month). From this document we understand that in the reign of Hammurabi Amurrum-šemi had bought 144 m^2 of uncultivated land from Watar-piša for 5 shekels (about 40 grams) of silver and used it for building. Soon after the accession of Samsu-iluna, when he proclaimed his *mîšarum*-edict, Watar-piša claimed that the land should be restored to him in accordance with the royal decree. The text illustrates perfectly how after the proclamation a sales contract could be annulled and the purchaser obliged to return what he had bought to the original owner. Because in this case buildings had been constructed on the land, Watar-piša asks to be compensated either with a similar parcel of uncultivated ground to the one he had sold or with silver. Amurrum-šemi prefers to adopt the second option and pays the agreed price for a second time. This document would be kept safely by him as proof of enduring ownership.

In this it can be seen that essentially the measures announced by the king under his *mîšarum*-decree were retroactive. Those measures aimed to restore legal, economic and social standards that had become downgraded. In our minds the notions of justice and social progress are closely linked. In ancient Mesopotamia it was justice that occupied prime position and any suggestion of injustice was seen to be a fundamental characteristic of disorder. It therefore follows that within the mind of the people of ancient Mesopotamia there was no notion of what we would call social progress. Instead, the measures the king instituted under his *mîšarum* were measures to bring back the original order. The rules of the game had not been changed, but everyone had been dealt a new hand of cards. So it should not be a matter of surprise to us that these measures had to be regularly repeated, for recurring effects can be attributed to the same causes. There is no suggestion that any subsequent announcement of an edict of grace indicated that an earlier one had been ineffectively applied.

On the contrary, there are several instances showing that the measures were applied positively. Some derive from the fact that in contracts drawn up shortly 'after the edict of the king', a specific reference to that edict is included. This is to show that the contract cannot be invalidated as a result of any measure in the edict that applied only to contracts concluded before it had been promulgated. Then there are some documents from several private archives in which the dates when certain loans were incurred can be correlated with the date of a *mîšarum*. Once the king had decreed that debts between private individuals were to be written off, a creditor would normally destroy his tablet stating the terms of the loan. But a number of loan documents have been found in private archives dated to months that precede the declaration of the *mîšarum*. It seems that in certain circumstances the creditor kept the tablet confirming the debt he was owed, but did not present it to his debtor. Such documents have been found dated by months before the *mîšarum* decreed by Hammurabi in Larsa just after he had annexed it in 1763. We also have similar documents from Year 42 (1749), but we know that in the middle of the following year, immediately following the death of his father, Samsu-iluna decreed a *mîšarum*.

The Ambivalent Status of the 'Code of Laws' of Hammurabi

Setting out the law in written form and displaying it in the middle of a city was one of the characteristic symbols of democracy in Ancient Greece. It explicitly demonstrated that the laws were the same for everyone. It is probable that a stele containing the text of the Code of Hammurabi was similarly on display in all the major temples of Babylonia, but there the situation was not exactly comparable. On the one hand Babylonian cities were very different from those of Ancient Greece, and on the other some of the punishments recorded in Hammurabi's laws vary according to the status of the individual. The famous stele of the Code, now preserved in Paris at the Louvre, was discovered during French excavations at the beginning of the twentieth century at Susa, an important archaeological site in south-western Iran. In the Old Babylonian period that stele was probably on display in Sippar. The text begins with a prologue, followed by about 275 different laws[13] (the word *dînum* could be translated 'verdict', 'legal dispute' or 'case' as well 'law'), which are followed by an epilogue. The laws are presented in a casuistic form, that is to say rather than stating general matters of principle to be applied by judges they are expressed as a conditional sentence and provide a solution to particular sets of circumstances. This is the same style used in that period for other collections of observations, such as when formulating medical symptoms and their appropriate treatments and when formulating divinatory phenomena and their various implications.

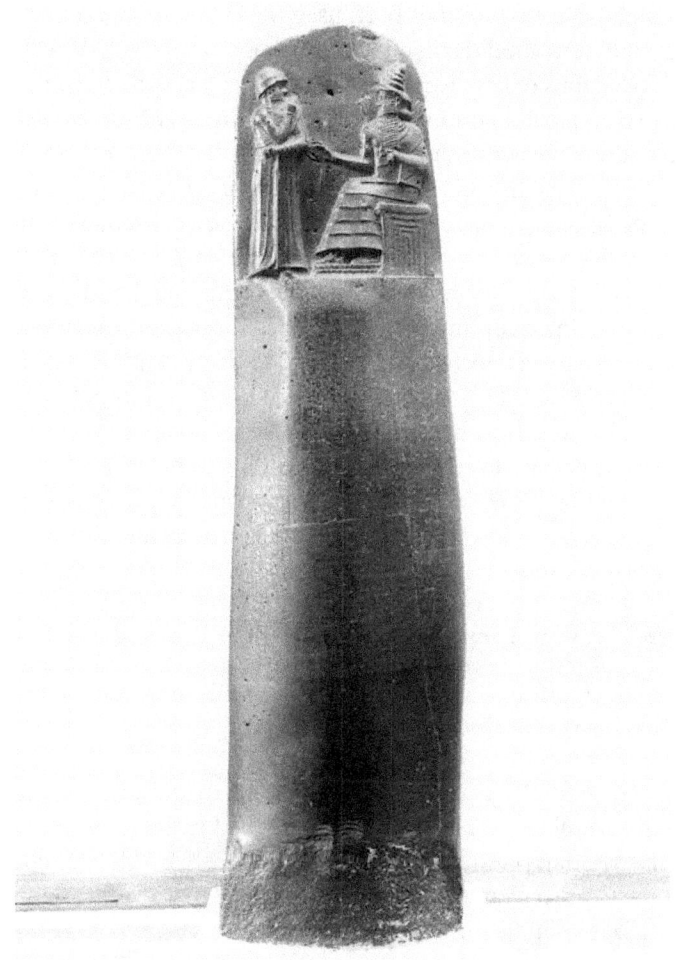

Fig. 34 The 2.25-metre high basalt stele of the 'Code of Hammurabi'. The text is written in horizontal columns on the front and on the back. In the twelfth century BC it was pillaged from Babylonia, probably from Sippar, by the ruler of Elam and taken to Susa in southwestern Iran as booty. French excavators found it there just over a century ago. At the head of the stele Hammurabi stands before the enthroned sun-god Šamaš, the god of justice, whose rays stream from his shoulders. The damage that can be seen at the base has destroyed the last few columns on the front. There is no trace of any dedicatory inscription, although the erasure must have been made deliberately to make room for such a secondary inscription.

Traditionally the term 'code' has been used for Hammurabi's collection of laws, but whether that term should still be used is a subject protractedly debated. Since none of the collections of laws we have can be said to have the spirit that we would associate with a 'civil code', continued use of the term can be said to be misleading. What is more, the term 'laws' may also need to be redefined, for there is some disagreement between legal historians and Assyriologists about the status of the Code of Hammurabi. In general, historians consider it to be a collection of laws to be applied in society. But many Assyriologists, noting the similarities of this text to other commemorative inscriptions in which the king is presented to the gods, prefer to emphasise that his intention in formulating these laws was to be remembered by future generations. It was normal for the king to document his military achievements in his inscriptions. He would also include the magnificent buildings he had had constructed, and exhort his successors to keep them well maintained and, if they should fall into ruin, to restore them according to his original plan. Similarly the Code commemorates Hammurabi as an exemplary judge, a model for all future kings, and it can be taken as a particular type of commemorative inscription. Hammurabi explicitly addresses posterity in a passage in the epilogue.

> May any king who at any time at all in the future lives in this land respect the words of justice (*awât mîšarim*) which I have inscribed on my stele. May he not modify the judgments that I have made in the land or the decisions that I have taken for the land.

The Stele discovered at Susa in 1901–2 is the principal text for the code, but there are also several clay tablets containing copied extracts. Some can be dated to the Old Babylonian period but others are obviously much later copies, which shows that the Code had assumed the status of a 'classical' text and formed part of the traditional syllabus for training scribes.

It is also of interest to note that the Code of Hammurabi had precursors. These shed light on the ongoing secular tradition of law-giving and are permeated with records of the king's own judicial activity. Clearly the Code itself was not the first attestation of its literary genre, but can be seen to result from an accumulative process. At least three comparable collections of laws can be attributed to earlier kings, two of which were written in Sumerian, those of Ur-Nammu of Ur (2111–2094) and of Lipit-Eštar of Isin (1936–1926). The third, of Daduša of Ešnunna, was written in Akkadian. Part of it was found on two tablets excavated at Tell Harmal (Šaduppum), and this is supplemented by a tablet from Tell Haddad (Me-Turan). In one way or another all these have influenced the content of the Code of Hammurabi. When the different texts are compared to see how traditional legal problems were solved, it can be seen that there is an inexhaustible possibility of cases differing is some detail or other.[14]

In both the laws of Ur-Nammu and those of Hammurabi the judgment proposed for a case of murder is the first situation to be mentioned. The sentence in Ur-Nammu is clear and simple.

> If a man has committed a murder this man shall be killed.

But in Hammurabi emphasis is placed on substantiating the evidence for the crime.

> If someone has accused a man suggesting that he has committed murder but has not been able to prove the matter, the accuser shall be put to death.

It seems, therefore, that not just an official person or group of people but also a private individual could present an accusation against someone before the judges, but that the accusation must be proven. Anyone making an accusation which he is unable to substantiate will suffer the same penalty as the one accused would have suffered had the case been proved. Even though Hammurabi does not explicitly state the normal penalty for a convicted murderer, it can be safely assumed that the legislation Ur-Nammu had previously enacted was still taken for granted and would be correctly administered by the courts in the reign of Hammurabi. By taking into account the laws of both the kings, a more comprehensive understanding of the legal system can be gained.

There is some evidence to suggest that some sentences in his Code derive from particular decisions Hammurabi himself took in particular cases brought before him. Law 21 states that a burglar will be hanged at the scene of his crime.

> If someone has broken into a house he will be put to death by hanging in front of the place he broke in.

But a particular incident of burglary forms the subject of a letter written by Hammurabi.

> The son of Ipquša the goldmith has told me the following. 'Last year thieves broke into my house and took away my goods. Now they have managed to come back again. They broke into my house but I caught those thieves.' He said that to me. So now I have sent this son of Ipquša to you. Put the thieves he seized in fetters and place them under guard and send them to me. Also send the witnesses for the son of Ipquša.[15]

We may well suppose that once Hammurabi had interrogated those thieves and the witnesses, that he gave orders for them to be executed 'in front of the place they broke in'. Thus it was that particular decision that was the reason behind the corresponding sentence to be included in the Code.

A recently published letter from Hammurabi's successor, Samsu-iluna, also sheds some light on how the Code came to be formed. Those responsible for the *nadîtum*, religious women attending to the duties of the temple of Šamaš, had earlier written to the king about two problem cases and he addressed his reply to the authorities at Sippar.

Introduction
Say to Sin-naṣir, Nuratum, Sin-idinnam, to the guild of merchants (*kârum*) of Sippar and to the judges of Sippar-Amnanum, to Awil-Nabium, to Sin-iddinam, to the *šangûm*-priests, to the judges, to the heads of the temples, to those in charge of the *nadîtum*-women, to the … judges and to the guardians of the gate of the cloister of Sippar-Yahrurum, Samsu-iluna (has said) this:

The first case
'Those in charge of the *nadîtum*-women of Šamaš at Sippar have informed me of this. "The people of Sippar have let their daughters enter the cloister but they have not provided any means of subsistence for them. They have become hungry and have been feeding from the stores of our lord. Even now the people of Sippar are continuing to let their daughters enter the cloister." That is what they have told me.'

Ruling by the king
If a *nadîtum* has not been provided with subsistence I have ordained that she is not to be allowed to enter the cloister. And if there is a *nadîtum* living in a cloister whose father or brothers have not provided any means of subsistence for her and have not drawn up documents for it I have ordained that pressure be put on the father and brothers to draw up documentation for her to be allowed into the cloister. And whatever he gives for his daughter he should bring into the presence of Sin-naṣir, Nuratum, Sin-iddinam, the *kârum* of Sippar and the judges of Sippar-Amnanum, Awil-Nabium, Sin-iddinam, the *šangûm*-priests, the judges, the heads of the temples, those in charge of the *nadîtum*-women, … the judges and the guardians of the gate of the cloister of Sippar-Yahrurum. He should write out a document for her and let her enter the cloister.

The second case
They have also told me about another matter. 'Mar-Šamaš, a man from Sippar, owes silver to the judge Awil-Sin and he has not repaid it. The judge has apprehended Mar-Šamaš and said: "If you keep hold of your goods[16] and I receive nothing, I shall take the slave of your daughter, a *nadîtum* of Šamaš, who is living in the cloister." That is what he said.' That is what I have been told.

Ruling by the king
A *nadîtum* of Šamaš who is living in the cloister and whose father and

brothers have provided subsistence for her and for whom they have drawn up a document[17] is not responsible for any debts or *ilkum*-service incurred by the household of her father and her brothers. Her father and her brothers will have to do their *ilkum*-service ... A creditor who apprehends a *nadîtum* of Šamaš because of some debts or some *ilkum*-service devolving on the household of her father and her brothers is an enemy of Šamaš.[18]

It can be seen that the king announces his verdict not as if it were a decision he took for this particular problem. If so he would have written something like 'Awil-Sin shall not seize the *nadîtum*, the slave of the daughter of Mar-Šamaš'. The verdict is formulated more anonymously, in the style of a law which is to have a general effect, one which the local authorities would be required to apply all similar problems. Such a style is typical of verdicts pronounced in the Code.

It should also be noted that the verdict includes an expansion of the problem that was actually raised. Those responsible for *nadîtum*-matters are said to have mentioned only a problem of debt with no word about *ilkum*-service. Furthermore, the specific problem described in this letter is not covered in the Code and it becomes obvious that the Code could not envisage every possible circumstance that could possibly arise. But conversely there must have been many occasions when an individual or a group of individuals in one way or another felt they had been cheated and felt the need to appeal to the king. His verdict on their problem would have been recorded and may sometimes have been added to official texts concerned with jurisprudence.

It is an attractive idea to think that a letter such as this might have enjoyed the status of a supplementary clause to the Code of Hammurabi. It assumes that over the course of time the text would have been updated, in the same way as happened with the *mîšarum*-edicts. But in fact no updated version has ever been found, and later manuscripts copy the text as one that was not to be altered. Hammurabi probably enjoyed such prestige that it was not acceptable or even desirable to try to make the text more complete. It was better to let the monument rest to glorify his judicial pre-eminence. The Epilogue contains strings of terrifying curses against any king who attempted to change what had been written and this will have been another factor discouraging modification.

Nevertheless, as can be seen from the document quoted above, judges had at their disposal copies of letters enabling them to become involved with jurisprudence. Such a letter could technically be called a rescript or an ordinance. It was known by the Babylonians as *ṣimdat šarrim*, usually translated as a 'royal decree', and it would have been stored in the archives of the cloister at Sippar and of the temple of Šamaš. Eventually the document would be recopied several times, which shows that the skill of jurisprudence did not fall into disuse.

In the following document Hammurabi himself orders Sin-iddinam to make his decision about a particular case conform to such ordinances.

> Sin-gimlanni, an overseer of five merchants, informed me of this. 'I gave something worth one mina of silver to the merchant Imgur-Sin for safe-keeping. I repeatedly asked him for it but he did not give it to me.' This is what he informed me about. Issue a written instruction that they bring the merchant Imgur-Sin to you. Investigate their problem. Make a judgment according to the ordinances (ṣimdatum).[19]

The 275 legal clauses in the text of the Code can be clustered loosely into subject groups, but no subdivisions of these groups are marked on the stele and the order in which the groups of clauses follow one another is not altogether clear. Occasional subheadings are found in three later manuscripts, such as 'verdicts concerning the *rêdûm*-soldiers and the *bâ'irum*-soldiers (before Law 26), and 'verdicts concerning fields, gardens and houses' (before Law 36). The original sequence has been loosely modified to make room for insertions. While these insertions can easily be linked to what has been said previously they clearly disturb the basic sequence. To give an overall view of the contents, headings can be proposed for the main sections of the Code. Much has been lost between Laws 66 and 102, and those clauses that can be restored in some way from parallel manuscripts are sequenced alphabetically rather than numerically. Some subjects recur in more than one section, such as theft (6–14 and 21–25), and slaves (15–20, 277–283 and 175–176).

Laws
1–5	the administration of justice
6–14	theft
15–20	slaves
21–25	more on theft
26–41	*rêdûm*-soldiers and *bâ'irum*-soldiers, and *nūaši biltim*, 'tribute payers'
42–H	farms and agriculture
?–126	silver
127–194	family law
195–214	wounds arising from accidents and violence
215–277	matters arising when professional services are required
277–282	more on slaves

****

To some extent the Code demonstrates how the king was able to administer justice for everyone everywhere in his kingdom. Wherever his judges were stationed, they were being shown through his wisdom how to reach a correct verdict, even in difficult cases. They would be inspired by the contents of the Code, which had been formulated in an impersonal way. In solving the cases submitted to them, they emulated the wisdom of the king himself. At least, according to words in the epilogue, the hope of Hammurabi seems to have been to make himself accessible to all his subjects.

> Let anyone who is aggrieved and has a complaint come before this statue of me, the king of justice, and let him read what is written on my stele, and let him attend to these very precious words of mine, and may my stele explain his complaint for him, so that he sees the appropriate solution and may he be satisfied.[20]

The requirement for a king to act as the judge for his people was also made by other gods on their chosen kings. The god Addu of Aleppo makes such an exhortation to Zimri-Lim, the king of Mari.

> When someone appeals to you about a legal complaint and says, 'Someone has done me wrong!', stand up and make a judgment for him, responding to him correctly. That is what I desire from you.[21]

The judges could consult official letters, such as the long letter of Samsu-iluna discussed above, which can be described as rescripts. They could then be sure that the judgments they made were in the spirit of the Code itself, even though the precise situation they were faced with had not been envisaged there. In this way, even if the king himself were not present to make a decision, their decision was indirectly his own work. Even so, there are in fact very few direct references to the Code in archived documents, which is a subject to be discussed later.[22]

Chapter 9

Hammurabi and his Subjects: Observations on Babylonian Society

In the last chapter we discussed in some detail the provisions of the Code. It represents one of the basic sources available to the historian and contains much information essential for making a detailed study of Babylonian society in the time of Hammurabi. However, the Code alone would be inadequate for drawing a proper picture and it needs to be read in conjunction with the different types of archived documents we have at our disposal, comprising letters, legal decisions and administrative records. By consulting these as well as the Code, we are able to draw up a reasonably comprehensible structure of three levels of Babylonian society and to show that they were not all the same size. There was a strong family basis to society, so that status as well as one's right to own family property and observe the traditions of family religion devolved from marriage and heredity. The lifestyle of the nomads contrasted with that of the sedentary population, some of whom lived in the towns and others in the countryside and this is a subject which will be given special attention.

The Three Levels of Society

According to some sentences in the Code, when it came to administering punishment, all levels of society were not treated equally. Distinctions were made according to whether someone was classed as *awîlum*, *muškênum* or *wardum*. The vast majority of the population was classed as *muškênum*. An *awîlum* belonged to a smaller and more privileged class of society associated with the palace aristocracy. Those who had no aspirations to own property but depended for a livelihood on someone else were classed as *wardum*, usually translated as a slave or a servant. The wealthier were expected to pay more silver than others for medical help. A surgeon was told to charge an *awîlum* approximately 40 grams of silver for his skilled services, but a *wardum*, at the bottom of the social ladder, would pay less than half that amount, about 16 grams of silver, and he also had to rely on his master to pay the bill. A *muškênum* would pay something in between, about 24 grams of silver.

> If a surgeon heals the broken bone of an *awîlum* or cures a damaged muscle the patient must give the surgeon five shekels of silver. If it is a *muškênum* he must give three shekels of silver. If it is someone's *wardum* the master of the slave must give two shekels of silver to the surgeon.[1]

Since *wardum* essentially expresses the idea of a person to be regarded as lower in status than the person with whom he is associated, 'slave' is not always the best equivalent to use. So instead the word servant is used when a governor writing to his king describes himself as *wardum*, or when a king uses the word to describe his relationship with his god. Social context counts for much when a translator selects which terms to use.

To prevent slaves from escaping, different kinds of chains and shackles were used. They are also said to have been 'branded with iron'.[2] Slave is clearly the correct term to use in these social contexts, but it must be remembered that in the palace-centric society of Babylon we should not think of a slave as someone deprived of his liberty. There would have been many other royal subjects who could not consider themselves free in the sense that citizens in Ancient Greece considered themselves free. The slaves were those individuals who were necessarily dependent on a master because they were not able to look after themselves. Circumstances could arise when the master would feel it was right to sell his slave. Some slaves were said to have been 'born in the house', meaning that they had inherited the status of slaves from their parents. There were others who had been forced into slavery as a result of war or of dire poverty. Such slaves had all their hair shaved off, save for a small lock, a distinctive mark of their new status. Once they were able to regain their earlier status, they would simply regrow their hair. The Code shows that it was not beyond the wit of some such to cheat the system.

> If a barber shaves away the lock of hair of a slave not belonging to him without the owner of the slave knowing they shall cut off the wrist of that barber. If a man tricks a barber to shave off the lock of hair of a slave not belonging, as for that man, they shall put him to death and hang him at his gate. The barber must swear, 'When I shaved I did not know' and he will go free.[3]

Someone who had been forced to become a slave would regain his original status when there was an occasion for the king to proclaim an *andurârum*, often translated as 'liberation' or 'emancipation', but 'restoration' would be a better term. A slave whose mother had been a free woman would be liberated by the *andurârum*, whilst a slave who was 'born in the house' could be returned to his (or her) original owner. If a statement in one letter reflects the generally accepted opinion, purchasers preferred such slaves.

> On the matter of the female slave about which you have written to me, buy her if she has been born in the house and if she is a weaver.[4]

Although it is not especially easy to pinpoint the role played by slaves in Babylonian society, their primary duties were to be the domestic servants and to do mundane chores, such as grinding grain for flour and washing the feet of the master of the house. Female slaves were responsible for weaving garments to clothe the members of the household. There seem to be no question of a substantial amount of production relying upon slave labour in a slave-based society, such as in Ancient Greece and Rome. Since there are relatively few references to slaves in documents concerned with dowries or with the administration of the estate of someone who has died, perhaps only a few households had slaves. There are only a few references to slaves being poorly treated, though letters sometimes refer to slaves attempting to escape, as this one addressed to Hammurabi does.

> The sons of Siyatum have informed me about this. 'A female slave has made off with her daughters from our house and she can now be found in Bad-tibira in the house of Ili-magir.' That is what they have informed me about. Now I am sending to you the sons of Siyatum. Let them have a written instruction that the slave and her daughters about whom they have written should be brought to you. Sort out the problem. If this slave really does belong to the sons of Siyatum and she has well and truly escaped, let the sons of Siyatum have back this slave and her daughters.[5]

The Code also refers to slaves attempting to escape, and anyone involved in the complicity of their crime, enabling their escape or concealing them from discovery, being put to death. Through his laws the king encourages his people to help to recapture escaped slaves, stipulating that there should be a reward of approximately 16 grams of silver, and threatens to punish anyone attempting to pervert the course of justice.

> If someone has opened the main gate for a male or a female slave of a person or of the palace he shall be put to death.
> If someone has sheltered in his house an escaping male or female slave of

a person or of the palace, and if he does not send him out when the herald cries out, the master of that house shall be put to death.

If someone has captured an escaping male or female slave in the countryside and brings him back to his master the master of the slave must give him two shekels of silver.

If this slave is not willing to identify his master he must take him to the palace. An enquiry will be made into his case and then he will be taken to his master.

If he keeps the slave in his house and later that slave is caught in his possession, that man will be put to death.

If the slave escapes from the hands of the one who has captured him that man must swear an oath to the owner of the slave and he will be acquitted.[6]

The passage is a good example of how a set of varying circumstances applying to one crime is presented in the Code as a sequence of varying sentences.

In Babylonian society to be a slave, whether male (*wardum*) or female (*amtum*), involved being treated differently from the two other classes of person, *awîlum* and *muškênum*. Different contexts demand different translations of the word *awîlum*. Usually it simply refers to an individual human being and can be translated 'someone'. But when *awîlum* is contrasted with *wardum* it is more appropriate to use a word conveying a superior social status, such as 'gentleman'. On other occasions, *awîlum* is contrasted with both *muškênum* and *wardum* to indicate someone holding a senior position in the palace administration. A possible English equivalent would be 'aristocrat' or 'nobleman', provided it is remembered that the word primarily indicates the status of one's occupation of employment rather than a noble title acquired by heredity. Under the monarchy of Hammurabi, occupying a position of high authority was usually the result of a personal favour of the king.

There has been much discussion about a proper translation of *muškênum*, which literally means someone who prostrates themselves. The cognate words in other Semitic languages are vaguely disparaging and it has even found its way into a European language such as French as *mesquin* ('stingy'). What is now becoming clear is that it indicates someone who was a subject of the king, but not part of the palace regime and someone who was not a *wardum*, in short, an ordinary individual. In several texts *muškênum* is contrasted with *ekallum* ('palace'), thus we conclude that the vast majority of the population belonged to this section of Babylonian society and that to be a *muškênum* implied neither affluence or poverty.

Families and Patrimonies

The basis of Babylonian society, as of most human societies, was the institution of marriage and a formally recognised family group. Marriage had consequences for the inheritance of status and patrimonies and also for aspects of a family's religious life. It embodied the principle of letting a father's authority over his daughter pass to her husband. Leaving behind her parental home and moving into the residence of her husband was the outward symbol of this change. The only exceptions were for widows, for women who had been consecrated to the service of a deity and for those known as 'prostitutes'.

On the occasion of a marriage, goods would be exchanged, with the father presenting a dowry to his daughter, and if the marriage contract gives details of the goods that comprised the dowry we can begin to appreciate their value. The dowry remained the wife's personal possession and became something that she could eventually pass on to her children. The family of the bridegroom would respond to these engagement presents with a bridal gift (*terhatum*) for the father of the girl. The obsolescent term 'troth' may better represent such reciprocation. For years *terhatum* has been translated as 'bride-price' and understood as the price paid for a girl's virginity. It is no longer possible to say that the wife was in any way purchased by her husband or by his father for him so it is no longer appropriate. After gifts had been exchanged the bridegroom would travel to the house of his future father-in-law and meet his bride. A ceremony would be held there, when the man would solemnly declare, 'You are my wife and I am your husband'. Then someone would knot together the fringes of the garments of the bride and groom and he would take her to her new home.

Normally the couple were considered as betrothed once the bridal gift had been given, but sometimes circumstances arose for a betrothal to be broken off. The *terhatum* Iddin-Ilaba gave to Ahuni, the father of his intended bride, was unusually in the form of a house, but when he later decided not to marry her, he demanded that the gift should be returned. Ahuni contested that, since he had actually purchased the house, the house could not be regarded as a *terhatum*. To demonstrate the strength of his argument in the presence of twenty witnesses he grasped a silver lance, apparently a sacred object. Iddin-Ilaba refused to agree and insisted that the girl should be thrown into the river. This phrase may mean that he considers the girl is now good for nothing since the engagement process had been improperly conducted. Alternatively he could be speaking ironically, implying that since she is now no good to him, he does not care what her father does to her. The document begins with a list of the names of 20 people, and is dated Hammurabi Year 45, Month 1, Day 10.

> These are the witnesses before whom Ahuni seized the silver lance and said. 'I have purchased the house absolutely properly. You have not given it to me as a *terhatum*'. Iddin-Ilaba said, 'I shall not marry your daughter. Tie her up and throw her into the river.'[7]

Normally a man had only one partner who enjoyed the legal status of a wife. Any other partners were concubines. If his wife did not produce children he could take a second wife, and she would hold a subordinate position to his first wife. Formally speaking, the first wife was regarded as the mother of any children born to the second wife. A husband could terminate a marriage unilaterally, but such an event is better described as repudiation rather than divorce. In the presence of witnesses he would symbolically cut off the fringe of his wife's garment and declare, 'You are no longer my wife'. This action effectively nullified what had been said and done in the marriage ceremony. The repudiated wife would then return to her father's house, but she was permitted to take back with her the dowry she was given when she was married.

Marital infidelity is a subject that is mentioned in three sentences in the Code. For a wife and her lover found together the normal punishment was that both be put to death. If the husband wished to pardon his wife, then her lover (referred to as the servant of the king) could also be pardoned. If the pair had not actually been caught together but had become the subject of rumours and the wife was eventually accused of carrying on an affair, she was obliged to submit herself to the river ordeal. If guilty, her unfaithfulness would have compromised her husband's status.

> If the wife of a man is surprised while lying with another man they shall be taken and thrown into the water. If the master of the wife will allow his wife to live the king will allow his servant to live. If a finger is pointed at the wife of a man for having a relationship with another man but she has not actually been caught while lying with him, she must submit herself to the ordeal of the river, for the sake of her husband.[8]

Birth determined whether society regarded someone as a free citizen or as a slave. But, as mentioned earlier, different circumstances in life could change one's social position. A slave could be liberated by his master and a free man could be enslaved after becoming impoverished, finding it impossible to pay his debts or being captured in enemy action. Many documents are concerned with determining the social status of individuals, such as a legal decision by Sin-iddinam, governor of Larsa. Ṣilli-Eštar had approached him about his young daughter Ahassunnu, whom he had asked the slave Kullupat to nurse. Then the owner of that slave, a herdsman named Dada, had effectively kidnapped the child. So the father of the girl went to Sin-iddinam with the request that he should determine who owned the child. He took the herdsman's wife with him, who had claimed that the girl was in fact a slave, the daughter of her own slave named Kullupat. The girl's father won his case by asserting his own claim while swearing an oath at the temple of Šamaš. The record states that the child was taken on the occasion of 'the opening of the great gate of Larsa', which suggests that she was kidnapped after 1763, when Hammurabi's siege of the city ended.

> Concerning Ahassunnu, whom Dada the herdsman, the son of Nur-ilišu, took from Kullupat her nurse at the opening of the great gate of Larsa: Ṣilli-Eštar has not stopped looking for her and he has seen her in the house of Dada, the son of Nur-ilišu. Ṣilli-Eštar has come to find Sin-iddinam and brought Ahatum, that man's wife. Ahatum has said, 'Ahassunu is not your daughter. She is the daughter of a slave from the house of my father-in-law.' Sin-iddinam has allowed Ṣilli-Eštar to swear by the god. Ṣilli-Eštar has sworn with these words at the gate of Šamaš, 'Ahassunu is my daughter and I gave her to be nursed by Kullupat.'[9]

The tablet, dated Hammurabi Year 41 (1752), Month 12, Day 3, closes with an oath and the names of four witnesses, .

As more and more information is gleaned from archived documents, it is becoming clear that heredity was the determining factor for a person's legal position, his social status and very often even his profession. Prosopographic

Fig. 35 A clay image of a carpenter apparently making a plough is one of the few representations of craftsmen to have been found. Now in the Louvre.

analyses can often show something like dynasties of succession, with some ministers and high officials under Hammurabi retaining their positions in the reign of Samsu-iluna, his son. The archives from Ur show that among the clergy, the same applied. We can safely suppose that it also extended to other professions, including the merchants, for it is perfectly natural for skills to be passed from father to son. Scribes in particular relied on their fathers to teach them their craft. What is often described as a school was simply the private house of a scribe where he would teach youngsters how to master his art. His own children would also be included, likely given his closest attention. That there were also opportunities to learn a trade as an apprentice is illustrated by a contract from Isin where a father entrusts his son to someone for two years to train as a cook. The rights and responsibilities of masters and parents in apprenticeships are alluded to in the Code.

> If a craftsman has taken a lad to bring up, and has taught him his skill, he cannot be reclaimed. But if he has not taught him his skill, once he has been brought up, he can return to the house of his father.[10]

Standard procedures for inheriting family property are not mentioned in the Code, but what actually happened is described in archival documents. We know that the practices were not precisely the same at Larsa, Isin and Sippar and assume that other centres may also have been different. After foreign communities had come under Babylonian administration, some local customs probably persisted from the time when they were politically independent. Even towards the end of the reign of Hammurabi differences appear. At Larsa, the inheritance was divided into as many parts as there were heirs plus one, with the oldest heir given twice as much as the others. The oldest heir also had more than the others at Isin, but what he received additionally was just one-tenth of the total amount of the inheritance. At Sippar a sense of egalitarianism prevailed, with the oldest heir treated the same as the rest and given no supplement at all. Whatever the local custom, once the inheritance had been divided into its constituent parts, the heirs received their portions by lot, but afterwards they would possibly come to an agreement among themselves to vary what each one kept.

Decisions about who would continue to live together after a death depended a great deal on the age of the father at death. From the archives discovered at the house known as 7 Quiet Street in Ur, we learn that Ku-Ningal, a purification priest died leaving five sons in Rim-Sin Year 34 (1789). No document was found about dividing the inheritance and it seems that the sons were treated as joint heirs, with two of them continuing to live in the house of their father after his death for half a century, until Samsu-iluna Year 12 (1738). The information we know about a house excavated in 1987 by a French expedition at Larsa and referred to as B.27

is similarly interesting. It is one of the larger residences on the northern part of the site, where some of the richer people of the city had been living. Many of the Larsa tablets now in museum collections derive from there, because that area had been the target of illicit pillaging in the early 1900s. The house occupied an area of about 500 m² and was divided into twenty rooms. Originally it had one large reception hall with a raised bench facing the entrance, but excavators identified two other similar benches erected in other rooms. It is clear that circumstances had arisen to make it necessary to subdivide the original house. What seems to have happened is that sometime in the middle of the reign of Rim-Sin, one of the rich citizens of Larsa had had the house constructed for himself. After his death his three sons decided to live together in their father's house, and each one had his own reception hall constructed in that part of the house that had been allocated to him. This may well have been perfectly normal with houses as large as this, but the situation would have been different in places like Ur and Nippur, where houses were much smaller.

If circumstances arose which compelled an heir to sell some or all of his inheritance, the community became concerned and a provision was introduced so that he did not lose his share of his patrimony forever. He was granted the right of repurchase. If his circumstances failed to improve enough for him to buy back what he had been forced to sell, one of the other heirs could do it for him.

Naturally an heir would expect to benefit from his inheritance but any claim on the estate for an outstanding debt introduced a negative aspect. A letter from Hammurabi describes how a father became responsible for a debt of about 750 grams of silver incurred by his son 'who had gone to his destiny', a phrase meaning that he had predeceased him.

> Iddiyatum has told me this. 'Sin-šemi lent 1½ minas of silver to to Sin-uselli, the son of Taribum. Afterwards Sin-uselli went to his destiny. Now Taribum has received the inheritance of Sin-uselli, his son, but Sin-šemi has not received the silver for the debt.' That is what Iddiyatum has told me. Examine the document that was sealed by Sin-uselli. Let Taribum, who has received the inheritance of his son, repay the silver according to the sealed document.[11]

Some family archives, where the records of inheritance from one generation to another were kept in safety, enable the ownership of property to traced back. Some houses in Babylon that were destroyed at the end of the first Dynasty in 1595 contained contracts which date back to the reign of Hammurabi and even to that of his father.

One significant element in preserving a family's rights of ownership was the practice of adoption. A husband and wife who had no descendants were faced with the agonising question about who would care for them and their property

Fig. 36   A typical tomb-chamber excavated at Tell Khoshi, probably the site of ancient Andarig. It is a good example of a vault constructed with inclined courses of baked bricks.

in their later life and after their death. In order to prolong, albeit artificially, the family line they would adopt a child, whom would be guaranteed the right to inherit as the eldest child, even if the couple subsequently had children of their own. The practice opened up the possibility of complex litigation on a number of different counts, so it is no surprise that Hammurabi makes provision in the Code for the rights of the adoptee and of the adoptive parents to be protected. An adopted child who seeks his natural parents could return to them, but a child that had been adopted as a baby (the phrase used is 'in its water') could never be reclaimed by them.

> If someone has adopted a child 'in its water' and has subsequently brought it up, that grown-up child shall not be reclaimed. If someone has adopted a child and after he has accepted him he seeks his father and mother, that grown-up child shall return to the house of his father.[12]

This subject comes up again in a letter written after the reign of Hammurabi.

> I have adopted from his birth the child of Akbarum, my wife's brother, for he is one of the troops under the command of the general Sin-tayyar, and I have been bringing him up until now. But Akbarum is in dispute with me

about this child that I have adopted since his birth and whom I have been bringing up.¹³

A *nadîtum*, a woman consecrated to the service of a temple, could also adopt a child. Even though a *nadîtum* serving in the temple of Šamaš at Sippar was not allowed to marry, she was allowed to adopt one of the younger girls who had been consecrated to service. That girl was given the specific duty of looking after her adoptive mother in her later life. A *nadîtum* serving in the temple of Marduk was allowed to marry but was not allowed to have children herself, so her husband would arrange to take a second wife, who would raise children for the couple.

Something similar to adoption is the subject of a few contracts. The adoptee was an adult and was obliged to pay an annual rent to his adopters in return for the inheritance he would expect to receive from them. It was not uncommon for disputes to arise as a result of these contracts. The adopters were presumably seeking an assurance of an income for the rest of their lives, comparable now to purchasing annuity.

****

The question of producing future descendants to perpetuate the line of the family must have been a dominant concern for everyone. But we also know, especially from documents found at the palace of Mari, that a cultic ceremony was performed, designed to maintain links with one's ancestors. The ritual was known as *kispum*, which made the focal point of the ceremony providing the deceased with whatever was felt necessary for them to survive in the realm of the spirits, where one entered at death. Although it is known primarily from the Mari palace records and has often been referred to as the cult of the ancestors, it seems to have been a ritual which was family-centric. A reference in one of the letters of Hammurabi suggests such an interpretation.

> Sin-uselli has informed me of this. 'My son Sukkukum has been missing for eight years and I do not know whether he is still alive. So I have regularly been observing the *kispum* as if he were dead.'¹⁴

The tomb chambers that were so often constructed underneath people's houses would also have symbolised for the resident family a sense of unity with their ancestors. The fact that these chambers had been incorporated into the foundation of so many houses must also have been a strong motivation for keeping the ownership of the house within the family. If it should happen that family pressures, such as those referred to above, forced the property to be sold, there would be strong reasons for repurchasing as soon as possible later. Even so, it must be noted that such chambers are not found in every Babylonian house.

That a family maintained a sense of unity in their personal religion and that the cult of a particular deity was venerated is suggested by the results of research on cylinder seals, a standard possession for a Babylonian. The usual style of the inscription on a seal follows the pattern 'Abum-waqar, son of Išme-ilum, servant of the god Šamaš'. All the members of a family would probably recognise themselves as servants of the same deity, and so the attention of a whole family, not just of one individual, was focussed on that deity.

A special sign of devotion would be for a family to decide to consecrate one of their daughters as a *nadîtum* to the temple of the principle deity of their town. The three religious centres we know most about are those of Marduk at Babylon, Ninurta at Nippur and especially Šamaš at Sippar. Here, the girls from the royal family were consecrated, such as the sister (or daughter) of Hammurabi of Babylon and even Erišti-Aya, a foreign princess who had come originally from Mari. We know something about the religious life of a *nadîtum* and also about the economic activities she would undertake. Rather than 'priestess' perhaps 'sister' or 'nun' would be a better term to use for *nadîtum*, since she played no part in the cult. Although she belonged to an organisation, there is no reason to suppose that she had been enlisted into a religious order or community.

Different Lifestyles

The daily life of the nomadic shepherd was obviously very different from that of the village rustic, and both were far removed from that of the citizen living in one of the larger towns. Even in such diverse circumstances they were all dependent on one other. The nomads, who made their living by raising flocks of sheep and goats, circulated in a fairly local area. Their animals needed watering several times a day so they were restricted to a small area of territory which often bordered on that of the sedentary population. From time to time a whole group of nomads would decamp to a different location, taking with them their animals and possessions and the whole of their community. This distinguishes them from transhumants, who delegate the responsibility of moving the animals to new pastures to a few shepherds from the community, while the main group remains at the campsite. To apply the more refined nomenclature of social anthropologists, who distinguish semi-nomadic groups as those that circulate around certain fixed points, from semi-sedentary groups that move location only once or twice a year, is not possible. Such local nomads are very different from the more wide-ranging wandering nomads who cover large swathes of territory. They traverse the deserts on camels, which can survive for days on end without water, but there is no evidence that the camel had been introduced into this area of the world before the end of the second millennium. The study of nomadism in the Middle East has been based on observations of the behaviour of the desert Arabs, who were excellent representatives of wandering nomads, but to draw inferences from that behaviour and transpose them to the local nomads of ancient Babylonia can be done only with considerable circumspection. What is better is to look for possible parallels in the descriptions of tribes who wandered around the region of the Middle Euphrates grazing their flocks during the nineteenth and early twentieth centuries. These descriptions are interesting in their own right and much can be learned from them to illuminate passages in ancient records such as those found at the palace of Mari.

When making comparisons between the beginning of the second millennium and more modern times, it is fundamentally important to ascertain what changes are likely to have occurred in the environment. Otherwise the ecological boundaries separating the nomadic from the sedentary populations will not be demarcated properly. Although scientific enquiry in this field has so far not produced definite answers, we can be reasonably certain that the pattern of rainfall has not changed greatly, though the tree cover used to be significantly greater. The evidence results from scientific assessments of the alluvial deposits of the watercourses, as well as from allusions in ancient texts. It is recorded that construction workers on land in the Middle Euphrates region gathered their substantial timber supplies from a large forest near a town called Halabit, modern Halabiye, to the north of Der ez-Zor. We also know that the deforestation of Jebel Sinjar occurred relatively recently, in the nineteenth century. Before then, according to texts from Mari and Tell Rimah, its slopes were covered with pistachio (also called terebinth). A change in rainfall would have had significance, but this general degradation of the vegetation has had disastrous consequences for the pasturelands, which would have been much more extensive in ancient times.

We are dealing with a society with two heterogeneous segments, the nomadic and the sedentary, which are mutually complementary economically speaking. The Assyriologist Rowton has described this type of society as 'dimorphism'. In principle, his analysis is helpful but subject to some qualifications. First of all, we must dispense with the preconception that nomadic breeders are the descendants of prehistoric hunters. Anthropological studies on early man prove that the nomadic way of life began only after the introduction of the agricultural practices. Nomads have obviously always needed supplies from the sedentary population and they in turn needed the breeders to supply some of their milk and meat and certainly their wool. Furthermore, nomads became an important source of seasonal labour and the sedentary farmers relied on them, especially at the time of harvest.

Political relationships between the sedentary population and groups of nomads were well documented at Mari, in particular regarding how they were governed. Under the control of the king of Mari a nomad group was known as *nawûm*, a word traditionally translated as 'steppe', but that is far from adequate since the meaning of the word is complex. It refers to the nomads themselves as well as to the terrain in which they roamed and the flocks roaming with them. The king selected a nomad chief, appointed him to a position of authority over each *nawûm* and authorised him to conclude treaties with any kingdom that was a vassal to the king of Mari, in the name of King Zimri-Lim. It goes without saying that the documentation we have derives in part from day-to-day disagreements that arose between the nomads and the sedentary population, especially about damages caused to the crops in the fields by nomads' straying animals. There is provision in the Code for the owner of a field to be compensated according to the size of his damaged field when a negligent shepherd allows his flock to wander over it. The stipulated rate of compensation is for the shepherd to pay about 6,000 litres of grain for every six hectares of field.

> If a shepherd has not arranged with the owner of a field to allow his flock to pasture but he does allow the flock to pasture without the knowledge of the owner of the field, the owner of the field shall harvest his field. The shepherd who has allowed his small animals to pasture in the field without the knowledge of the owner of the field must give an extra 20 *gur* of barley grain for every *bur*.[15]

Problems also arose between different nomadic groups and between them and the sedentary population about rights of access to water sources. Sometimes matters grew out of hand and the crisis provoked the nomads to raid the land occupied by the sedentary population. Then it was necessary to raise the alarm by a system of bonfires and the people and their animals were taken into the safety of the walled town. Letters can show bitter animosity arising between people of different lifestyles. A good example of this is the extraordinary antagonism expressed by a nomad chief who had been called up to join forces with the king of Mari against another who displayed all the signs of torpidity.

> Before my departure I spoken in this way, 'You must come with me. Zimri-Lim has decided to make an expedition.' But you are content to eat and drink and sleep and not to come with me. Lying around idle and sleeping will not get your colour up. I can swear to you that as for me, I was never idle for a whole day without getting out of my house. I have a stifling feeling until I get outside to get some air.[16]

****

J.-R. Kupper, in his thesis published in 1957, produced one of the most influential studies of the nomads. It was the first attempt to assemble all the evidence from the archives of Mari about the subject available at the time. He suggested dividing the nomads into four groups, three of which could be seen as close to the sedentary population in varying degrees. The Hanaeans had organised themselves into clans and can be considered as the group best integrated into the state, often listed as members of the contingents enlisted for the king's military adventures. The Benjaminites were less settled and much more turbulent, with a king at the head of each of their five tribes. The most independent group were the Suteans, who avoided contact with the sedentary population and survived by pillaging and trading slaves. They frequented the territory between Tadmor (Palmyra) and the Middle Euphrates. The fourth group, the Habiru, are best considered separately for they do not represent an ethnic unit. It is about these that most has been written since their name in Akkadian corresponds to the Hebrew of the Bible. The name they are given in the Bible and in Akkadian suggests that they are 'emigrants' and it is supposed that for one reason or another the sedentaries among them had left their towns, whilst the nomads among them had fled their clans to live on the fringes of society more or less outside the law.

The ideas advanced by J.-R. Kupper must now to be substantially revised in the light of more recent texts that have been published. It is clear that the division he made between Hanaeans and Benjaminites is not quite as clear as he had thought, for quite often Benjaminites are subsumed under the designation of Hanaeans. From an etymological standpoint J.-M. Durand has shown that the name of the Hanaeans means 'those who dwell under a tent', which could correlate to 'Bedouin'. Therefore, it can be assumed that they, like the Habiru, embodied a distinctive lifestyle rather than that they belonged to a particular ethnic group. We now know that the greatest distinction to be seen in the texts is between the Bene Yamina and the Bene Sim'al, the Benjaminites (or Yaminites, 'sons of the south') and the Bensim'alites (or Sim'alites, 'sons of the north'). The word *sim'al* usually means 'on the left' and *yamin* 'on the right', but in geographical contexts the words means 'north' and 'south'.[17] The names of the four points of the compass depended on the idea that as one looked towards the rising sun, it was appropriate to use the word 'on the left' for North and 'on the right' for South. The Bene Sim'al mentioned in the Mari archives in the eighteenth century BC were probably nomads wandering around the Jebel Sinjar and in the Habur triangle, while the Bene Yamina were settled in the area of the Middle Euphrates.

Another development stimulated by Kupper in recent research on the nomads clarifies the difference between describing nomadism as a way of life and as a society bound to tribal divisions. Some clans are known to be 'living in the steppe' while others had settled in particular localities. These two elements of the population are contrasted often in the Mari texts as Akkadians and Bedouin (the so-called Hanaeans), and in the Babylonian texts as Akkadians and Amorites. Some of the sedentary groups seem to have been directly descended from those early settlers from the migrations of the third millennium, with some nomads who had recently adopted a settled way of life. There are indications that the settled poulation, whether living in the towns or in the countryside, had not completely lost their memories of tribal affiliation. What held true for the common men also held true for the kings, as was noted earlier.

****

Fig. 37   A plan of the small fortified town of Šaduppum (modern Tell Harmal; see photograph in Fig. 26) where extensive excavations have been conducted by Iraqi archaeologists. The temple (marked with A), consecrated to the principal deity of the town, Bel-gašer, is separated from the residence of the governor of the locality by a street.

Compared to the nomads, a sense of unity among the sedentary population was preserved both for those dwelling in the towns and for those in the countryside. Ever since the time of the 'urban revolution' in the fourth millennium, the ideals of Babylonian civilisation consisted of a society based in towns and this worked out in practice for those who had settled in the 'Land Between the Two Rivers.' The centrality of the town to the countryside and the outlying villages was embodied in its high defensive walls offering security for those within them. At any cause for alarm, instructions were sent for the people to gather themselves and their flocks into a fortified place. Many documents from Mari and some from other sites in Babylonia carry such instructions. In the fifteenth year of his reign (1632), King Ammi-ṣaduqa sent a series of messages to the authorities in Sippar-Yahrurum warning about the enemy who was lurking in the area. They were ordered to gather their flocks into the town and not to allow the gates to be opened during the day unless the strictest security was observed. The severity of the situation was emphasised by sending heralds who 'by the command of the palace' would take up position at the great gates of Sippar and keep the gate under observation.[18]

One enemy tactic to overcome the defences of a town wall and attack those inside who were relying on its protection was to block the gate. This ensured that those inside were incarcerated and unable to travel and maintain communication. This must have been the background to this statement:

> The enemies are blocking the gate. I am not able to come up to you.[19]

The town gate was an obvious focal point. In daily life it was the place where the taxes due for commercial goods being brought into the city were collected. It was the obvious place to do this since there was not a site that could be called a market square or agora. Identity checks were made at the gate before persons were allowed to pass through into the town. There was no automatic admittance granted to soldiers sent by an allied town. One message concerns some Babylonian soldiers sent to Uruk after the alliance made by the king of Uruk with the father of Hammurabi:

> It is not permitted for soldiers to be brought into the town. The soldiers must pass the night outside the walls.[20]

The cultivated land could reach right up to the town walls. One letter referring to a field states that it abutted on to the walls.[21] In a letter from Mari, gardeners were summoned to catch two escaping slaves and this suggests that there was horticultural activity between the town walls of Mari and the Euphrates. The slaves had managed to avoid detection from the palace guards, apparently by using the *harem* ('the house of the queen') as their means of escape. They then made for the gate of the town dedicated to the god Itur-Mer. There they took advantage of some weakness in the wall and were able climb over and jump down outside. But once the alarm was given the gardeners were able to catch them.

> Two palace servants went out through the 'house of the queen' towards the gate of the god Itur-Mer. They went up to the middle surrounding wall. Yari'p-Dagan told me about it without delay. I went up and set off in pursuit and then they jumped over the wall just where there are some gaps. I shouted to the gardeners outside and they caught them.[22]

Archaeologists have tended to concentrate on those areas of Mesopotamian sites where prestigious buildings such as temples and palaces could be found. Only rarely have they concentrated on domestic buildings. This is understandable, for the more prestigious the building, the more likely it will be to unearth prize finds such as statues. But excavating domestic quarters provides the indispensable evidence for getting to know the kinds of homes in which people lived and the interactions of urban society. Until recently it was only really at Ur and Nippur that serious attention was paid to excavating the domestic areas of a town. In fact in the course of a few decades much more frequent subtle refurbishment and reorganisation is likely to have been carried out in domestic quarters, rather than in public buildings and to trace these changes requires very delicate excavation techniques. It is gratifying to note that since 1980 more attention is being paid to domestic buildings. In this connection the recent surveys and excavations at Larsa and Maškan-šapir should be mentioned as well as the more complete work at smaller towns such as Šaduppum and Harradum.

Raw dried clay was used for bricks to construct ordinary houses. In the more prestigious dwellings the lower courses of the walls were made of baked bricks, to prevent erosion. The beams of the flat roof were covered with a mat of twisted reeds on to which was laid a covering of clay mixed with chopped straw. Every year it was necessary to redaub the walls and the roof with a mixture of clay as protection against the winter rains. Some houses had panelled doors made of planks of wood, but these were extremely costly and it was much more usual to have simpler doors made from woven palm leaves. A contract for the sale of a house will often mention the beams and the doors as features affecting the value.

In general what is most noticeable about the houses in Babylonian towns is their very basic amenities. When Woolley was excavating two areas of Ur, the largest dwelling he found occupied no more than 170 m^2 of ground. The houses in the town were also built very close together, which can most easily be explained by the high price of land, a consequence of the fact that the space available within

Fig. 38 Traditional reed buildings, known in Arabic as *zarifeh*, are common in Southern Iraq. As early as the fourth millennium BC they feature in Mesopotamian iconography.

the town walls for building was limited. That is why the recent excavation of an area in the north-east of the town of Larsa proved so special. There, many of the houses occupied between 500 and 1,000 m² of ground and included about twenty different rooms. What had been excavated was a part of the town where splendid, large, private residences had been built by the merchants, apparently to display how successful they had been in their businesses. The excavators also noted that the houses were not joined by any party-wall. They were detached houses and it is easy to imagine the merchant and his family walking in a well-kept garden in the surrounding space. It must have been a Babylonian equivalent of Hampstead in London. But such elegance was reserved for only a few privileged folk. Most people would not have lived like that, but in tiny houses with simple, functional rooms around a central courtyard. They would reach them through back streets with tortuous alleyways and cul-de-sacs. Archaeologists are unsure how many, if any, would have had an upper storey.

When estimating the population of an ancient town it is usually assumed that then the density of the population was about the same as it is in the villages of the area today. But that can vary between 100 to 400 persons per hectare, which means any figure is likely to be far from accurate. The uncertainty is compounded because it is hardly ever possible to be sure of the actual boundaries of an ancient town.

Where one lived in a town affected the structure of one's social life. An area within a town was called *bâbtum*, meaning a neighbourhood, ward or community. Sometimes it functioned like a parish council, with those in authority called 'heads', but the size of a typical *bâbtum* or how many people lived in it is not known. Nor is it known if the heads were given more precise titles, for how long they held office or what status they enjoyed. Occasionally a letter or the record of a legal decision provides an example of the kind of things they were expected to do, such as acting as an expert source of information if there was a dispute about the price of a piece of land. Recent work at Larsa has shown that people of a similar social standing or profession, such as the merchants, tended to live in the same *bâbtum*. Similarly, the houses of the clergy at Ur were often sited very close to the religious centre of the town and were dominated by the great temple of the moon-god, Nanna or Sin. In a Babylonian town the merchants, who were often foreigners, lived in a neighbourhood called *kârum* ('quay'), but the commercial importance of boat traffic, mentioned earlier, meant that the word came to mean 'the merchant's neighbourhood'. When it was necessary to provide temporary accommodation for outsiders who were travelling through, some of the houses in the town could be requisitioned.

The Code states that legal decisions could be made by the *bâbtum*. If someone's claim that he had been robbed turned out to be false, then he was considered to have brought disrepute on his neighbourhood and he would be required to pay compensation.

> If someone says, 'Something belonging to me has been lost' when nothing belonging to him has been lost, if he has called into question his neighbourhood, his neighbourhood shall make an official declaration before the god that nothing belonging to him has been lost, and he shall give double the amount of all he was claiming to his neighbourhood.[23]

The Code also had a role to play in sorting out marital problems. A woman who was known to have been frittering away her goods on loose living would be thrown into the river, not necessarily to undergo the ordeal, in which her guilt or innocence would be determined by the river as judge, but to be drowned.

> If a woman has shown that she disapproves of her husband and has told him, 'You may not have sex with me any more', her allegation shall be examined by her neighbourhood. If she has conducted herself well and has not committed any fault but her husband has gone out and has greatly wronged her, this woman is not to be blamed. She can take her dowry and go away to the house of her father. But if she has not conducted herself well and has gone out, wasted away her house and has wronged her husband, that woman shall be thrown into the water.[24]

****

A more complete description of Babylonian society would look at village life, but we have virtually no idea about rural social structure. No site of an ancient village in the historical period has ever been selected for a full-scale excavation. Every year the rivers would burst their banks and flood the surrounding countryside and the villagers would always have been at the mercy of these inundations, but we have no evidence for saying much more than this. It is one of the most prominent gaps in the results of Mesopotamian archaeology. Listing the villages named in archival documents attempts to fill in the picture, but those names can only rarely be located. From texts from Mari we know the names of several villages on the 15 kilometre-wide flood plain along a 40 kilometre stretch of the Euphrates valley as well as supplementary information, such as whether the village was located on the right or the left bank and the name of the next village downstream or upstream. But surface surveys have failed to reveal the site of any Old Babylonian village in that region. They were probably scattered settlements with temporary building structures which could be easily replaced on some other site once the flood had receded. The archaeologist intent on finding relics of rural life faces a task very different from one concerned with urbanism.

Some places in the countryside around Sippar were said to have forts and towers. They were probably some type of fortified farm, but the amount of protection they offered would have been extremely limited. When Ammi-ṣaduqa heard that the enemy was prowling around Sippar-Yahrurum, he despatched an order for the inhabitants to collect their working oxen and take refuge within the town walls.

Some texts refer to hiring seasonal labourers, a typical need of all farming communities, especially at the time of harvest, when all available manpower has to be mobilised. 'The Farmer's Almanac' is a Sumerian school text which lists different jobs to be done on the land in the different seasons of the year. Because in Southern and Central Iraq rainfall was so meagre, efficient crop production depended on irrigation. This is why the Code includes some detailed provisions about maintaining the dykes in good order.

> If someone has been negligent about reinforcing the dyke of his field, and he has not reinforced his dyke, and a burst occurs in the dyke and it floods a section under irrigation, the man at the dyke where the burst has occurred will have to compensate for the grain which he has caused to be lost. If he is not able to compensate for the grain he will be sold, he and his goods. The members of the section under irrigation from which the water has washed away grain will share.[25]

The regulation implies that the water level of the two rivers could rise unexpectedly. This would have disastrous consequences unless every effort were made to protect the crops that had already been sown. So agricultural land was set a little lower than the level of the Tigris and the Euphrates and the main canals dug from them and then the irrigation waters would spread by gravity. That is why there was a dangerous risk of the fields being overwhelmed by floods.

Chapter 10

The Palace Economy

The Babylonian economy depended partly on 'large organisations' (as defined by the American Assyriologist A. Leo Oppenheim), such as the palace and the temples, and partly on individuals. Some researchers take the view that in the time of Hammurabi the palace dominated all economic and social affairs while others claim to have found evidence of the emergence of individual property rights in the Old Babylonian period. There is ample documentation available for both viewpoints but it comes from scattered locations and the detail it provides is unclear. Why certain archives have been found in certain places that provide substantial information for particular sites has been largely fortuitous, but as for elsewhere, any information we have is inadequate. There are a number of texts which were written in the palace at Babylon but the official archives in the capital, if they have survived, are still to be discovered. What information we have mostly comes from letters and receipts for goods officially delivered by the administration in the capital, which have been discovered in private houses in a number of different places. Such documentation sheds some light on how economic matters were actually dealt with in the kingdom of Babylon during the time of Hammurabi.

According to J.-P. Vernant, a 'palace economy' meant that *all* elements of economic life were controlled by the palace.

> Social life seems to have been centred around the palace, which had to play different roles at the same time: religious, political, military, administrative and economic. Within this system, which can be called a palace economy, all the elements of power and all the elements of sovereignty are concentrated and merged in the person of the king. All sectors of economic life and all spheres of

social activity are subject to his control and regulation through the mediation of a professional class of scribes anchored in tradition, which involved a complex hierarchy of palace functionaries and royal inspectors ... There would be no space in an economy of this type for any private commerce.[1]

It is naturally interesting to try to discover, from what we know of the prevailing situation in Babylon under Hammurabi, the extent to which his regime corresponded to this model. But first a fundamental misunderstanding must be dispelled. The palace was not simply a commercial agent, involved with the three elements of production, consumption and exchange. It was also a regulatory authority. Special emphasis must be placed on its role as entrepreneur, with regard to its production and selling of goods, rather than on its role as a consumer and purchaser, for these aspects are not sufficiently documented in the material we have at our disposal.

The Palace as a Producer

Many modern archaeologists, like ancient authors, place great emphasis on the products of skilled craftsmen. Certainly they were of considerable importance in an economic context and for the military superiority and the prestige they could confer. But we should not forget that the produce of agriculturalists was essential for providing the basic resources for Babylon.

The term 'royal domain' may be understood comprehensively to mean all the property of the sovereign throughout the kingdom, but it may also indicate a particular specified area. In fact it consisted of different developments in various areas of the kingdom. One of our principal sources for the 'royal domain' of Hammurabi is the correspondence of Šamaš-hazir, his 'chief of the landholdings'. The archives of Šamaš-hazir were found at Larsa, during clandestine excavations at the beginning of the last century. He was the chief administrator of royal land in the 'lower region', that is to say the southern part of the ancient kingdom of Larsa after it was annexed by Hammurabi. These documents show how that land, the royal domain in the region of Larsa, was managed shortly after it had come under the control of the king of Babylon. Further information can be found in the correspondence of Sin-iddinam, the governor of Hammurabi. Because the documents came to light through clandestine digging, it is not certain but at least probable that they came from these men's archives in their houses in Larsa. Some other administrative archives, especially those concerned with managing palace fields in the region of Lagash, which are full of interesting facts and figures, supplement the information in those letters.

Some of the land in the royal domain was described by the Babylonians as 'fields at the disposition of the palace'. It was cultivated by sub-contractors who

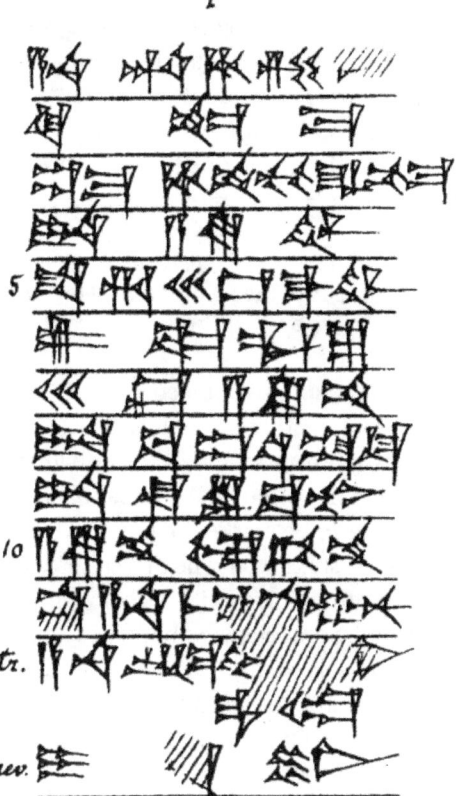

Fig. 39 A letter from Larsa, now in the Louvre, from Hammurabi to Šamaš-hazir. It was first copied by F. Thureau-Dangin.

were required to pay dues every year, partly in produce and partly in silver. The palace authority was responsible for providing oxen and agricultural equipment as necessary and also for attending to the maintenance of the irrigation channels. A similar system operated for the palm groves, and was the basis for the production of barley, sesame, vegetables and dates. Such land can be referred to, albeit anachronistically, as a 'reserve'.

Other palace land was allotted in the form of tenancies. It is impossible to estimate what proportion of the available land was allotted in this way, but we know it included fields, orchards and houses and that it was land that the king had assigned to particular individuals. In return they were obliged to perform a specific duty of service (*ilkum*), which could mean military service or some kind of skilled labour. Such landholdings are sometimes described as subsistence holdings, because they were granted instead of food rations.

The fields varied very much in size, between 6 and 36 hectares. The term 'fief' has often been used for such a landholding, however this is a mistake, for the documentations shows that the system was significantly different from the fiefs of mediaeval society. Why some individuals were granted a subsistence holding while others were granted food rations is not known, but we know of a few cases where a person moved from the one type of grant to the other.

One assignment of land by Hammurabi was given to a stonecutter.

> Of the fields at the disposition of the palace, give Sin-imguranni the stonecutter a parcel of 20 hectares of the fallow land by the gate in Larsa, a good quality field with water close by.[2]

Not all letters of this type are quite so detailed. Describing the quality of the soil and mentioning that water was readily available was just as important as specifying the total area available for cultivation. Once an individual had received a letter of assignment from the king he would take it to Šamaš-hazir, who would have to decide where precisely it was to be marked out. A surveyor would demarcate the boundary with a cord, then a stake would be driven into the ground in the centre of the plot in the presence of the beneficiary. This would symbolise that he had taken possession of the land. Someone who had been assigned a subsistence field could either cultivate it himself, assuming he lived nearby, or he could arrange with a local farmer to cultivate it for him for a fixed annual rent. Beneficiaries frequently complained that the tenant farmers did not pay the rent and kept the whole produce of the field for themselves.

In the Code of Hammurabi, in the laws concerned with landholdings granted to a *rêdûm*-soldier and to a *bâ'irum*-soldier, it is forbidden for someone to appropriate land that had been granted to a tenant.

> The field, the garden and the house of a *rêdûm*, a *bâ'irum* or a state tenant shall not be sold. If someone purchases the field, the garden or the house of a *rêdûm*, a *bâ'irum* or a state tenant the tablet he has shall be broken and he will lose his money. The field, the garden or house shall revert to the owner.[3]

Furthermore, it was forbidden for a beneficiary to assign these lands as provision for his wife after his death, that is as a jointure, or to his daughter as a dowry. These terms could be seen simply as restricting rights to ownership, but in fact their real purpose was to offer a measure of protection. If a tenant farmer had a poor year and found he was unable to pay his debt, his creditor was prevented from taking possession of his land and removing his source of livelihood to regain his capital. The next sentence in the Code makes this clear.

> A *rêdûm*, a *bâ'irum* or a state tenant shall not make any written assignment to his wife or to his daughter about his field, his garden or his house which are tied to his service and he shall not give them for a debt.⁴

Disputes about landholdings were frequent and are the topic of very many letters from Hammurabi to Sin-iddinam and Šamaš-hazir. A typical one deals with solving the problems of Epeš-ilim.

> Speak to Sin-iddinam. This is what Hammurabi says. 'Epeš-ilim, a palace guard, has given me this information. "The son of Lu-Asalluhi has argued with me about the field that Šamaš-hazir, the one in charge of landholdings, had assigned to me, and he has removed my grain. And Etel-pi-Marduk has argued with me about my orchard and he has removed my dates." That is what I have been told. So now I am sending Epeš-ilim. Write for his opponents to be summoned to you. If he has been deprived of his field and of his orchard unjustly give him back his field and his grain, and likewise with the orchard and the dates.'⁵

It is important to gather information from the dry and austere accounting tablets that have been found, for from them we learn how the flocks of sheep and the herds of cattle belonging to the palace were managed. Those primarily responsible were known as shepherds but they delegated the day-to-day tasks to subordinate agricultural labourers. They were entrepreneurs who were required to produce a certain number of beasts as well as a specified amount of silver every year. Animals that had died accidentally were meticulously recorded in the accounts and knackers were ordered to salvage all useful material, such as wool, skin and tendons, from the carcasses. The amount of silver that was expected to be raised from every carcass was stipulated.

The cattle took most looking after. When they were required for work in the fields and there was no time for them to graze, it was important to be sure they had sufficient grain and fodder for nutrition. Since these were dear commodities it was important that they were kept working. Oxen were essential for agricultural work. They were used routinely for hauling heavy carts over short distances and seasonally for ploughing and for threshing the grain after the harvest. Donkeys would be used to carry smaller loads. Although no beast would manage more than about 90 kilograms, they were able to carry their loads a much longer distance. The Assyrian merchants used caravans of donkeys to transport clothing material and tin to central Anatolia, a journey of over 1,000 kilometres lasting about three months.

The palace kept a very precise account of all the payments that these entrepreneurial agricultural labourers completed, but sometimes there were serious shortfalls. It is not surprising to find that there were times when they were late

Fig. 40 A palm-grove in the region of Nasiriyeh. Palm trees have the advantage of hardly ever being affected by salinity in the irrigation water. Today, as in ancient times, various kinds of vegetables are grown in the shade between the trunks of the trees.

in delivering the dues they had to give to the palace. Hammurabi had to write to Sin-iddinam with a request to chase the late payments. He would have had the assistance of two *rêdûm*-soldiers.

> I have written to Namtilani-idug several times about collecting the late payments from the shepherd and the agricultural workers. Now I am sending you two *rêdûm*-soldiers. Give them orders in writing so that without delay they can collect the late payments from the shepherd and the agricultural workers.[6]

A set of documents from the beginning of the reign of Samsu-iluna concerns some palm groves for which late payments had accumulated so greatly that the sovereign was forced to clear the books by enacting a *mîšarum* edict.

It has been established without doubt that the entrepreneurs were responsible for the day to day management of palace property, but the way they were repaid is still a matter of debate and the details in the accounting records do not enable us to establish the status they held. One view is that they were managers dependent on the state, but they can also be seen as private individuals working for their own profit. If they were independent the palace was adopting a system of delegating the responsibilities of palace personnel to outsiders. Such outsourcing would relieve the palace of the problems of finding extra workers for important jobs that arose only seasonally. It is also noteworthy that they became occupied with work for the temple and for wealthy citizens as well as the work on palace land. The image created is one of independent entrepreneurs to whom the palace could appeal for service since they had been integrated into the palace administration as managers. The inscriptions on their cylinder seals usually begin with the name of the contractor followed by the name of his father. Some of the seals that have been found describe the man as a servant of a god, but none of the seals describe the contractor as a servant of the king, which would have been taken to mean that he was a palace functionary. This observation has been used to buttress the arguments against assuming that the men the palace entrusted with the management of its fields, palm-groves and flocks enjoyed the status of palace functionaries.

****

When considering the status of craftsmen the people trained to process agricultural products must also be included. Less documentation about them in the Old Babylonian period is available than we had for the earlier period of Ur III. For the twentieth century we have the archives of the royal workshops at Isin and for the eighteenth century those from the palace of Mari. Other archives, such as those from Larsa and Uruk, have more limited significance. This textual material is a valuable supplement to the evidence of archaeology. The Mari documents include very meticulous descriptions of the work of goldsmiths and silversmiths and these can be linked to the evidence from medallions from Larsa and at Dilbat. But since it was common practice for precious metal to be reused not very much has remained, meaning textual evidence is indispensable when considering material that could not have survived, such as textiles and perfumes. Hardly any complementary evidence for clothes comes from iconography, for statues, paintings and seal engravings show gods and kings in their official dress, not everyday apparel.

Some texts give details about working arrangements for the craftsmen. The attendance registers from the workshops in Isin show that craftsmen worked there only part-time, which suggests that for the rest of the time they worked on their own account. At Larsa under Hammurabi many workers were paid with subsistence fields, but almost nothing else is known about them. Some production of textiles were done by women working in private houses, but this activity was also practised on a larger scale in the workshops of the palace. At Mari we know that girls who had been captured were made to produce what was woven in the workshops there. Living conditions in the workhouse could not have been easy. Priority would have to be given to ensure that basic materials were always available for the craftsmen who depended on them, especially materials such as precious and non-precious metals brought in from outside. Tin was a strategic commodity, used as an alloy with copper to make bronze for stronger weapons. A complex network of activity involved transporting tin from mines in Afghanistan to areas such as Anatolia where copper was available. The merchants from Ashur played an intermediary role in this profitable trade and other towns, such as Ešnunna and Susa, found themselves in a position to control this tin route and, as previously mentioned, used that to check the trade. The collections of agricultural instruments found at Kutalla suggest that copper was used more widely than bronze for manufacturing tools. Maintaining the irrigation system required adequate tools for the workmen,. If they were not available they would complain to the official responsible who would have to make a requisition.

> Please send me quickly twelve copper spades and six copper hoes. I have reclaimed from Apil-Šamaš and Apilša some copper hoes. Now, without having been able to work the copper, I have not been able to obtain any. And the hired workmen complain, for you need a hoe and a spade when working on a channel.[7]

After they had been used copper tools, especially sickles, were weighed to assess the wear. Different manufactured materials have been associated with different regions. Some would have been indigenous but others must have been manufactured locally copying a foreign style. 'Cretan boots' were worn in Mari but they are more likely to have been made in Mari following a Cretan design than to have been imported from the Aegean. Not all muslin comes from Mosul!

*****

The question that now arises is how the economic affairs of the kingdom at large were managed against this background of the management of royal property. The German Assyriologist, J. Renger, has suggested that a great part, perhaps the greater part, of the population depended on what was allocated to them by the palace. Some were given actual food rations and others were given cultivable land in return for their obligatory duties. Such a view means that the amount of independent private work was negligible and even throws into question whether there was any land in private ownership. Most of the relevant information is again derived from documents from the ancient kingdom of Larsa during the time of Babylonian supremacy. Many contracts have been found there dating from the time of Hammurabi and his successor

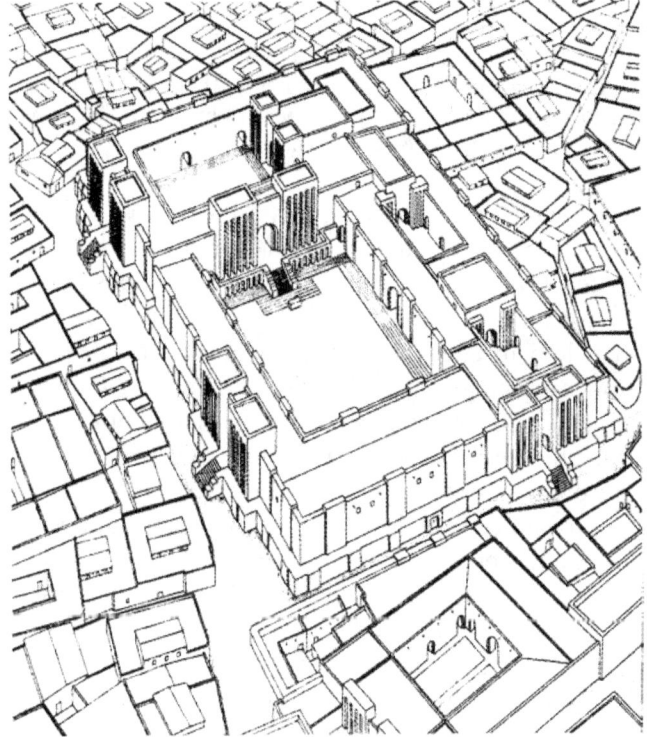

Fig. 41 A reconstruction by Seton-Lloyd of the temple of the goddess Kititum at Nerebtum. The archives found in this building illustrate various aspects of the economic life of a Mesopotamian temple.

and hardly any concern sales of land. This has been interpreted as evidence that Hammurabi instigated a general appropriation of the land and fixed property at Larsa, all taken by the king as a right of conquest. Renger has subsequently proposed a different, more radical explanation of the facts. In the south of Iraq there were no fields in private ownership, but houses and orchards could belong to individual citizens. This idea does not seem well-founded. Palm groves were extremely important to the economy in the south and to exclude them from state ownership seems strange. The distinction between land that produced grain as the property of the state and orchards which could be taken into private ownership is reminiscent of Soviet ideas. Furthermore, it conflicts with what is stated in some of the texts. An appeal was sent to Hammurabi by someone living in a village near to Larsa, because Šamaš-hazir had granted a field to a soldier, that was his by right of inheritance. The king accordingly wrote to his administrator:

> Sin-išmeanni, the man from Kutalla who looks after the Tilmun-palms, has told me, 'Šamaš-hazir has dispossessed me of the field of the house of my father to give it to a *rêdûm*.' That is what he has told me. Can he be dispossessed of a field to which he has a permanent right? If this field is part of his patrimony then give it back to Sin-išmeanni.[8]

The expression 'the field of the house of my father' gives the clear impression that we are here dealing with an unwarranted encroachment on to property that had been privately inherited. It could be that if collections of family archives ever become more complete, they may show that the supposed confiscation of land by the Babylonians after their conquest never happened. Certainly legal documents drawn up under Hammurabi and Samsu-iluna mention fields as well as houses and orchards as property to be shared among heirs. We can therefore assume that in Larsa before and after the Babylonian conquest some arable land was privately owned. What had been the royal domain of the kings of Larsa now became the royal domain of Hammurabi and it was only on this land that the victor imposed his rights of conquest.

The provision made for temple officials seems to have been similar to that for palace officials. Their fresh food rations consisted of redistributions from what had been offered to the deities, but they could also hold land for producing their own food. On occasions the king allocated a field for producing food to a temple official, which raises questions about whether it was the palace which controlled the ownership of temple land. A letter from Lu-Ninurta, the minister of Hammurabi, suggests that such an allocation of land could have constituted a transfer from the royal domain. He writes to remind Šamaš-hazir that he was prohibited from removing a field and allocating it to someone called Ili-iqisham on the domain of the temple of the god Sin.

The Palace as a Commerical Centre

International commerce in rare materials was naturally conducted through the palace. It collected goods needed in the court and unobtainable in the alluvial plains of Babylonia. This trade involved basic materials such as wood, metal and

Fig. 42 The stairway leading up to the main temple of Šamaš at Larsa. This photograph shows the restoration undertaken by the Cassite kings in the second half of the second millennium, after the building which had been erected in the time of Hammurabi had fallen into ruins.

precious stones. This activity was unquestionably important, but the involvement of the palace in selling on foodstuffs is also important and is easily forgotten. The archives from Larsa in the time of Hammurabi and Samsu-iluna (1763–1738) and those from Babylon in the time of Ammi-ditana and Ammi-saduqa 100 years later (1683–1626) provide some particularly helpful information.

All kinds of goods at different times and from different sources were traded by the palace. Wool, arriving when the flocks owned by the palace were sheared, was constantly mentioned. But we also read in documents from the time of Hammurabi and Samsu-iluna of fish caught by soldiers in the southern marshes, of dates and vegetables from the palm groves and of cereals. Credit-worthy entrepreneurs would collect this merchandise from the palace, transport it to their own towns and sell it on to retailers. When the palace made a claim to the entrepreneurs for the goods supplied they would pay with the silver which they had collected from their customers.

The word *tamkârum*, used to denote an entrepreneur, has been traditionally translated 'merchant'. The status of a *tamkârum* held when conducting this commerce is as controversial as that of the agricultural entrepreneurs referred to earlier. They could have been palace functionaries or private sub-contractors to whom the palace outsourced trading in supplies that were surplus to requirements. It is sometimes recorded that the king gave a subsistence field to the 'head of the merchants', which supports the idea that they were functionaries. Furthermore, he can describe himself as 'a servant of the king' on his seal. But this relates only to the 'head of the merchants' and may not have been the same for the ordinary *tamkârum*. The temples as well as the palace could use the services of a *tamkârum* to trade their surplus and this fact has been taken to support the idea that they were private entrepreneurs.

We know that all the merchants of a town congregated in the *kârum*, the trading district and the centre of commercial activity. The *kârum* was an independent institution and could be asked by the palace and by the temples to market their goods. Sometimes one of the merchants is described as 'of the palace', which implies that he but not all of his colleagues was an integral member of the palace personnel. It cannot be justifiably argued that all merchants were officially agents of the palace. The palace managed its commercial activity in a similar way to how it managed its agricultural labourers: by outsourcing the work to independent sub-contractors. Assyrian merchants worked together as permanent members of a firm, but their Babylonian colleagues did not. The associations they formed were relatively short-lived. Once the accounts were settled a trading group was dissolved. Those who had sponsored the enterprise with their capital would get it back with an agreed rate of interest, with the profit would be distributed equally among all those involved in the partnership.

A merchant from the village of Kutalla, about 14 kilometres away from Larsa, kept a document in his archive in which the judges make a decision in the temple of Šamaš, the principal deity of the neighbouring large town, about who should own a plot of land. It is an interesting case in which two members, in the process of dissolving a partnership, dispute over a plot of land. Iribam-Sin claimed that he had made the purchase with money from the partnership. But his cousin, Ṣilli-Eštar, maintained that he had bought it from his own resources, the funds having come from his mother, and he won the case. Two documents were issued, one about how the land was to be divided and the other confirming the rights of ownership. Both texts are dated in the same month of the same year (Hammurabi Year 34, Month 12 = 1759 BC), but since the day of the month is not mentioned it is unclear whether the dispute over the ownership of the land led to the dissolution of the partnership, or whether there was disagreement about how to divide the assets. The names of nine witnesses are listed on both documents.

> Ṣilli-Eštar, the son of Ili-shukkal, and Iribam the son of Ubar-Sin formed a partnership. They have gone to find judges for its dissolution. The judges have sent them to the temple of Šamaš. In the temple of Šamaš the judges have reached a decision. They have reimbursed the financial sponsor and have acquitted them of their supplementary rights. The share of Iribam-Sin is a male slave, Lustammar-Šamaš, with a chain and a female slave, Lishliman. The share of Ṣilli-Eštar is a male slave, Ibšina-El, and a female slave, Geštinanna-lamassi. They have arranged the division. In the temple of Šamaš and in the temple of Sin they have made a declaration under oath. They have made up their accounts together. They will not return and will not bring one another to court. Neither will have any rights over whatever the one has handed over to the other.[9]

The second document implies that the dissolved partnership had regrouped with more than the two people involved. The interests of Ṣilli-Eštar and Iribam-Sin now seem to be shared together with all their brothers. The basic unit used for land measurement, a *sar*, is about 36 m².

> Concerning the house covering an area of 1 *sar* and a warehouse covering an area of 2 *sar*, which Ṣilli-Eštar and his brother Awil-ili, the sons of Ili-šukkal, have bought from Sin-muballiṭ and his brothers, the sons of Pirhum: Ṣilli-Eštar has made the following declaration in the temple of Šamaš. 'This has certainly been purchased with silver from my mother and has not been purchased with silver from the partnership.' Iribam-Sin and his brothers, the sons of Ubar-Sin, have no rights over the house and the warehouse. They will not dispute this in the future. They have sworn by the king Hammurabi.[10]

The Palace as a Regulating Authority

Babylonia could be described as a pre-monetary economic society in the time of Hammurabi. Silver was used in various forms as a circulating currency and would be paid by weight when concluding a business transaction. It was also used as an item of exchange. Documents known as tariff lists give a value in silver for basic commodities such as wool, oil and dates. No tariff list has yet been found from the time of Hammurabi, but there are one or two places in the Code where prices and professional charges are stipulated. According to Laws 257–258, the annual wages for a hired labourer would be 8 *gur* of grain (a *gur*, a measure of cubic capacity, was something like 2,400 litres). Paying a man to look after cattle cost less, 6 *gur* (1,800 litres) per year. The daily rate for hiring oxen and a chariot with a driver was said to be 180 litres of grain, but to hire just the chariot would cost much less, 40 litres of grain (Laws 271–272). That wages could be fixed in this way by the king has suggested to those who take a state-centred view of the Babylonian economy that the palace occupied a dominating position over the market, which would have amounted to a real monopoly.

That idea needs further investigation, especially when wool is the commodity under consideration. For the state to have exerted a monopoly three principal factors have to be assumed. First, the palace must have owned all the sheep. In fact, some flocks did not belong to the palace. Hammurabi's sister, a *nadîtum* in the temple, is said to have owned flocks, and more ordinary people, such as the soldier named Ubarum, entrusted tiny flocks of a dozen or so sheep to a shepherd. Then there are the temples, such as that of Nanna at Ur and of Šamaš at Sippar, which owned very large flocks. Secondly, it seems on balance, that the palace wool trade was managed for the palace officials by entrepreneurs, who had an independent status like that of the *tamkârum*, as previously discussed. Finally there is the argument about price. The palace by virtue of its monopoly is supposed to have fixed the price of wool at a level which would not vary over 150 years, from the reign of Hammurabi to the end of his dynasty. But looking again at the actual documentation of sales including references to more recently discovered texts we can see that this was not the case. The price of wool, like that of all other products, was gradually increased during that period. One talent of wool (about 30 kilograms) fetched six shekels of silver (about 50 grams) on average around 1750, but by 1600 it fetched ten shekels. There is no basis to support the theory of a palace monopoly for the wool trade. On the contrary, we have some evidence from letters that there was some private trade in wool. There are relatively few documents compared with the abundant evidence for palace trade because private transactions were unlikely to have been sales on credit. Documentation for private sales settled instantly are unnecessary, whereas for the palace, working on a credit basis, had to have contracts issued and written accounts prepared.

Some Assyriologists still follow K. Polanyi, preferring the idea that a non-market economy existed during the time of Hammurabi. Those ideas were formulated theoretically without the benefit of the documentation that is now available. Many of the texts published in recent years show very clearly that fluctuating prices characterised the market. It is all too easy to use these terms anachronistically and to allow misunderstandings to arise. To read from an actual letter just how transactions were conducted will make things clearer. Two commercial agents wish to sell some oil but, because they cannot find a purchaser, see no way out of their situation. They therefore write for new instructions.

> Master, we have come to Yabliya as your letter told us to. But as for the oil there is no silver and no grain. Even though the herald has made an appeal no-one has given us any grain and we have not received any silver.[11]

It has also been suggested that the palace may have exercised control on the economy by fixing wages, since there are sentences in the Code referring to varying scales of pay. A higher rate applies at the beginning of the year than that applying at the end.

> If someone has hired a paid worker he must give him six grains (26 mg) of silver a day from the beginning of the year to the end of the fifth month, and he must give him five grains (22 mg) of silver from the sixth month to the end of the year.[12]

But it should be remembered that the beginning of the Babylonian year was in the spring. The first five months would be filled with intensive agricultural activities so it was fitting for labourers, who would be hard to find, to be paid at a higher rate. These tariffs were not just a ruler's pious thoughts as they are sometimes referred to on a document. Alammuš-naṣir, under whose orders textile workers were employed, wrote to someone who had received complaints from them, stating that that 'the salary of a hired labourer is inscribed on the stele'.[13] This is probably a reference to a copy of the Code which was intended to be displayed in public and which contained references to such matters. It would be completely anachronistic to suggest that the palace controlled the labour market insofar as it was able to fix the amount a salary could increase. The Code exemplifies concepts of justice and authority, not of power over the market and the economy. The evidence from the documents recovered from the archives shows that in fact salaries were higher than those stipulated in the Code. It gave minimum wage rates and to pay a man less would have been unjust.

That the sovereign could redress problems by proclaiming an 'edict of grace' (*mîšarum*) is also relevant. It was usual for him to do this at the beginning of his reign, but if the economic situation deteriorated too far he could proclaim other such acts later in his reign. Any arrears of payments due to the palace would then be excused and non-commercial debts would be written off for the debtors.

****

One of the lessons of this chapter has been to stress the importance of exercising sound judgement about the interpretation of sources. It would be very easy to be deluded by the tiny number of private documents that have survived. It is quite natural that much should have been recorded about the affairs of the central institutions, such as the palace and the temples, because their complex management necessitated written sources. This does not justify rushing to the conclusion that the extent to which they exerted control over the economy corresponded to the number of official documents found. Small traders and producers would have easily carried on their work without written documentation. The way in which the economy was conducted in the reign of Hammurabi is not really comparable to the model of a palace economy described by J.-P. Vernant. Certainly there existed a 'complex hierarchy of palace dignitaries', but it would be wrong to infer from this that the king 'controlled and meticulously regulated all sectors of economic life and all levels of social behaviour'. There was room for a private sector in commerce. The palace should not be seen as a monolithic entity. The royal estate was not a continuous stretch of territory. In many towns the provincial administrative centre was referred to as 'the palace'. Furthermore, in the first half of the second millennium, the contribution of the temples to economic life was not inconsiderable. And of course there were some wealthy individuals, each of whom had his own estate (*bîtum*) which was managed in the same way as that of the palace but on a smaller scale. All these reasons persuade us to abandon the term 'palace economy' in favour of 'estate economy'.

Conclusion

The Legacy of Hammurabi

During excavations at Sippar, inscribed building cones were found expressing Hammurabi's aspirations for posterity.

> I placed my good name in the mouth of the people, so that they would say it every day like the name of a god, and in the future it would never be forgotten.[1]

It seems appropriate to conclude with an assessment of Hammurabi's claim to eternal recognition and to examine the extent to which his fame stretched beyond his long reign over the kingdom of Babylon.

Every king of Mesopotamia hoped that his name would not melt away into obscurity after his death and some attention was usually paid by his successors to a sovereign after he had died. Hammurabi was similarly concerned that he should not be forgotten by posterity, as he states explicitly in the Epilogue to the Code. That such a hope could be fulfilled would have been quite reasonable for the decades immediately following his death, but the memory of Hammurabi survived for more than a millennium. What made him famous was his Code of Laws. Many later documents have been found which are copied extracts from the text as a whole and they cover a period of fourteen centuries after his death. None of the earlier collections of laws, such as those of Ur-Nammu, Lipit-Eštar of Isin and Daduša of Ešnunna, were copied so much by later generations. It is well-known that after the twenty-first century scribes recopied the Code of Ur-Nammu in their schools in the Old Babylonian period, but no manuscript can be dated later than the middle of the second millennium. The long tradition of copying the laws of Hammurabi distinguishes him from his predecessors.

In the seventh century Asshurbanipal built up his famous library at Nineveh and several copies of Hammurabi's laws were found there, even though they would not have played any role in the legal system of the time. Scribes were required to copy out the text as part of their academic training. Some of these late copies have scribal comments added in an effort to explain matters of philological interest. The text of the Code may well have been regarded as a fine example of Classical Babylonian writing, in the same way as Latin writers later came to regard the prose of Cicero as a model. In a late Babylonian exegetical document, the text of the Prologue was quoted and subjected to an erudite philological examination and used as a starting-point for more esoteric speculation.

As was mentioned earlier, the stele on which the laws are inscribed was excavated from Susa, taken there in the twelfth century BC by an Elamite king as a trophy of battle. Although the sovereignty of Hammurabi never extended so far east, a scribe copying the text in the sixth century believed that Hammurabi himself had erected the stele in Susa. This adds to the impression that for many centuries after his death Hammurabi was endowed with an aura of distinction, an aura easily surpassing the prestige he would have enjoyed when he was alive. By contrast Herodotus, writing at about the same time, made no mention of the name of Hammurabi among those still remembered as famous.

The person of Hammurabi also emerges in the context of what has by convention come to be called 'the cult of the ancestors'. Apparently it was a cultic practice observed by private individuals and also by the royal family. A famous document from the reign of Ammi-ṣaduqa, the great-great-grandson of Hammurabi, lists all the kings who had preceded him on the throne of Babylon, going back as far as his nomadic ancestors at the beginning of the second millennium. At an important part of the *kispum* ritual, he invokes the deceased with the words:

> Come, eat this, drink this, and bless Ammi-ṣaduqa, son of Ammi-ditana, king of Babylon!

The same Ammi-ṣaduqa had a statue of his ancestor made and we know he consulted oracles about manufacturing this statue.

In the sixth century BC, Neo-Babylonian kings made great efforts to restore the ancient sanctuaries in various Babylonian towns. While carrying out this work they maintained the tradition of reading any of the foundation inscriptions of earlier rulers they unearthed. Nabonidus records that, several decades before he became king, Nebuchadnezzar carried out some restoration work at Larsa, but he had not been able to find evidence of any king before Burnaburiaš, a Cassite of the fourteenth century. He continues his narrative by recounting how, by the intercession of the god Marduk, a strong wind arose and blew away sand which had accumulated around the ruins of the temple, exposing a lost inscription.

> I saw an inscription including the name of Hammurabi, the king from of old, who, seven hundred years before Burnaburiaš, had rebuilt on the ancient foundations the Ebabbar temple for the god Šamaš and the ziggurat.

After describing his restoration of the temple and the attention he had paid to the original plans Nabonidus continues:

> I read the inscription, including the name of Hammurabi, on an alabaster tablet which was found within. I placed it together with an inscription including my own name to stay there permanently.[2]

A document like this shows that Hammurabi was still considered important in later times. The same treatment could have been applied to inscriptions of even earlier rulers, such as Sargon and Naram-Sin, the kings of Agade.

The traditional way in which the scribes were trained was another factor to stimulate the veneration of Hammurabi by later generations. They were required to copy out royal inscriptions as an exercise, with certain Balaṭu had to copy the dedicatory inscriptions on some musical instruments that had been presented to a temple by the king of Babylon after Mari had been conquered. The instruments have never been found, but the inscriptions on them have survived in this copy made fourteen years after the death of Hammurabi.

Copies of two more inscriptions of Hammurabi come from much later, from the sixth century in the Neo-Babylonian period. One of them includes a colophon, in which the scribe states that the original came from a temple in Babylon and that he had placed his copy in the sanctuary of Nabu in Borsippa, with the intention that the patron deity of scribes would grant him happiness and the answer to his prayers. From the first millennium we also have a copy of a medical text about treatments for the eyes which the scribe claims dates back to the time of Hammurabi. There are similar inscriptions on other documents referring to other ancient kings, such as the copies of amulet inscriptions from the time of Naram-Sin of Agade and Rim-Sin of Larsa.

A tablet found in the temple of Nabu in Kalhu shows that the memory of Hammurabi was kept alive among Assyrian literati in the first millennium BC. A scribe copied what are supposed to be a series of questions addressed to the gods by the king of Babylon about certain military expeditions which he planned to undertake. Similar texts concern some of the later kings of the First Dynasty of Babylon. We also find a scribe writing from Babylon in the seventh century to the king of Assyria, who was almost certainly Assurbanipal. He claims to be sending him a copy of two damaged tablets in his possession related to Hammurabi.

> An ancient tablet made by King Hammurabi as well as an inscription which was even older than the time of Hammurabi.[3]

The latest reference to Hammurabi in cuneiform literature is the mention of his name in a bilingual hymn from the library of the temple of Ebabbar in Sippar from the Achaemenid period, a text to which reference has been made earlier.[4]

Despite all this, we must acknowledge that the later tradition does not accord to Hammurabi the same level of prestige it accords to Sargon, who was considered to have played a more crucial part in the course of Mesopotamian history. Furthermore, there is no evidence for any later reflection on the achievements of his reign, as was the case for the kings of Agade and, to a lesser degree, those of the Ur III Dynasty. We do not have any 'historical omen' concerning him, as we have for some other rulers who in our perception have less importance. Even so, there was no question of his ever being forgotten. In the eighth century there was a governor of Suhum, in the Middle Euphrates region, who claimed to be descended from Tunamissah, who in turn is said to be 'the son of Hammurabi, the king of Babylon', a fact clearly cited as a matter of pride. None of the attempts to equate King Amraphel in Genesis 14 with Hammurabi can be supported with any clear evidence and so they should be disregarded.[5]

To decide whether Hammurabi really deserves the prominence given to him by historians today is hard. Samsi-Addu, who was ten years older, could easily be considered equally important, though as yet no monograph on him has been published. Yet the great impact made on the history of Babylonia by various key points in the reign of Hammurabi cannot be lightly dismissed. What has done more than anything else to push him into the role of a leading actor on the Ancient Mesopotamian stage has been the discovery of his Code of Laws, a seminal document for a wide range of modern professions.

Notes

Time Chart

1. His name is placed in brackets because, although he was traditionally supposed to be the first sovereign of the dynasty, he was probably an illustrious Bedouin chief who was not resident in Babylon.

Part One: The Conqueror

1. Most of them were first published in the series *ARM*. For the re-edition see *LAPO* 16–18 (J.-M. Durand, *Documents épistolaires du palais de Mari* (three volumes). Littératures anciennes du Proche-Orient 16–18. Paris, 1997–2000).
2. The version of the year names of Hammurabi used in this book are taken from M.J.A. Horsnell, *The Year Names of the First Dynasty of Babylon*. Vol. II. Hamilton, 1999.
3. In principle the Babylonian year began in the springtime, with the vernal equinox and was divided into 12 lunar months. Although the correct order of the names of the Babylonian months is known, it is more convenient in modern scholarly literature to refer to them by number (i, ii, iii, etc.). Because the months followed the phases of the moon they would be only 29 or 30 days long. In order to synchronise the lunar with the solar calendar it was necessary to allow for an intercalary month, so that some years stretched to thirteen months.

4. M. Civil, 'Sur les "livres d'écolier" à l'époque Paléo-Babylonienne', in J.-M. Durand and J.-R. Kupper (ed.) *Miscellanea Babyloniaca. Mélanges offerts à Maurice Birot* (Paris, 1985) pp. 67–78 (esp. p. 72, lines 44, 48).
5. *ARM* xxvi/2 381: 5–10.

Chapter 1: From the Accession of Hammurabi to the Death of Samsi-Addu (1792–1775)

1. See further p. 111, and the chronological table on p. xii.
2. *ARM* 4: 26 (= *LAPO* 17: 534): 9–20.
3. CT 48:15; see D. Charpin, 'Lettres et procès ...', pp. 89–90, no. 45, for a translation and commentary.
4. M.7412: 8–10; the text is mentioned in *FM* 5 (second part: p. 111, note 289) but it has not yet been published.
5. *ARM* 1: 129 (= *LAPO* 17: 544).
6. *ARM* 5:14 (= *LAPO* 18: 916): 3′–14′.
7. A.1289+ (= *LAPO* 16: 281): 25′–28′.

Chapter 2: From the Death of Samsi-Addu to the Victory over Elam (1775–1764)

1. On this question see further Chapter 7, p. 134.
2. FM 6:14: 12'–17'.
3. Apparently an idiom meaning 'forming an indissoluble unit'.
4. *ARM* 26/2, 449: 5–23. These reminders of the past recalled by Hammurabi accord with what we know to have been the previous state of relations between Mari and Babylon.
5. *ARM* 26/2, 449: 25–50.
6. *ARM* 26/2, 449: 51–68.
7. *ARM* 28, 25: 24–31.
8. A. 482, cited by G. Dossin, 'Les archives épistolaires du palais de Mari', Syria 19 (1938), pp. 117–118 (= *Recueil* G. Dossin 1983, pp. 114–115); for a commentary see *MARI* 4, p. 323 note 131.
9. A. 3618: 21'–27' is a letter from Yasim-Dagan, as yet unpublished, but cited in my study CDOG 2, p. 122 note 37.
10. *ARM* 26/2, 363: 4–25.
11. *ARM* 26/2, 367: 9–26.
12. *ARM* 26/2, 368: 9–18.

13. *ARM* 26/2, 365: 3–15.
14. *ARM* 26/2, 369: 17'–20'.
15. *ARM* 26/2, 303: 49'.
16. *ARM* 26/2 379: 29–34 (with a modified translation).
17. *ARM* 6, 53: (= *LAPO* 16: 320).
18. A. 4626 (= *LAPO* 16 286): 8'–11'.
19. M. 6435+ (= *LAPO* 16 290).
20. *ARM* 2, 21 (= *LAPO* 16 350): 22–25.
21. *ARM* 26/1, 100BIS: 29–34.
22. J.-M. Durand, 'L'empereur d'Élam et ses vassaux', in H. Gasche, M. Tanret, C. Janssen and A. Degraeve (ed.) *Cinquante-deux réflexions sur le Proche-Orient ancien offertes en hommage à Léon De Meyer*. Mesopotamian History and Environments Occasional Publications 2, Ghent 1994, pp. 15–22.
23. A. 3669+: 17'–20', published by D. Lacambre, 'La bataille de Hirîtum', *MARI* 8 (1997) p. 449.
24. A. 257 (= *LAPO* 16 300).
25. A. 405; an unpublished letter from Ibal-pi-El, quoted in FM 5, p. 228.

Chapter 3: The Great Conquests (1764–1759)

1. *ARM* 26/2, 385: 8'–13'.
2. *ARM* 26/2, 385: 13'–15'.
3. *ARM* 26/2, 385: 43'–44'.
4. *CH* iii: 70–iv:6.
5. *ARM* 26/2: 383: 6–12.
6. *ARM* 26/2: 381: 4'–6'.
7. *ARM* 26/2: 386: 3'–5'.
8. This clearly refers to the palace.
9. *ARM* 27: 156: 2'–7'.
10. *ARM* 26/2, 374: 12–21.
11. *ARM* 27, 161: 8–9.
12. *AbB* iv, 115: 5–6 and 11–19.
13. Literally 'came down to Larsa'.
14. *AbB* iv, 115: 5–6 and 11–19.
15. *AbB* xiii,10; See D. Charpin, 'Lettres et procès ...' p. 86 no. 42.
16. A. 2962, re-edited in FM v, pp. 254–256.
17. The text is cited on p. 88, note 26.
18. D. Frayne, *RIME* 4, p. 346, no. 11: 27–30.

Chapter 5: The King and The Gods

1. The formally abbreviated Latin legends on British coins have similarly changed. On a Georgian coin we find D G M B FR ET H REX F D BR ET L D S R I A TH ET EL, 'By the grace of God, King of Great Britain, France and Ireland, Defender of the Faith, Duke of Brunswick and Luneburg, High Treasurer and Elector of the Holy Roman Empire', whereas the 2002 crown commemorating the Golden Jubilee of Elizabeth II reads, AMOR POPULI PRAESIDIUM REG, 'The love of the people is the Queen's protection'.
2. *CT* 21 40–42 iv: 5–14; See Nathan Wasserman, 'CT 21, 40–42, A Bilingual Report of Oracular Signs with a Royal Hymn of Hammurabi' (RA 86 (1992), 1–18), particularly p. 6.
3. D. Frayne, *RIME* 4, p. 349, no. 13.
4. D. Frayne, *RIME* 4, no. 7.
5. D. Frayne, *RIME* 4, no. 8.
6. Ibid., p. 80.
7. A. 2968, see M. Guichard, *RA* 98 (2004), 16–25.
8. The name of this tribe, literally to be translated 'The sons of the right', i.e. of the south, is very similar to the Biblical name Benjamin.
9. ARM 26/2, 385: 5'–6'. Bene Sim'al can be translated literally as 'The sons of the left', i.e. of the north.
10. CH i:1–49; cf. Martha T. Roth, *Law Collections from Mesopotamia and Asia Minor* (Atlanta, 1995) 76.
11. At the time of writing Marduk, the local god of Babylon, did not enjoy such a superior status, though of course later, in the second half of the second millennium, he did acquire his position at the top of the Sumero-Akkadian pantheon.
12. cf. D. Frayne, *RIME* 4, p. 360 no. 2002.
13. See below pp. 84–5.
14. *ARM* 26/2 371: 9–30.
15. *ARM* 26/1 209: 8–13.
16. *ARM* 26/1 185-bis (= *LAPO* 18 1145): 18–26.
17. *ARM* 26/1 212 (= *LAPO* 18 1146): 1'–9'.
18. D. Frayne, *RIME* 4, p. 344, no. 10.
19. *ARM* 26/1 160: 7'–20'.
20. Such suspicions, it will be remembered, were raised by Cicero.
21. *ARM* 26/1 102: 13'–29'.
22. *ARM* 26/2 385: 13'–15'.
23. See N. Wasserman, 'CT 21, 4042 – A bilingual report of oracular signs with

a royal hymn of Hammurabi', RA 86, 1992, pp. 1–18; see further A. Fadhil and G. Pettinato, 'Inno ad Hammurabi da Sippar', Orientis Antiqui Miscellanea 2, 1995, pp. 173–187.
24. *ARM* xxvi/2 469 = *LAPO* 16, 287: 10–15.
25. The leash symbolised divine authority to be the ruler of the people.
26. D. Frayne, *RIME* 4, p. 353, no. 16.
27. On occasions divine statues would be moved on a cart, and so it is possible that this richly decorated throne would be used when such transport was appropriate.
28. *RIME* 4, E43.6.2: 51–55, p. 335.

Chapter 6: The Government of the Kingdom

1. A. 2119 (*LAPO* 17 442) 13–21.
2. *ARM* xxvi/2 449: 12–15.
3. A. 3158 (*LAPO* 18 1008) 4–12.
4. *ARM* xxvi/2 401: 33–34.
5. M. 6060 (= *LAPO* 16 297): 19'–25'.
6. *ARM* xxvi/2 375: 4–19
7. *ARM* xxvi/2, 369: 6–7.
8. *ARM* xxvi/1, 104: 5–17.
9. *ARM* xxvi/1, 13: 7–9.
10. *LAPO* 18 1110 (= *ARM* x 147).
11. *AbB* xiii 8.
12. M. Anbar and M. Stol, "Textes de l'époque babylonienne ancienne III', RA 85, 1991, p. 19, no. 8.
13. J-R. Kupper, 'Lettres de Kiš', RA 53, 1959, pp. 30–31, D, 16: 7–11.
14. Law 23.
15. *AbB* x 19: 9.
16. D. Charpin, 'Lettres et procès ...', p. 103 no. 60.
17. Law 16.
18. This text, A. 510, was referred to by J.M. Durand in ARM xxvi/1, p. 28 n.104, and p. 407 n. 149, but it is not yet published.
19. 'Cylinder I'.
20. *VS* 17 41: 173–177; see J.J. van Dijk, 'Une insurrection générale au pays de Larsa avant l'avènement de Nur-Adad', *Journal of Cuneiform Studies* 19, 1965, pp. 1–25.
21. The dedicatory inscription of Lu-Nanna has been mentioned above, see p. 111.

Chapter 7: War and Peace as Means of Conquest

1. *ARM* xxvi/2: 468: 21'–26'.
2. *ARM* vi 28 (= *LAPO* 17 573): 13–15.
3. *CTN* iv 63: 2–7.
4. Law 26.
5. Law 33; see M. Roth, 'Hammurabi's Wronged Man', *Journal of the American Oriental Society* 122, 2002, pp. 38–45, esp. p. 41 n. 24.
6. *ARM* xxvii 161: 45–52.
7. *ARM* xxvi/2 363: 9–15.
8. *LAPO* 17, pp. 332–337.
9. *FM* vi 10.
10. A. 2539 (as yet unpublished).
11. *FM* vi 12: 6–10.
12. *FM* vi 13: 18–30.
13. A. 3591: 15'–16'; see M. Guichard, 'Au pays de la Dame de Nagar', in *FM* ii, Paris, 1994, pp. 256–257.
14. Ibid., p. 70.
15. *AbB* xiii 25.
16. *ARM* ii 22 (= *LAPO* 17 585): 23–31.
17. *ARM* ii 31 (= *LAPO* 17 591): 7'–18'.
18. *CTN* iv 63: 9–12.
19. *FM* vi 16: 7–18.
20. *FM* vi 17: 7–31.
21. Law 32.
22. That particular decisions taken by the king may lie behind particular sentences in the Code is mentioned further in Chapter 8.
23. *AbB* ix 32.
24. Laws 27–29.
25. Laws 134–135.
26. *ARM* ii 23 (= *LAPO* 17 590): 7–8.
27. *ARM* ii 70 (= *LAPO* 16 352): 4'–11'.
28. *ARM* xxvi/2 370: 4'–9'.
29. *ARM* xxvi/1 101: 27–28.
30. *ARM* xxvi/2 384: 68'–69'.
31. *ARM* ii 76 (= *LAPO* 16 404).
32. *ARM* xiv 122 (= *LAPO* 16 368): 13–20.
33. *ARM* xxviii 14.
34. *ARM* xxvi/2 384: 29'–33' and 42'–60'.
35. A.430+, not yet published, but quoted in my study in *CDOG* 2, pp. 118–119.

36. *ARM* xxvi/2 372: 49–54.
37. *ARM* xxvi/2 384: 63'–65'.
38. *ARM* xxvi/2 347: 9–16.
39. *ARM* xxvi/2 404: 17–18.
40. Some details of the sacrificial ritual concluding a treaty in the Hebrew Bible are given in Genesis 15: 9–10 and Jeremiah 34: 18–19. There the animal was split into two and the parties to the agreement passed between the separated halves. This has been understood as symbolic of the fate destined for anyone who failed to maintain the terms of the treaty.
41. A. 361; see Fig. 31.
42. *ARM* xxvi/2 372: 56–57.
43. A. 2968+; M. Guichard, RA 98, 2004, pp. 16–25.
44. See J.-M. Durand, '*Assyriologie*', Annuaire du Collège de France, 2000–1, pp. 693–705.
45. *ARM* xxvi/2 468: 8'–9'.
46. *ARM* xxvi/? 373: 30–33.
47. *ARM* xxvi/2 385: 1'–7'.
48. A. 3838, quoted in N. Ziegler, 'Les enfants du palais', Ktèma 22, 1997, p. 56 n. 55.
49. Epilogue l: 92ff.
50. Epilogue xlvii: 9ff.

Chapter 8: Hammurabi, the Legislator and the Judge

1. D. Frayne, *RIME*, p. 148 no. 7: 50–56.
2. In France, according to the ordinance of Montils-lès-Tours (1454), Charles VII assumed the title '*Roi fontaine de Justice*', and bequeathed it to his successors. In Britain it used to be that the monarch himself, wherever he happened to be, would administer justice in 'The Court of the King before the King Himself'. After the Magna Carta, that court always sat at Westminster Hall in London and eventually sat without the monarch being present. The name survives today in the Queen's Bench Division of the High Court of Justice.
3. A campaign that was mentioned earlier, see pp. 26–27.
4. D. Charpin, 'Lettres et procès ... ', p. 78, no. 36.
5. See below, Chapter 10, p. 265; D. Charpin, 'Lettres et procès ...', p. 110, no. 69 and p. 111, no. 70.
6. *CT* 45, 18: 12ff.; see also ANET^3 p. 544 (text B).
7. *CT* 48, 11; se R.A. Veenker, 'An Old-Babylonian Legal Procedure for Appeal. Evidence from the *ṭuppi lā ragāmim*', Hebrew Union College Annual

45, 1974, pp. 1–15.
8. Law 2.
9. *AbB* xiii 105.
10. A. 1945: 12–27; see S. Lafont, 'Un "cas royal" à l'époque de Mari', *RA* 91, 1997, pp. 109–119.
11. Other details about the *mîšarum* have already been mentioned in Chapter 5.
12. D. Charpin, 'Lettres et procès … ', p. 90 no. 46.
13. By tradition the laws are numbered from 1 to 282 but the final number should probably be lower. It is uncertain how many were included between Law 65 (the last one legible on the front of the stele, before 5, 6 or 7 columns were effaced) and Law 99 (the first one legible on the back of the stele). Fragmentary copies of the laws on clay tablets go a long way to restoring what was in this gap but so far no full restoration has been possible.
14. Such as the verdicts for Laws 17–20, see below, pp. 222–223.
15. *AbB* xiii 12; for another translation and commentary see 'Lettres et procès …', p. 85 no. 41.
16. Meaning 'if you fail to reimburse me by refusing to sell your goods'.
17. The document would be a written undertaking to support her for life.
18. D. Charpin, 'Lettres et procès …' pp. 86–88, no. 43.
19. *AbB* 13: 27.
20. Epilogue xlviii: 3ff.
21. *FM* vii 38: 7'–11'.
22. See p. 199.

Chapter 9: Hammurabi and His Subjects: Observations on Babylonian Society

1. Laws 221–223.
2. It may be that some other metal was actually used for the branding, since at that time iron was regarded as a precious stone.
3. Laws 226–227.
4. *AbB* vi 4: 24–26.
5. *AbB* xiii 18.
6. Laws 15–20.
7. D. Charpin, 'Lettres et procès … ', p. 92 no. 48.
8. Laws 131 and 132.
9. D. Charpin, 'Lettres et procès … ', p. 100 no. 57.
10. Laws 188–189.

11. *AbB* xiii 22.
12. Law 185.
13. *AbB* vii 103.
14. *AbB* xiii 21: 3–9.
15. Law 57.
16. A.1146 (= *LAPO* 16 38): 11–19.
17. The name Yemen is used in Arabic to indicate the southern part of the Arabian peninsula.
18. *AbB* xii 9: 6–9.
19. *AbB* ix 160: 10–11.
20. W 204473 i: 16, published by A. Falkenstein, 'Zu den Inschriftenfunden der Grabung in Uruk-Warka 1960–61', *Baghdader Mitteilungen* 2, 1963, pp. 1–82.
21. *AbB* x 164:7.
22. *FM* ii 17, published by N. Ziegler, 'Deux esclaves en fuite à Mari', in D. Charpin and J.-M. Durand (ed.) *Recueil d'études à la mémoire de Maurice Birot, Florilegium marianum* II, Mémoires de NABU 3, Paris 1994, pp. 11–21 (see p. 17).
23. Law 126.
24. Laws 142–143.
25. Laws 53–54. What would be shared is not made explicit, but presumably it was the proceeds from the sale of the offender.

Chapter 10: The Palace Economy

1. J.-P. Vernant, *Les origines de la pensée grecque*, Paris, 1962, p. 18.
2. *AbB* iv: 1.
3. Laws 36–37.
4. Law 38.
5. *AbB* xiii: 43.
6. *AbB* xiii: 9.
7. *AbB* x 69:1–10.
8. *AbB* iv: 16.
9. D. Charpin, 'Lettres et procès …', p. 110, no. 69.
10. Ibid., p. 111, no. 70.
11. *AbB* 12 95: 4–8.
12. Law 273.
13. A. 3529; see M. Roth, *Law Collections from Mesopotamia and Asia Minor*, Writings from the Ancient World 6, Atlanta, 1995, p. 6 and p. 10 n. 1.

Conclusion: The Legacy of Hammurabi

1. See D. Frayne, *RIME* 4, text no. 2.
2. H. Schaudig, *Die Inschriften Nabonids von Babylon und Kyros' des Grossen*, Alter Orient und Altes Testament 256, Münster, 2001, p. 402 (2.11 1 ii 20–25) and p. 405 (2.11 1 iii 27–31).
3. S. Parpola, *Letters from Assyrian and Babylonian Scholars*, State Archives of Assyria 10, Helsinki, 1993, text no. 155.
4. See p. 76 and pp. 86–7; see also A. Fadhil and G. Pettinato, 'Inno ad Hammurabi da Sippar', Orientis Antiqui Miscellanea 2, 1995, pp. 173–187.
5. See most recently *FM* v: 26.

Bibliography

The content of the English edition of this book corresponds more or less exactly to the original French edition of 2003. But the author has updated this Bibliography seeking to place greater emphasis on material that is available in English.

I. GENERAL SURVEYS

Mesopotamian civilisation in general

P. Amiet, *The Art of the Ancient Near East*, New York, 1980.
A. Benoît, *Les civilisations du Proche-Orient*, Les manuels de l'École du Louvre, Paris, 2003.
D. Charpin, *Writing, Law and Kingship in Old Babylonian Mesopotamia* (translated by Jane Marie Todd), Chicago University Press, Chicago, IL, 2010.
D. Charpin, *Reading and Writing in Babylon* (translated by Jane Marie Todd), Harvard University Press, Cambridge, MA, 2011 (revised version of the original French *Lire et écrire à Babylone*, Presses Universitaires de France, Paris, 2008).
F. Joannès (ed.), *Dictionnaire de la civilisation mésopotamienne*, coll. Bouquins, Paris, 2001.
G. Leick (ed.), *The Babylonian World*, New York and London, 2007.
K. Radner and E. Robson (eds), *The Oxford Handbook of Cuneiform Culture*, Oxford, 2011.
M. Roaf, *Cultural Atlas of Mesopotamia and the Ancient Near East*, Oxford, 1990 (several reprintings).

J. M. Sasson, J. Baines, G. Beckman and K. S. Rubinson (eds), *Civilizations of the Ancient Near East*, 4 vols., New York, 1995; reprinted in 2 vols., Peabody, 2000.

More specific studies
D. Charpin and J.-M. Durand (eds), *Mari, Ébla et les Hourrites... Deuxième partie*, Amurru 2, Paris, 2001.
J.-M. Durand (ed.), *Mari, Ébla et les Hourrites: dix ans de travaux. Actes du colloque international (Paris, mai 1993). Première partie*, Amurru 1, Paris, 1996.
F. R. Kraus, *Vom mesopotamischen Menschen der altbabylonischen Zeit und seiner Welt*, Amsterdam and London, 1973.
J. N. Postgate, *Early Mesopotamia. Society and Economy at the Dawn of History*, London and New York, 1992.
R. Pruzsinszky, *Mesopotamian Chronology of the 2nd Millennium B.C. An Introduction to the Textual Evidence and Related Chronological Issues*, Österreischen Akademie der Wissenschaften phil.-hist. Klasse 56, Vienna, 2009.

Websites
http://www.archibab.fr, the ARCHIBAB project, for a collection of archival documents.
http://etcsl.orinst.ox.ac.uk, Electronic Text Corpus of Sumerian Literature, for literary texts in Sumerian.
http://www.seal.uni-leipzig.de, Sources of Early Akkadian Literature, for literary texts in Akkadian.
http://oracc.museum.upenn.edu/qcat, the Open Richly Annotated Cuneiform Corpus, for Sumerian royal inscriptions.

II. SPECIFIC SURVEYS

The following works have been selected to help the reader find extra information on the subjects covered in specific chapters of this book.

Introduction

A.-M. Christin (ed.), *A History of Writing: From Hieroglyph to Multimedia*, 2002 (especially the articles of D. Charpin, J.-M. Durand and M. Guichard).
D. Collon, *First Impressions. Cylinder Seals in the Ancient Near East*, London, 1987.
J.-M. Durand, D. Charpin et al., 'Tell Hariri / Mari: textes', in *Supplément au Dictionnaire de la Bible* 14, Paris, 2008, col. 214–356.

D. R. Frayne, *Old Babylonian Period (2003-1595 BC)*, Royal Inscriptions of Mesopotamia. Early Periods 4, Toronto, 1990.

F. R. Kraus, then K. R. Veenhof (eds), *Altbabylonische Briefe*, 13 vol. (proceeding), Leiden, 1964- (the translations of these Old Babylonian letters are given in English in several of these volumes).

C.B.F. Walker, *Cuneiform*, Reading the Past, London, 1987.

The documents from Mari

Archives royales de Mari (31 vols., proceeding).

Florilegium marianum (12 vols., proceeding).

MARI, annales de recherches interdisciplinaires (8 vols.).

J.-M. Durand, *Les documents épistolaires du palais de Mari*, vols. I, II and III, coll. *Littératures anciennes du Proche Orient* 16-17-18, Paris, 1997, 1998 and 2000 (a selection of 1200 letters, with new translations and commentaries in French).

W. Heimpel, *Letters to the King of Mari. A New Translation, with Historical Introduction, Notes, and Commentary*, MC 12, Winona Lake, 2003 (English translations of ARM 26/1, 26/2 and 27).

Chapters 1-4

D. Charpin, 'Histoire politique de la Mésopotamie (2002-1595)', in P. Attinger and M. Wäfler (eds), *Mesopotamien: Die altbabylonische Zeit, Annäherungen* 4, Orbis Biblicus et Orientalis 160/4, Fribourg and Göttingen, pp. 25-480.

D. Charpin, 'La politique hydraulique des rois paléo-babyloniens', *Annales, Histoire, Sciences sociales* 57/3, 2002, pp. 545-59.

D. Charpin and N. Ziegler, *Mari et le Proche-Orient à l'époque amorrite: essai d'histoire politique*, Florilegium marianum V, Mémoires de NABU 6, Paris, 2003.

A. Goddeeris, 'The Emergence of Amorite Dynasties in Northern Babylonia during the Early Old Babylonian Period', in W.H. van Soldt, R. Kalvelagen and D. Katz (eds), *Ethnicity in Ancient Mesopotamia, Papers Read at the 48th Rencontre Assyriologique Internationale, Leiden, 1-4 July 2002*, PIHANS 102, Leiden, 2005, pp. 138-46.

Chapter 5

D. Charpin, 'Prophètes et rois dans le Proche-Orient amorrite', in A. Lemaire (ed.), *Prophètes et rois. Bible et Proche-Orient*, Paris, 2001, pp. 21-53.

D. Charpin, *Le Clergé d'Ur au siècle d'Hammurabi (XIXe-XVIIIe siècles av. J. -C.)*, Hautes Études Orientales 22, Geneva-Paris, 1986.

F. Rochberg, 'Old Babylonian Celestial Divination', in A. K. Guinan et al. (eds), *If a Man Builds a Joyful House: Assyriological Studies in Honor of Erle Verdun Leichty*, Leiden and Boston, 2006, pp. 337–48.

Chapter 6

M.-Th. Barrelet and J.-M. Durand, 'La "figure du roi" dans l'iconographie et dans les textes depuis Ur-Nanše jusqu'à la fin de la 1ère dynastie de Babylone', in P. Garelli (ed.), *Le palais et la royauté (Archéologie et Civilisation). XIXe Rencontre Assyriologique Internationale, Paris, 29 juin–2 juillet 1971*, Paris, 1974, pp. 27–138.

D. Charpin, 'L'exercice du pouvoir par les rois de la Ière dynastie de Babylone: problèmes de méthode', in G. Wilhelm (ed.), *Organization, Representation and Symbols of Power in the Ancient Near East*, Winona Lake, in press, pp. 21–32.

D. Charpin, '"Le roi est mort, vive le roi!" Les funérailles des souverains amorrites et l'avènement de leur successeur', in R. van der Spek (ed.), *Studies in Ancient Near Eastern World View and Society Presented to Marten Stol on the occasion of his 65th birthday*, Bethesda, 2008, pp. 69–95.

J.-M. Durand, 'L'organisation de l'espace dans le palais de Mari', in E. Lévy (ed.), *Le système palatial en Orient, en Grèce et à Rome*, Strasbourg, 1985, pp. 39–110.

D. Fleming, 'Kingship of City and Tribe Conjoined: Zimri-Lim at Mari', in J. Szuchman (ed.), *Nomads, Tribes, and the State in the Ancient Near East. Cross-Disciplinary Perspectives*, Oriental Institute Seminars 5, Chicago, IL, 2009, pp. 227–40.

B. Lion, 'Des princes de Babylone à Mari', in D. Charpin and J.-M. Durand (eds), *Florilegium marianum II, Recueil d'études à la mémoire de Maurice Birot*, Mémoires de NABU 3, Paris, 1994, pp. 221–34.

J. Margueron, *Recherches sur les palais mésopotamiens à l'Âge du Bronze*, Bibliothèque archéologique et historique 107, Paris, 1982.

A. Seri, *Local Power in Old Babylonian Mesopotamia*, Studies in Egyptology and the Ancient Near East, London, 2005 (see also D. Charpin, 'Économie, société et institutions paléo-babyloniennes: nouvelles sources, nouvelles approches', *Revue d'assyriologie et d'archéologie orientale* 101, 2007, pp. 147–82).

N. Ziegler, *Florilegium marianum IV, Le Harem de Zimri-Lim*, Mémoires de NABU 5, Paris, 1999.

N. Ziegler, 'Les enfants du palais', *Ktèma. Civilisations de l'Orient, de la Grèce et de Rome antiques* 22, 1997, pp. 45–57.

Chapter 7

D. Charpin, 'Hammurabi and International Law' and 'Controlling Cross-border Traffic', in D. Charpin, *Writing, Law and Kingship in Old Babylonian Mesopotamia*, Chicago University Press, Chicago, IL, 2010, pp. 97–114; 115–26.

J.-M. Durand, 'Unité et diversités au Proche-Orient à l'époque amorrite', in D. Charpin and F. Joannès (eds), *La circulation des biens, des personnes et des idées dans le Proche-Orient ancien. Actes de la XXXVIIIe Rencontre Assyriologique Internationale (Paris, 8-10 juillet 1991)*, Paris, 1992, pp. 97–128.

M. Guichard, 'Les aspects religieux de la guerre à Mari', *Revue d'assyriologie et d'archéologie orientale* 93, 1999, pp. 27–48.

J.-R. Kupper, 'Béliers et tours de siège', *Revue d'assyriologie et d'archéologie orientale* 91, 1997, pp. 121–33.

B. Lafont, 'Relations internationales, alliances et diplomatie au temps des rois amorrites', *Amurru* 2, 2001, pp. 213–328; summarised in English in 'International Relations in the Ancient Near East: The Birth of a Complete Diplomatic System', *Diplomacy and Statecraft* 12/1, 2001, pp. 39–60.

F. Lerouxel, 'Les échanges de présents entre souverains amorrites au XVIIIème siècle d'après les Archives royales de Mari', in D. Charpin and J.-M. Durand (eds), *Recueil d'études à la mémoire d'André Parrot, Florilegium marianum* VI, Mémoires de NABU 7, Paris, 2002, pp. 413–64.

N. Ziegler, 'Aspects économiques des guerres de Samsî-Addu', in J. Andreau et al. (eds), *Économie antique. La guerre dans les économies antiques. Entretiens d'archéologie et d'histoire*, Saint-Bertrand-de-Comminges, 2000, pp. 14–33.

N. Ziegler, 'Samsî-Addu et ses soldats', in P. Abrahami and L. Battini (eds), *Les armées du Proche-Orient ancien (IIIe-Ier mill. av. J.-C.). Actes du colloque international ogranisé à Lyon les 1er et 2 décembre 2006*, Maison de l'Orient et de la Méditerranée, BAR International Series 1855, Oxford, 2008, pp. 49–56.

Chapter 8

For the Code of Hammurabi

G. R. Driver and J. C. Miles, *The Babylonian Laws Volume II, Transliterated Text, Translation, Philological Notes, Glossary*, Oxford, 1955 (still the most classical edition of the Code of Hammurabi).

M. Roth, *Law Collections from Mesopotamia and Asia Minor*, Writings from the Ancient World 6, Atlanta, 1995 (an excellent modern translation).

B. André-Salvini, *Le code de Hammurabi*, coll. 'Solo', Louvre - R.M.N., Paris, 2003.

Other sources

D. Charpin, 'Les prêteurs et le palais: les édits de *mîšarum* des rois de Babylone et leurs traces dans les archives privées', in A.C.V.M. Bongenaar (ed.), *Interdependency of Institutions and Private Entrepreneurs (MOS Studies 2). Proceedings of the Second MOS Symposium (Leiden 1998)*, PIHANS 87, Leiden, 2000, pp. 185–211.

D. Charpin, 'Lettres et procès paléo-babyloniens', in F. Joannès (ed.), *Rendre la justice en Mésopotamie*, Paris, 2000, pp. 69–111.

D. Charpin, 'The "Restauration" Edicts of the Babylonian Kings and their Applications', in D. Charpin, *Writing, Law and Kingship in Old Babylonian Mesopotamia*, Chicago University Press, Chicago, IL, 2010, pp. 83–96.

S. Démare(-Lafont), 'La valeur de la loi dans les droits cunéiformes', *Archives de philosophie du Droit* 32, 1987, pp. 335–46.

S. Lafont, 'Les actes législatifs des rois mésopotamiens', in S. Dauchy, J. Monballyu and A. Wijffels (eds), *Auctoritates. Xenia R. C. Van Caenegem Oblata. La formation du droit et ses auteurs*, Iuris Scripta Historica XIII, Brussels, 1997, pp. 3–27.

W. F. Leemans, 'King Ḫammurapi as Judge', in *Symbolae iuridicae et historicae Martino David dedicatae. Tomus alter: Iura orientis antiqui*, Leiden, 1968, pp. 107–29.

E. Lévy (ed.), *La codification des lois dans l'Antiquité. Actes du colloque de Strasbourg 27–29 novembre 1997*, Travaux du Centre de Recherche sur le Proche-Orient et la Grèce antiques 16, Paris, 2000.

M. Roth, 'Hammurabi's Wronged Man', *Journal of the American Oriental Society* 122, 2002, pp. 38–45.

K. R. Veenhof, 'The Relation between Royal Decrees and Laws in the Old Babylonian Period', *Jaarbericht van het vooraziatsich-egyptisch Genootschap Ex Oriente Lux* 35/36, 1997–2000, pp. 49–84.

Chapter 9

M. Civil, *The Farmer's Instructions. A Sumerian Agricultural Manual*, Aula Orientalis-Supplementa 5, Barcelona, 1994.

D. Charpin, *Le Clergé d'Ur au siècle d'Hammurabi (XIXe-XVIIIe siècles av. J.-C.)*, Hautes Études Orientales 22, Geneva-Paris, 1986.

D. Charpin, 'The Transfer of Property Deeds and the Constitution of Family Archives', in D. Charpin, *Writing, Law and Kingship in Old Babylonian Mesopotamia*, Chicago University Press, Chicago, IL, 2010, pp. 53–70.

M. Roth, 'Mesopotamian Legal Traditions and the Laws of Hammurabi',

Chicago Kent Law Review 71/1, 1995, pp. 13-39.

M. Stol, 'The Care of the Elderly in Mesopotamia in the Old Babylonian Period', in M. Stol and S. P. Vleeming (eds), *The Care of Elderly in the Ancient Near East*, Leiden, 1998, pp. 50-117.

C. Nicolle (ed.), *Nomades et sédentaires dans le Proche-Orient ancien. Compte rendu de la XLVIe Rencontre Assyriologique Internationale, Paris, 10-13 juillet 2000*, Amurru 3, Paris, 2004.

K. R. Veenhof (ed.), *Houses and Households in Ancient Mesopotamia. Papers read at the 40e Rencontre Assyriologique Internationale, Leiden, July 5-8, 1993*, Publications de l'Institut historique et archéologique néerlandais de Stamboul 78, Leiden, 1997.

R. Westbrook, *Old Babylonian Marriage Law*, Archiv für Orientforschung Beiheft 23, Vienna, 1988.

Chapter 10

A. C. V. M. Bongenaar (eds), *Interdependency of Institutions and Private Entrepreneurs (MOS Studies 2). Proceedings of the Second MOS Symposium (Leiden 1998)*, Publications de l'Institut historique et archéologique néerlandais de Stamboul 87, Leiden, 2000.

D. Charpin, *Archives familiales et propriété privée en Babylonie ancienne: étude des documents de 'Tell Sifr'*, Hautes Études Orientales 12, Geneva-Paris, 1980.

P. Clancier, F. Joannès, P. Rouillard and A. Tenu (eds), *Autour de Polanyi. Vocabulaires, théories et modalités des échanges*, Colloques de la Maison René-Ginouvès 1, Paris, 2005.

M. de J. Ellis, *Agriculture and State in Ancient Mesopotamia*, Occasional Publications of the Babylonian Fund 1, Philadelphia, 1976.

S. Lafont, 'Fief et féodalité dans le Proche-Orient ancien', in E. Bournazel and J.-P. Poly (eds), *Les féodalités, Histoire générale des systèmes politiques*, Paris, 1998, pp. 517-644.

M. Stol, 'State and Private Business in the Land of Larsa', *Journal of Cuneiform Studies* 34, 1982, pp. 127-230.

Conclusion

V. A. Hurowitz, 'Hammurabi in Mesopotamian Tradition', in Y. Sefati et al. (eds), *'An experienced scribe who neglects nothing'. Ancient Near Eastern studies in honor of Jacob Klein*, Bethesda, 2005, pp. 497-532.

R. Pientka-Hinz, 'Midlifecrisis und Angst vor dem Vergessen? Zur Geschichtsüberlieferung Ḫammu-rapis von Babylon', in K.-P. Adam (ed.), *Historiographie in der Antike*, Berlin and New York, 2007, pp. 1–25.

Index

Abum-waqar: 172
Adab: 72
Adad: 85, 88, 116
Addu, city-god of Aleppo: 159
Afghanistan: tin mines, 190
Agade: 15
Ahum-waqar: 146
Ahuni: 165
Akkadian: 5, 9, 16, 23, 60, 72, 175; literature, 6, 15; personal names, 14, 24, 100; writing techniques, 5–6
Alammuš-naṣir: 197
Aleppo: 26–7, 37, 43, 47, 50, 66, 93, 128, 130; hepatoscopy, 81; worship of Addu, 159
âlik idî: 128
Amat-Šamaš: 95
Amenophis IV: 113
Ammi-ditana: 193
Ammi-ṣaduqa: 77, 111, 177, 181, 193; ancestors, 23, 200; decree, 150
Amorites: 6, 23, 50, 72, 77, 83, 94, 98, 101, 110, 116–17, 176; kings, 15, 24, 66, 76, 85, 92–3, 96, 105; military tactics, 119, 121
Amurru: 80
Amurrum-šemi: 151
An: 71, 78
Anam of Uruk: letter to Sin-muballiṭ, 92
Anatolia: Boghazköy archives, 113; copper reserves, 190; trading routes, 187
Ancient Greece: 2, 146, 152, 162; slave labour, 163
Andarig: 38–9, 47, 96, 120; besieged by Zimri-Lim, 39
Annunitum: 24
Anšan (Tall-i-Maliyan): 27
Apil-Sin: 24–5, 44
âpilum: of Marduk, 81–2; of Dagan, 82
Arbele: see Urbilum
Aristotle: 2, 146
Ašlakka: 37, 39, 62
Ašnakkum: 32
Asqur-Addu, king of Karana: 69, 135
Assur: 26, 38

Assurbanipal: 200, 202
Assyrian king list: 78
Atamrum, king of Andarig: 47, 49, 62, 134–5; siege of Razama, 125
Atra-hasis: 15–6
awîlum: 161–2, 164
Aya: 89

bâbtum: 180
Babylon: 18, 23, 24, 29, 32, 35, 37, 40, 42, 49, 71, 79, 83, 88, 123, 133, 136, 184; alliance with Ekallatum, 29; alliance with Mari against Elam, 20, 40; conflict with Ešnunna, 62–3; 'Nebuchadnezzar's Museum', 66; palace archives, 19; temple, 65; temple of Marduk, 172
Babylonia: 23–6, 35, 55, 71, 73, 81, 98, 107, 143, 146, 192, 195; borders, 24, 77, 139; economy, 195–6; hepatoscopy, 81; military forces, 115–16; transport network, 114; Upper and Lower Region, 105–6
Baghdad: 3, 104, 116, 181
Bahrain: 31
bâ'irum: 126–7, 158, 186–7
Balaṭu: 201
Bedouin: 3, 117, 137, 175–6
Beltani, wife of Rim-Sin: 92
bêltum: 93
Belum-kima-ilim: 133
Bene Sim'al: 37, 175
Bene Yamina: 37, 39, 42, 78
Benjaminites: 175
Bible: 175, 202

bītum: 91–2
Borsippa: 9, 24, 71; palace, 104; temple of Nabu, 9
Bunu-Eštar: 39–40
Burnaburiaš: 201

Code of Hammurabi: 9, 56, 107, 109–10, 143, 154–9, 161–2, 166, 168, 170, 174, 180, 195–7, 200, 202; *bâ'irum* and *rêdûm*, 126–7, 158, 186–7; divine ordeals, 149; Epilogue, 111, 141, 154, 157, 199; *ilkum*, 117; maintaining dykes, 181–2; Prologue, 65, 67, 71, 78; slavery, 162–4; stele, 111, 154; war, 140
Cult of ancestors: 136
Cuneiform: 4–5, 13, 20

Daduša of Ešnunna: 17, 26, 28, 30; alliance with Samsi-Addu of Ekallatum, 30; laws, 199
Dagan: 82, 94
Der: 26, 116, 118
Dilbat: 24, 71, 127, 189; archives, 19; Hurrian names, 70
Dildaba: 104
Ditanu: 96
Diyala: 16, 125
Durand, J.-M.: 6, 175

E-abzu, temple of Enki at Eridu: 10
Ebabbar: 202
Ekallatum: 26, 38, 133; alliance with Babylon, 29
ekallum: 104
Ekur: 15; worship of Enlil, 83
Elam: 20, 38, 44–6, 49–50, 55, 81, 86, 88, 98–9, 114, 118, 121,

123, 125, 131, 139–40, 200;
conquests, 127, 130–1;
emperor, 1, 27, 38, 43–8,
50, 130, 139; *sukkal*, 27,
49, 58, 120, 130
El-Amarnah: 113
Emar: 27
Emutbalum: 61
Enki: 10
Enlil: 9, 78, 83, 88, 101
Epeš-ilim: 187
Eridu: 10, 71
Erra: 24
Erra-nada: 82; *šukkallum*, 98
Ešnunna (Tell Asmar): 26, 29, 38,
42, 46, 60, 72, 77, 91–2, 101,
116, 118, 120, 122, 126–7,
131; besieged, 43; captured
by Elamites, 44, 47, 51;
conflict with Babylon,
62–3; Daduša stele, 110;
destroyed by flooding, 71;
palace, 102; trade, 190
Eštar: 24, 43, 71, 80, 121–2, 136
Euphrates: 25–8, 37–8, 62, 65, 173,
175, 177, 181, 202;
defining borders, 27, 40,
139; river transport, 30

German Oriental Society: 17–8
Gilgameš: 15
Gula: 146
Gungunnum: 57

Habiru: 175
Habur triangle: 26, 37, 46, 121, 135,
175
Hadni-Addu: 96
Halabit (Halabiye): 173
Hali-Haldun: 99
Hammurabi of Babylon: 2–3, 17,
19–20, 30, 32, 36, 40, 44,
49, 53, 56, 58, 75, 79, 80,
89, 97, 99, 117, 124, 132,
135, 137, 141, 145–6, 150,
152, 155, 158, 167, 192, 199,
201–2; agricultural
projects, 60; alliance with
Samsi-Addu and Ibal-pi-
El II, 31–2; alliance with
Ṣilli-Sin, 139; building
works of, 27; capture of
Rapiqum, 29;
correspondence: with
Ibal-pi-El, 134; with Rim-
Sin, 45; with Šamaš-hazir,
187; with Sin-idinnam, 61,
184, 187–8; with Zimri-
Lim, 37, 40–1, 43, 48, 55,
84–5, 88, 114, 131, 139;
destruction of Malgium,
28; family, 18, 20, 23–5, 71,
76–7, 94–6, 177, 196;
military activities, 1, 8–9,
31–2, 85–6, 109, 114, 119,
125; *mîšarum*, 27, 30, 60;
occupation of Larsa, 60;
reign, 1, 8, 18, 24–5, 35, 55,
69–73, 77, 123, 140, 149–
51, 164, 169–71, 183–4,
191, 193, 195–6, 198, 202;
royal epithets, 76;
support for Mari, 38;
territory conquered, 44,
51, 61–2, 72, 80–1, 91,
104, 190; wives, 92; year
names, 12, 29, 35, 50, 59–
60, 63–4, 66, 110, 121
Hammurabi of Kurda: 43, 52
Hanaeans: 175–6
Hanat: 30, 37
Hardum: 149

Haya-sumu, king of Ilan-ṣura: 135
Herodotus: 200
Hiritum: 46, 50, 124
Hit: 41–3, 48, 85, 114; bitumen wells, 114–5
Homs, 27, 140
Hulalum: 32
Hurrian: 6; names, 70

Ibal-El: 137
Ibal-pi-El, general at Mari: 52, 99, 116, 128, 131, 133; correspondence: with Hammurabi of Babylon, 134; with Zimri-Lim, 91–2
Ibal-pi-El II, king of Ešnunna: 31, 39, 42, 44, 49, 124; alliance with Hammurabi of Babylon and Samsi-Addu, 31–2; alliance with Zimri-Lim, 32–3, 122; capture of Rapiqum, 38; disloyalty to Išme-Dagan, 32; military campaigns, 31, 38; peace treaties, 37–8, 138
Iddin-Ilaba: 165
Ikun-pi-Sin: 133
Ilan-ṣura: 32, 47, 135
ilkum: 117, 135, 185–6
Iltani: 69, 94–5
Inanna: 92
Inib-Šamaš: 99
Iribam-Sin: 194–5
Išar-Lim: 132–3
Išhi-Addu, king of Qatna: 93, 134; correspondence with Išme-Dagan, 134
Isin: 27–8, 71, 78, 83, 101, 104, 146, 189; archives, 101–2; captured by Sin-muballiṭ, 25; palace of Enlil-bani, 102; rivalry with Larsa, 25; worship of Gula, 146
Išme-Dagan, king of Ekallatum: 29, 32–3, 43, 50, 52, 61, 99, 111, 123, 129, 131–2, 134; correspondence with Išhi-Addu, 134; family, 26, 28, 31; loss of territory, 33; refuge in Babylon, 38, 65
Išme-ilum: 172
Itur-Asdu: 42, 111
Itur-Mer: 178

Jebel Sinjar: 26, 32, 38–9, 61–2, 120, 135, 173, 175

Kahat: 37
Kalhu: 201
Karana: 69, 95–6, 135
Karkar: 72
Karkemiš: 27
kârum: 180, 194
Kazallu: 45–6, 72
Keš: 71
Kiš: 9, 10, 19, 70–1, 77, 104, 107
Kiš-Dilbat-Marad: 67
kispum: 24, 78, 171, 200
kittum: 150
Ku-Ningal: 168
Kupper, J.-R.: 175–6
Kurda: 37, 39, 43, 100, 130
Kurdistan: 140
Kutalla: 190, 194
Kutha: 24, 71

Lagaš-Girsu: 72
Larsa: 9, 23, 26, 35 42, 46, 55–6, 59–60, 71, 81, 83, 92, 98, 101, 106, 118, 140, 152, 179, 191–2, 194; archives, 184, 189, 193; besieged, 119,

124; captured by Hammurabi of Babylon, 1, 9, 80, 91, 104–5, 167, 184, 190; excavations, 125, 169, 178, 189; governor, 121; kingdom known as Emutbalum, 61; military defences, 57; palace of Nur-Adad, 101; restoration work, 201; rivalry with Isin, 25; temple of Šamaš, 111, 194;

La'um: correspondence with Zimri-Lim, 130
Lebanon: 31
Lipit-Eštar of Isin: 16; laws, 78, 154, 199
lipit napištim: 138
lîtum: 105
Livy: 2
Louvre: 9, 80–1, 110–1
Lu-Nanna: 111
Lu-Ninurta: 19, 98, 149, 192
Lugal-Marad: 24

Malgium: 26–8, 36, 55, 57, 65, 67, 72, 124
Mankisum: 26, 28–9, 50, 52, 63; annexed by Apil-Sin, 24–5, 44; annexed by Ešnunna, 4; besieged, 44
Marad: 24, 28, 146
marat šarrim: 94
Marduk: 29, 50, 56, 78, 81–2, 201; temples, 171–2
Marduk-naṣir: 98
Mari: 3, 19–20, 20, 29–30, 37, 40, 42, 49, 51, 55, 65, 72, 86, 96–9, 101, 103–4, 105, 110, 114–16, 118, 123, 128, 131, 133–6, 149, 173–4, 177,

190; alliance with Babylon against Elam, 20, 40; archives, 1, 6, 12, 17, 27, 35, 65, 81, 85, 92, 140, 175–6, 181, 189; borders, 38, 139; captured by Hammurabi of Babylon, 1; census, 118; destroyed, 66, 69; divisions of the kingdom, 105; excavation, 18; governor, 47; 'judge', 105; palace, 69, 80, 105, 119, 171, 173, 189; return of Zimri-Lim, 32

mashatum: 48
Maškan-šapir: 25, 28, 56, 61, 72, 86, 95, 106, 109; annexed by Nur-Adad of Larsa, 57; excavations, 178; in Emutbalum, 61; revolt, 57
Mesopotamia: 1–2, 6–7, 20, 23, 27, 95, 116; Northern Mesopotamia, 35; Upper Mesopotamia, 26–7, 32, 38, 50, 120, 124, 137
Me-Turan: 154
mina: 30
mîšarum: 27, 30, 60, 80, 107, 145, 150, 152, 157, 188–9, 197
Mulhan: 38
muškênum: 161–2, 164
Mut-Hadqim: 38, 132
Mutiabal: 45
Mutu-Numaha: 96–7

Nabu: 24, 85, 201
nadîtum: 81, 94–5, 101, 149, 157, 171–2, 196
nâgiru: 109
Namhu: 96
Naram-Sin, king of Agade: 15, 201

Nebuchadnezzar: 66; restored Larsa, 201
Nergal: 56
Nin-egal: 92
Nin-Isina: 78
Nin-pirig: 88
Ninurta: 9, 83, 172
Nippur: 14–5, 16, 56, 169, 178; worship of Ninurta, 83, 172
Nur-Adad, king of Larsa: 57, 111, 145
Opis: see Upi
Oppenheim, A. L.: 183
Ordeal: 148–9

Palestine: 140
Parrot, A.: 3, 66
Polanyi, K.: 196
Puzur-Gula: 146

Qabra: 124, 140
Qarni-Lim, king of Andarig: 38–9, 96
Qaṭna (Tell Mishrife): 26–7, 43, 50, 58, 101, 124, 131; hepatoscopy, 81
Qaṭṭara (Tell al-Rimah): 32, 113, 173; archives, 69; palace, 102
Qaṭṭunan, 105

rabiânum: 107
Rapiqum: 27, 29, 36–7, 42; captured by Hammurabi of Babylon, 29, 81; captured by Ibal-pi-El II, 38; fortifications, 70–1; recaptured by Daduša of Ešnunna, 30
Razama: 47, 124–5
rêdûm: 115, 117, 188; in Code of Hammurabi, 126–7, 158, 186–7

Renger, J.: 190–2
Rim-Sin, king of Larsa: 35, 44–5, 55, 59–61, 67, 80, 100–1, 168–9, 201; controlled territory, 27–8; correspondence with Hammurabi of Babylon, 45; family, 56, 95; wives, 92
Rim-Sin-Šala-baštašu, wife of Rim-Sin: 92
Roman Empire: slave labour, 163

Šaduppum (Tell Harmal): 154
Saggaratum, 105, 116
Sakirum: 48
Šala: statues, 88
Šamaš: 46, 48, 56, 88–9, 110, 116, 146, 172; symbol of justice, 80, 145; temples, 81, 94, 111, 157, 171–2, 194, 196
Šamaš-hazir: 146, 149, 184, 192; correspondence with Hammurabi of Babylon, 187
Šamaš-rabi: 148
Samsi-Addu of Ekallatum: 24, 29–32, 36, 42, 122, 124, 128, 202; alliance with Daduša of Ešnunna, 30; alliance with Hammurabi of Babylon and Ubal-pi-El II, 31–2; death, 1, 31, 35, 38; family, 26, 94, 121; 'Great King', 26; military campaigns, 31, 65; seal, 110; Šehna, 26; territory, 26–8
Samsu-iluna: 18, 99, 107, 156, 168, 188, 192–3; *mîšarum*, 150, 152

šandabakkum: 98
šâpir nârim: 106
šâpir rêdê: 116
šâpirum: 105
šâpiṭum: 105
Sargon of Agade: 15, 201
saskum: 48
Šehna (Tell Leilan): 26, 44, 47, 101, 113; capitulated to Zimri-Lim, 38–9; palace, 102; renamed by Samsi-Addu as Šubat-Enlil, 26
Šerda: 88–9
Šibtu: 93, 104; correspondence with Zimri-Lim, 82–3
Ṣilli-Eštar: 166, 194–5
Ṣilli-Sin, king of Ešnunna: 52–3, 94, 127, 137; alliance with Hammurabi of Babylon, 139; gifts from Zimri-Lim, 62
Simat-Eštar, wife of Rim-Sin: 92
Sin (Nanna): 88, 100; priestesses, 94; temples, 180, 192, 196
Sin-bel-aplim: 133; *šukkal ubâri*, 98
Sin-idinnam: 82, 98, 106, 111, 146, 158, 166; correspondence with Hammurabi of Babylon, 61, 184, 187–8; inscriptions, 111
Sin-kašid, king of Uruk: 23, 140; alliance with Sumu-la-El, 23; wives, 140
Sin-muballiṭ: 24–5, 100, 107; correspondence with Anam of Uruk, 92; death, 79; family, 24, 56, 76–7, 107; territory, 25
Sippar: 89, 95, 104, 152, 156, 168, 181; archives, 19; Ebabbar, 202; excavations, 9, 199; fortifications, 71; temple of Šamaš, 94, 110, 157, 171–2, 196
Sippar Amnanum (Tell ed-Der): 17, 104; Great Sippar, 104
Sippar-Yahrurum: 177, 181
Šitullum: 50
Šu-iliya, king of Isin: 100
Šu-nuhra-alu, secretary of Zimri-Lim, 98
Šubartu: 10
Šubat-Enlil: see Šehna
Suhum: 30, 38, 37, 42, 105
šukkallum: 98–9
Šulgi, king of Ur: 111
Sumer: 25, 64, 83
Sumerian: 9–10, 14, 16, 23, 27, 60, 66, 72, 154; literature, 15–7, 20
Sumu-abum: 76–7
Sumu-ditana: 96–7
Sumu-la-El: 18, 23, 77, 140; alliance with Sin-kašid, 23
Susa: 9, 27, 59, 111, 152, 154, 190
Šušarra (Tell Shemshara): 102, 113
Suti: 25, 128, 175
Syria: 3, 23, 58, 124, 140

Ṭab-eli-matim, 'grand servant' of Hammurabi of Babylon: 99
tâmîtu: 85
tamkârum: 194
Taurus: 26
têbibtum: 118
Tell Asmar: see Ešnunna
Tell al-Rimah: see Qaṭṭarah
Tell ed-Der: see Sippar Amnanum
Tell Haddad: see Me-Turan
Tell Hariri: see Mari
Tell Harmal: see Šaduppum
Tell Leilan: see Šehna

Tell Mishrife: see Qatna
Tell Shemshara: see Šušarra
terhatum: 165
Terqa: 94, 105, 116
Thucydides: 2
Tigris: 24–8, 30, 38, 44, 50, 65, 67, 70, 72, 85
Tilmun: 31–2
Tišpak: 102–3
ṭuppi lā ragāmim: 147–8
ṭupšar sakkakkim: 98
Tur-Abdin: 26, 31
Turukkû: 70; deportation to Dilbat, 127; semi-nomadic characteristics, 123
Tuttul: 32, 65, 72; palace of Yasmah-Addu, 102

Ugarit: 47, 113
Upi (Opis): 52; annexed by Apil-Sin, 24, 44; annexed by Ešnunna, 44; Elamite siege, 44, 46, 124
Ur: 10, 16, 71, 88, 169, 178; archives, 168; temple of Nanna, 196
Ur III Dynasty: 15, 23, 72, 98, 202
Ur-Nammu: laws, 154–5, 199
Ur-Utu: tablets 17
Uraš: 24
Urbilum (Arbele): 30
Uruk: 27–8, 71, 101, 104, 177; archives of, 189; palace at, 102; seized by Sin-muballiṭ (1803), 25
Vernant, J.-P.: 183–4, 198

Warad-Sin: 57, 148
wardum: 92, 161–2, 164
Watar-piša: 151

Yabliya: 38
Yagid-Lim: 96, 119
Yahdun-Lim: 96, 104
Yamhad: 109, 117
Yamutbal: 57
Yansib-Addu: 41
Yarim-Addu: 44, 53, 55, 59
Yarim-Lim, king of Aleppo: 37, 47, 49, 103, 128
Yasim-sumu: 98
Yasmah-Addu, king of Mari: 19–20, 26–8; 32, 93, 104, 118

Zababa: 9, 24, 77
Zabala: 9, 72, 88
Zalmaqum: 50, 65, 121
Zagros mountains: 26, 31, 116
Zarpanitum: 88
Zimri-Addu: 57–8, 122
Zimri-Lim, king of Mari: 3, 18–20, 27, 32, 37, 39, 40, 42, 49, 51, 58, 62, 64, 78, 82, 84, 86, 95–6, 98–100, 104–5, 107, 109, 118–9, 125, 128–30, 133–5, 137, 140, 149, 159, 174; alliance with Ibal-pi-El II, 32–3, 122, 138; Ašlakka as a base of operations, 39; belonging to Bene Sim'al, 37; correspondence: with Hammurabi of Babylon, 37, 40–1, 43, 48, 55, 84–5, 88, 114, 131, 139; with Ibal-pi-El, 91–2; with Šibtu, 82–3; with La'um, 130; family, 47, 93, 96, 103–4; inner circle, 109; military forces, 38, 49–50, 58, 85, 116–7; siege of Andarig, 39